The Kindly Flame

Such ones ill iudge of loue, that cannot loue,
Ne in their frosen hearts feele kindly flame:
For thy they ought not thing vnknowne reproue,
Ne naturall affection faultlesse blame,
For fault of few that haue abusd the same.
For it of honor and all vertue is
The roote, and brings forth glorious flowres of fame,
That crowne true louers with immortale blis,
The meed of them that loue, and do not liue amisse.

    THE FAERIE QUEENE, IV, *Proem*, ii

The Kindly Flame

A STUDY OF THE
THIRD AND FOURTH BOOKS OF
SPENSER'S *FAERIE QUEENE*

By THOMAS P. ROCHE, Jr.

PRINCETON, NEW JERSEY
PRINCETON UNIVERSITY PRESS
1964

Copyright © 1964 by Princeton University Press
ALL RIGHTS RESERVED
L.C. Card: 63-18649

Publication of this book has been aided by
the Research Fund of Princeton University and by
the Ford Foundation program to support
publication, through university presses,
of works in the humanities and social sciences

Printed in the United States of America
by Princeton University Press, Princeton, New Jersey

For Rosemond Tuve

She will outstrip all praise
And make it halt behind her.

Preface

"But by occasion hereof, many other aduentures are intermedled, but rather as Accidents, then intendments. As the loue of Britomart, the ouerthrow of Marinell, the misery of Florimell, the vertuousnes of Belphœbe, the lasciuiousnes of Hellenora, and many the like." Spenser's statement in the letter to Ralegh has caused many critics and readers to despair of finding a structural principle in the third and fourth books of *The Faerie Queene*, and it is true that there is little material continuity in the narrative. It would be fruitless to cite the number of times that one has read or heard the opinion that in Books I and II Spenser was in control of the structure and that in III and IV he became confused, indifferent, or careless. Books I and II do have narrative continuity; Books III and IV do not. In Books I and II the structure is simple; in III and IV it is not. All four have structure. In each case the structure is dictated by Spenser's allegorical treatment of the virtue of that particular book. In the legends of chastity and friendship, in place of the simple Red Cross narrative of the legend of holiness, we find the stories of Britomart and Arthegall, Amoret and Scudamour, Belphoebe and Timias, Florimell and Marinell. It is the purpose of this book to show that the legends of chastity and friendship require the complicated narrative structure to exemplify Spenser's conceptions of these virtues.

The method of inquiry is a close examination of the text. Lest the minutiae of such detailed reading obscure the general purpose of the study the introductory chapter is divided into two sections. The first is an attempt to explain my method of reading texts allegorically with examples from the middle books of the poem. I feel that this primer is necessary because my method of reading allegory is less common than it should

PREFACE

be and because too often apparent agreement about particular readings merely masks more basic theoretical disagreements that crop up later to plague both reader and critic. The second section takes the long view and explains the basic plan of the whole poem, relating Arthur's quest to the tasks of the individual knights, distinguishing between England and Faeryland, and explaining the time scheme of the poem. With this background the reader is in a better position to evaluate my treatment of Books III and IV. The main chapters of the book deal with the adventures of Britomart, Belphoebe and Amoret, and Florimell as separate entities in order to show Spenser's skill in depicting moral virtue, without the cumbersome difficulty of wondering how and why one adventure is followed by another. The conclusion attempts to show that these individual narrative episodes do in fact fit together to form a complex allegory and that the apparently random selection of narrative episodes does comprise a unified structure. One can only hope that the exposition will show that the accidents of Spenser's allegory are similar to the accidents of existence: they illuminate the essence that is the form of their being.

Several other peculiarities of the book remain to be discussed. The major ideas and organization were completed in my Princeton doctoral thesis, September 1958. The years that have elapsed since the completion of the thesis and of this manuscript have brought many contributions to Spenserian scholarship. Most of these I have read, but since my ideas were already somewhat solidified, I have decided not to mention the most recent scholarship unless it directly contradicts or corrects my own ideas. This position is not entirely gracious, but my book is intended primarily for those Spenserians who are already familiar with the scholarship, and they will be able to make the proper adjudications. I also did not want to add unnecessarily to the footnotes, which at times are heavily weighted with documentation and opinion. In a

PREFACE

field where scholarly battles have often obscured the poem I felt it more beneficial to avoid extraneous skirmishes. Again, to relieve the burden of footnotes laden with references to Greek and Roman classics I have used wherever possible the editions of the Loeb Library. Unless otherwise cited, references to the classics are to this invaluable aid to the laboring scholar.

Finally I would like to thank those who have helped me in the completion of the book. Some will be surprised at my gratitude; others, I fear, may be annoyed either at their inclusion or omission. To the latter my first thanks. Of those to whom I am consciously indebted I shall begin with my parents and Beatrice Putney Westerfield, who first made me aware of literature. My aunt and uncle, Dr. and Mrs. Harold Moore, and my cousins, Mr. and Mrs. Raymond Gillmor, with real faith, eased the burden of the long years of research. To Professors Harold Bloom, Sherman Hawkins, and Rosemond Tuve I owe continued friendship, inspiration, and suggestions only sometimes noted lest they overshadow. Professors Walter Davis, Clay Hunt, and James Thorpe I thank for their frank and helpful criticism of the manuscript. Professor Charles Ryskamp courageously challenged the Print Room of the British Museum in search of the Holbein illustration. Mr. Peter Marinelli generously gave me several footnote references, but his modesty refused citation. I am also indebted to the staffs of the Princeton University Library, the British Museum, and the Warburg Institute of London, and to the 1900 Fund of Williams College, the Annan Fund, and the Research Fund of Princeton University. To Miss Wesley Samuels, my typist, and Mr. Burr Wallen, my indefatigable research assistant, I give my thanks and best wishes for their new careers. Finally, my deepest thanks to Miriam Brokaw, a more gracious editor than any book deserves.

T.P.R.

Princeton, New Jersey

LIST OF ABBREVIATIONS

AJP   *American Journal of Philology*
CP   *Classical Philology*
ELH   *English Literary History*
JEGP   *Journal of English and Germanic Philology*
JWCI   *Journal of the Warburg and Courtauld Institutes*
MLN   *Modern Language Notes*
PL   *Patrologia Latina*, ed. J. P. Migne
PMLA   *Publications of the Modern Language Association*
SEL   *Studies in English Literature*
SP   *Studies in Philology*
TSE   *University of Texas Studies in English*
TLS   *Times Literary Supplement*
UTQ   *University of Toronto Quarterly*

ACKNOWLEDGMENTS

Grateful acknowledgment is made for permission to quote from other works:

From THE COLLECTED POEMS OF HART CRANE. By permission of Liveright, Publishers, N.Y. Copyright (C) R, 1961, by Liveright Publishing Corp.

From "The Oven Bird" from COMPLETE POEMS OF ROBERT FROST. Copyright 1916, 1921 by Holt, Rinehart and Winston, Inc. Copyright renewed 1944 by Robert Frost. Reprinted by permission of Holt, Rinehart and Winston, Inc.

From "The Sea and the Mirror," Copyright 1944 by W. H. Auden. From "The Truest Poetry is the Most Feigning," Copyright 1954 by W. H. Auden. From "The Shield of Achilles," Copyright 1952 by W. H. Auden. Reprinted by permission of Random House, Inc.

Contents

PREFACE — vii

INTRODUCTION: FAERYLAND AS FICTION — 3
  i. The Nature of the Allegory — 3
  ii. The Nature of Faeryland — 31

CHAPTER I: THE IMAGE OF BRITOMART — 51
  i. Britomart as Chastity — 53
  ii. The Quest Defined — 66
    a. Castle Joyous — 67
    b. The House of Busyrane — 72
    c. Britomart and Arthegall — 88

CHAPTER II: BELPHOEBE AND AMORET — 96
  i. Belphoebe and the Three Queens — 97
  ii. The Two Venuses — 101
  iii. The Birth — 103
  iv. Amoret's Education — 116
    a. The Garden of Adonis — 117
    b. The Temple of Venus — 128
    c. The Original Ending of 1590 — 133
  v. Belphoebe and Timias — 136
  vi. Conclusion — 149

CHAPTER III: FLORIMELL AND MARINELL — 151
  i. Florimell and the Chaste Helen — 152
  ii. The False Florimell — 162
  iii. The Marriage of the Thames and Medway — 167
  iv. Marinell and the Reluctant Achilles — 184
  v. *Potentia Amoris* — 189

CONCLUSION: STRUCTURE AS MEANING — 195

INDEX — 213

The Kindly Flame

But vnto them besydes, I add my owne readinge and out of them both togeather with comparison of tymes, lyknes of manners and customes, affinitie of wordes, & names . . . and many other lyke Circumstances I doe gather a likeliehoode of truth not certenlie affirminge anythinge but by conferringe of tymes, languages monumentes and suchlike, I doe hunte out a probabillitie of thinges which I leaue vnto your iudgment to beleaue or refuise.

—View of the Present State of Ireland

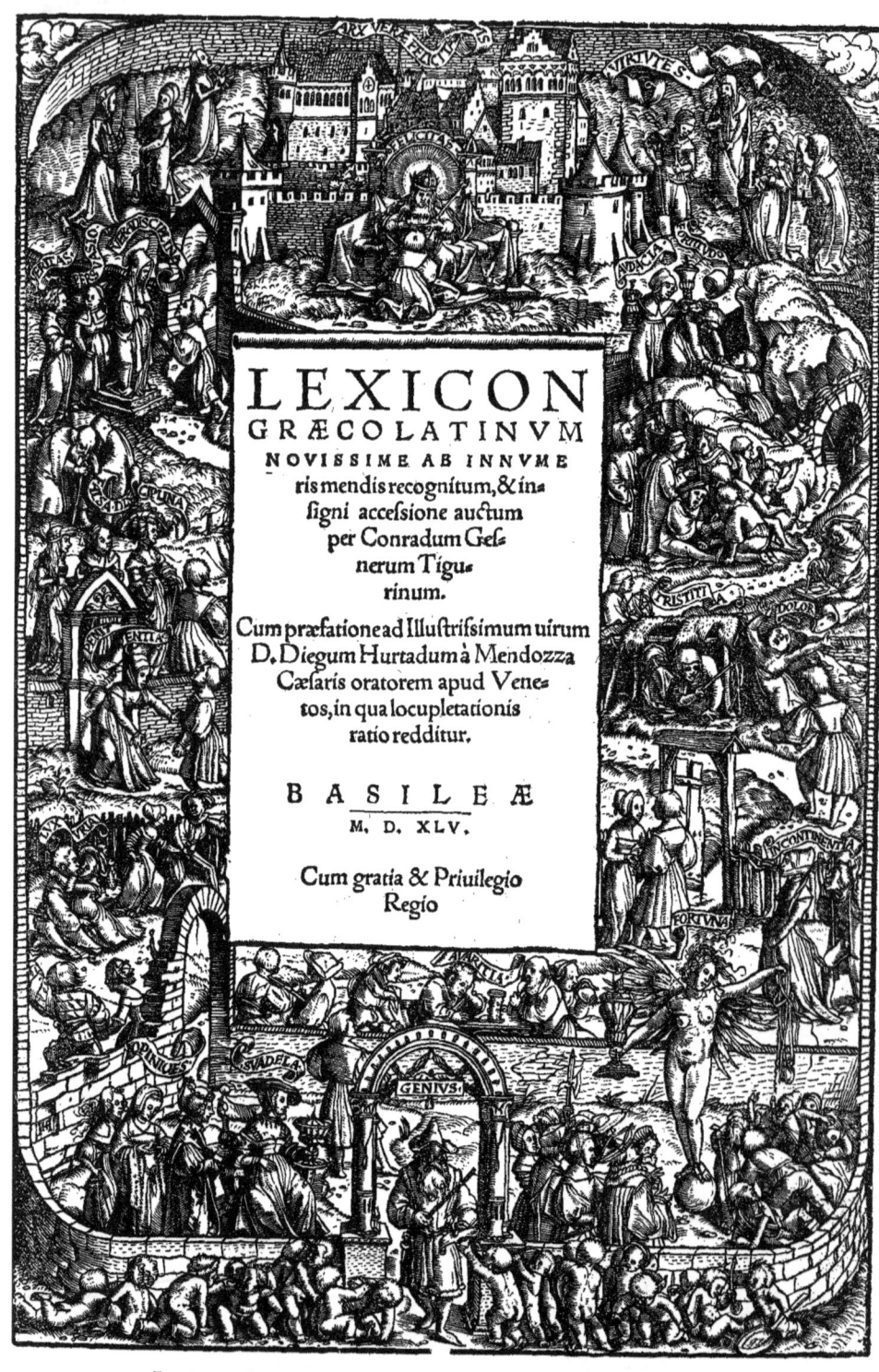

Lexicon Graeco Latinum, Basle, 1545, with the Holbein "Genius" title-border (from the collection of Mr. and Mrs. Philip Hofer, Cambridge, Mass.).

Introduction: Faeryland as Fiction

i · THE NATURE OF THE ALLEGORY

IN Books III and IV of *The Faerie Queene* Spenser breaks the pattern of expectation set up by the narrative structures of Books I and II, turning from the epic structure of Virgil to the episodic romance structure of Ariosto. The shift in narrative technique has been attributed to Spenser's ineptitude in handling the virtues of chastity and friendship or to his returning to an earlier plan to make use of material already written.[1] These explanations, it seems to me, do not suggest recognition of the amazing brilliance and vitality of Books III and IV or of Spenser's superb ability to integrate apparently disparate materials. They rest on the judgment that "the narrative" and "the allegory" have somehow gone awry, all coherence gone, as if narrative and allegory were two separate and parallel functions of the poem we find before us. In what sense can we complain that Books III and IV do not "present a continuous story on the allegorical level"?[2] How can a story be told on any level but that of story? Stories may delight, and they often instruct, but they always tell us about some action. It is with the action of the narrative that any inquiry into allegory must begin.

Prince Arthur goes in search of the Faerie Queene, Guyon meets Mammon and captures Acrasia. This action is embodied

---

[1] Josephine Waters Bennett, *The Evolution of "The Faerie Queene,"* Chicago, 1942, pp. 138ff. *The Works of Edmund Spenser: a Variorum Edition*, ed. Edwin Greenlaw, C. G. Osgood, F. M. Padelford, *et al.*, 11 vols., Baltimore, 1932-1957, vol. 3, pp. 310-329 (hereafter cited as *Var.* 3.310-329). All quotations from the works of Spenser are taken from this edition and will be cited in the text.

[2] Joshua McClennen, "On the Meaning and Function of Allegory in the English Renaissance," *Univ. of Michigan Contributions in Philology*, No. 6, April 1947, p. 9.

INTRODUCTION

in a narrative, whose words present to the reader the meaning that the author wanted this action to convey. The allegory is part of the meaning presented by the narrative and may either be intended by the author or discovered by the reader or both.[3] At no point is the allegory independent of the action as presented in the narrative. If the critic grants independence to the allegory, chaos is come again, for he is in fact denying the primacy of that golden world we enter when we read literature.

Renaissance rhetoricians showed their awareness of the dependence of allegory on narrative by defining it as "continued metaphor," the use of which "serueth most aptly to ingraue the liuely images of things, and to present them vnder daepe shadowes to the contemplation of the mind, wherein wit and iudgement take pleasure, and the remembrance receiueth a long lasting impression. . . ."[4] Here the emphasis is decidedly on "the liuely images of things" that give rise to the allegorical meanings, that is, on the tenor of this continued metaphor which the vehicle (narrative) illuminates. Only through the "daepe shadowes" of particulars can the universals, which are the repository of allegorical meanings, be presented to the human mind. This is not to say that the universal allegorical meanings are stuffed into the particulars of the narrative. The allegory is contained by the narrative in the same way and to the degree that universals are contained by particulars. Particulars figure forth universals; the narrative figures forth the allegory. The narrative presents itself and under the guise of its deep shadows lures the mind toward a vision of those lively images it em-

---

[3] I am aware that I am begging a rather large question of aesthetics in this definition, but I want to include as allegory both the intentional allegory of *The Faerie Queene* and the probably unintentional allegory of the Song of Solomon.

[4] Henry Peacham, *The Garden of Eloquence*, Scholars' Facsimiles and Reprints, Gainesville, Fla., 1954, p. 27. Cf. also Ambrogio Calepino, *Dictionarivm Octo Lingvarum*, Basle, 1584, s.v. "allegoria"; Thomas Wilson, *The Arte of Rhetorique*, ed. G. H. Mair, Oxford, 1909, p. 176.

bodies, toward those universals that are the ground and form of *these* particulars.

In this sense, of course, reading narratives allegorically does not differ in the least from reading them symbolically, and we have no way of distinguishing a proper reading of *The Faerie Queene* from a proper reading of *The Scarlet Letter*, or *The Golden Bowl*, or *Finnegans Wake*. However, to bring allegorical reading within shouting distance of symbolic reading tends to correct our jaded and erroneous opinions about the relation of the allegory to the narrative text. No one would think of saying that the scarlet letter equals   or that the golden bowl means   or that Anna Livia Plurabelle represents   —without relating these statements to the text that complicates, enriches, and makes them significant. Yet how few critics of Spenser feel obliged to carry their remarks beyond this "predicate nominative" stage of criticism? In part our modern oversimplification of allegorical reading is due to the common and traditional metaphor of rind and pith to explain the relation of the allegorical senses to the narrative text. Sir John Harington, for example, despite the implications of the metaphor, does not doubt that the relation is "organic":

"First of all for the litterall sence (as it were the vtmost barke or ryne) they set downe in manner of an historie, the acts and notable exploits of some persons worthy memorie; then *in the same fiction*, as a second rine and somewhat more fine, as it were nearer to the pith and marrow, they place the Morall sence, profitable for the actiue life of man, approuing vertuous actions and condemning the contrarie. Manie times also *vnder the selfesame words* they *comprehend* some true vnderstanding of naturall Philosophie, or somtimes of politike gouernement, and now and then of diuinitie: and these same sences that *comprehend* so excellent knowledge we call the Allegorie, which *Plutarch* defineth to be when one thing

5

is told, and *by that* another is vnderstood." [Italics mine except for Plutarch][5]

The senses are contained (*wrapped* or *comprehended*) in the narrative, and *by that* do we come to understand the fuller significance of the text. Harington is talking about the way an Elizabethan discovered meaning in narrative poems, and for this purpose the metaphor of rind and pith is valid. He is not talking about the enjoyment of poetry, the pleasure of entering that golden world of narrative—unless we are to visualize the Elizabethan reader surrounded by empty nutshells or orange peels. In general, critics have not been careful to observe that Harington and the other Renaissance writers who use this metaphor are not thinking of two separate and divided entities; the allegorical senses reveal themselves when one "gets into" the work. As soon as the critic begins to talk about poets telling stories *on the allegorical level,* he confuses the tenor and vehicle of this continued metaphor and misses the beauty and economy of the allegorical mode. To leap at random from the concrete embodiment of the universal in the narrative to an abstract statement of it can only flatten out the narrative and dull the experience that the allegorical narrative is attempting to create in the reader. Like other men the readers and writers of allegory cannot serve two masters.

At this point one should beat a hasty retreat from the kinship with modern symbolic reading lest we trick ourselves into applying the criteria of the novel or the drama to an entirely different type of literature. Red Cross is a character, but he is neither "round" nor dramatic. Guyon's bloody babe should not raise the question of what to do with our orphans, nor should Busyrane's wounding Britomart arouse the slightest trace either of pity or of fear. *The Faerie Queene* is symbolic, but its allegorical narrative is not trying to do any of these things.

[5] Sir John Harington, *Orlando Furioso*, London, 1591, sig. ¶iiij. Reprinted in G. Gregory Smith, *Elizabethan Critical Essays*, 2 vols., London, 1937, vol. 2 pp. 201-202.

Allegorical reading (or more simply allegory) is a form of literary criticism with a metaphysical basis. It postulates a verbal universe at every point correspondent with the physical world in which we live, that is, a Realistic view of language. The history of allegorical interpretation of the Bible and secular literature is too long and complicated to relate here, but by the time of the sixteenth century allegory had attached itself firmly to the image of the universe created by Ptolemy and Dionysius the Areopagite and familiarly known as the "Elizabethan world picture." According to this theory there are in reality three worlds: the *sublunary*, the fallen world in which we live, subject to change and decay; the *celestial*, the unchanging world of the planets and stars; the *supercelestial*, the dwelling of angels and the Godhead. These three worlds are held together by God's Love and are analogically correspondent. Thus, in the sublunary world fire burns, while in the celestial world its analogue the sun not only burns but by its burning nourishes life, and in the supercelestial world the seraphim burn with love for their Creator.[6] The three worlds are a progression away from the material and toward the spiritual, and just as our image of the purely spiritual seraphim is drawn from our knowledge of the visible fire and sun, so too is our knowledge of universal truths drawn (in part) from our reading of the imitation of the visible worlds. Pico makes this quite clear in the introduction to his *Heptaplus*:

"For euen as the ... three worlds being girt and buckled with the bands of concord doe by reciprocall libertie, interchange their natures; the like do they also by their appellations. And this is the principle from whence springeth & groweth the discipline of allegoricall sense. For it is certaine

---

[6] *Iohannis Pici Mirandvlae ... omnia ... opera*, Venice, 1557, sig. **4. "Elemētaris urit: coelestis uiuificat: supercoelestis amat." The quotation may also be found on p. 188 of *De Hominis Dignitate, Heptaplus, De Ente et Uno*, ed. Eugenio Garin, Florence, 1942.

that the ancient fathers could not conueniently haue represented one thing by other figures, but that they had first learned the secret amity and affinitie of all nature. Otherwise there could bee no reason, why they should represent this thing by this forme, and that by that, rather then otherwise. But hauing the knowledge of the vniuersall world, and of euery part thereof, and being inspired with the same spirit, that not onely knoweth all things: but did also make all things: they haue oftentimes, and very fitly figured the natures of the one world, by that which they knew to bee correspondent thereto in the others."[7]

The basis of allegorical reading is this analogical nature of the universe. In an hierarchical universe where each thing has a fixed place the relationship of any two things in the same world or sphere may adumbrate the relationship of two other things in another world or sphere. The original pair do not lose their identity or relationship by such adumbration; they simply call attention to other possible relationships through the fact that they themselves are related in such a way. The analogies are validated by the fact that the whole hierarchical structure with its often unseen web of interrelationships is contained within the mind of God, Who sees the relationship of all things one to another. In allegorical reading a further step is taken: since words represent things, words must represent this basic analogical relationship.

The whole matter will be made clearer by returning to Harington's *Apology for Poetry*. Immediately following his definition of allegory is an example: "*Perseus* sonne of *Iupiter* is fained by the Poets to haue slaine *Gorgon*, and after that

---

[7] The translation is that of the English translator of Pierre de la Primaudaye, *The French Academie*, London, 1618, p. 671. De la Primaudaye in his discussion of the division of the universal world simply translates the second proemium to Pico's *Heptaplus*. The original Latin text is on sig. **4 of the Venice, 1557, edition and on p. 192 of the Garin edition. The passage also occurs in Fornari's *Della Espositione Sopra L'Orlando fvrioso Parte Seconda*, Florence, 1550, vol. 2, p. 3.

conquest atchieued, to haue flowen vp to heauen." Harington gives an euhemeristic interpretation as the "Historicall sence" and continues with several more senses:

"Morally it signifieth thus much, *Perseus* a wise man, sonne of *Iupiter* endewed with vertue from aboue, slayeth sinne and vice, a thing base & earthly; signified by *Gorgon*, and so mounteth vp to the skie of vertue: It signifies in one kinde of Allegorie thus much; the mind of man being gotten by God, and so the childe of God killing and vanquishing the earthlinesse of this Gorgonicall nature, ascendeth vp to the vnderstanding of heauenly things, of high things, of eternal things; in which cōtemplacion cōsisteth the perfection of man: this is the natural allegory, because mā [is] one of the chiefe works of nature: It hath also a more high and heauenly Allegorie, that the heauenly nature, daughter of *Iupiter*, procuring with her continuall motion, corruption and mortality in the inferiour bodies, seuered it selfe at last from these earthly bodies, and flew vp on high, and there remaineth for euer. It hath also another Theological Allegorie; that the angelicall nature, daughter of the most high God the creator of all things; killing & ouercomming all bodily substance, signified by *Gorgon*, ascended into heauen: the like infinite Allegories I could pike out of other Poeticall fictions, saue that I would auoid tediousnes."[8]

The final, almost parenthetical comment is worth the consideration of any one piecing out the Elizabethan idea of allegory. Many poetical fictions adumbrate more than one allegorical meaning, and these meanings, as the Perseus example shows, need not conform totally with every detail in the narrative (vehicle of the continued metaphor). Perseus, the son of Jupiter, may become in an allegorical reading the

---

[8] Harington, *Orlando Furioso*, 1591, sig. Piiij-Piiij^v. Reprinted in Smith, vol. 2, pp. 202-203. For an earlier interpretation of the Perseus myth that follows the method employed by Harington but finds different meanings see Giovanni Boccaccio, *Genealogie Deorum Gentilium*, ed. Vincenzo Romano, 2 vols., Bari, 1951, vol. 1, p. 19 (Book I, chap. 3).

INTRODUCTION

daughter of God, as in the "more high and heauenly Allegorie." Perseus is not the name or personification of the heavenly or the angelical natures; he is an allegorical representation of these beings because in his narrative he is the offspring (not son or daughter) of Jupiter, and hence because of the poetic statement of this particular adventure the whole statement may adumbrate these and any other heavenly mysteries that follow this particular pattern. There is no relation between narrative statement and allegorical meaning except the "secret amity and affinitie of all nature." When the structural patterns of the narrative coincide with the structural patterns of any other events of nature or supernature, we as readers are entitled to view the conformity or analogy as an allegorical meaning.

This, I take it, is what Elizabethans meant when they called allegory a "continued metaphor." They do not mean a point-for-point correspondence between the narrative events and any meanings they may derive from the narrative; that is, the continuity is not vertical but horizontal. In reading a metaphorical statement one does not jump from the vehicle to the tenor at every stage; such reading calls to mind the old adage about changing horses (or vehicles) in midstream. This point is best illustrated by turning to proverbial statements, which the Renaissance rhetoricians saw did not drag along the problems of imaginative literature. "A bird in the hand is worth two in the bush." Try a vertical or one-for-one translation: An opportunity in the (bank?) is worth two opportunities in the (neighbor's bank? other hand?). One sees at once the distortion of translation and the enormous difficulty of arriving at a satisfactory equivalent for the orignal statement, yet no one (I think) would miss the point. If this is the case with such a simple metaphorical statement, surely the allegorical narrative will demand more complicated reading.

To see the difference, let us consider two passages from

The Faerie Queene. The two passages I have chosen are allegorically worlds apart. The one—the flight of Florimell in Book III, canto 1—is the beginning of a new narrative, clearly indebted to the first canto of *Orlando Furioso,* where Angelica rushes madly away from her rash of lovers. The narrative is brisk, and we are apparently not to fret about "allegorical meanings." The other is the key allegorical episode in Book IV, Spenser's continuation of Chaucer's Squire's Tale with its insistent allegorical demands from Agape and her three sons Priamond, Diamond, and Triamond. The allegorical intention is obvious, but the conceit is extremely dark. On the surface they are both simple narratives, but one cannot help feeling the vast difference in the narrative of Florimell's scattering Britomart and her companions and of Cambell's encounter with Triamond. The difference felt in reading these two episodes can be attributed to Spenser's allegorical intentions, and these intentions are embodied in the narrative itself. How, then, do the two narratives differ?

The opening of Book III differs markedly from the opening of Book I. The gentle knight, lovely lady, milk-white lamb, and lagging dwarf passing by present an iconic, two-dimensional vision like that of a medieval processional. Within the first five stanzas we know the purpose of their journey and the sad history of the lady's parents. All is simplicity and clarity. Book III begins with ambiguity. Arthur and Guyon, having finished their work with Acrasia, meet a knight and an aged squire. The strange knight and Guyon fight, but Guyon is dissuaded from a further trial—by the Palmer, of whose presence the reader has not been aware. In a moment Florimell flashes by pursued by the "griesly Foster," and we begin to realize that there were six people riding together after the opening encounter: Arthur and Timias, Guyon and the Palmer, Britomart and Glauce. Neither Florimell nor Glauce has been named; Britomart has been identified simply as a "single damzell." As quickly as the group

INTRODUCTION

was assembled, it is dispersed, and we are left with Britomart riding on unknowingly to Malecasta's castle (apparently with Glauce, although she is never again mentioned in the early adventures of Britomart). Britomart comes upon a single knight beset by six knights, who twenty-two stanzas later we are told is Red Cross. Things are not what they seem, but this is not the thematic development of the novelist nor the ineptitude of Spenser as a narrator. It is the method of allegory.

Sometimes there is an evocation of the setting; here there is not. Sometimes there is a careful delineation of character; here there is not. Sometimes there is a decided "point of view"; here there is not. The manner of the narrative is dictated not by a set of rules but by the effect the poet wants to create, and in this respect the allegorical poet is freer even than his modern descendant the novelist. We do not need to know where the characters are nor who or how many they are nor how we are to view them. The narrative will tell all, until the poet wants to focus the meaning. Then he may bring in these other ways of declaring meaning. The technique of the allegorical narrative lulls the reader into its meaning. If the reader should feel on occasion a paucity of allegorical significance, he may be absolutely right. Many things are necessary to keep a story going, or to get it started, which is the case with the opening episode of Book III.

This is all very pedestrian, but Spenser's technique as a poet has fared so badly in the hands of the critics that it may be worthwhile to examine his skill in handling a simple narrative passage. Harington's translation of Ariosto presents Angelica's flight from her own point of view. Everything in the description points to her inner fears.

But follow we *Angelica* that fled.

That fled through woods, and deserts all obscure,
Through places vninhabited and wast,

FAERYLAND AS FICTION

> Ne could she yet repute her selfe secure,
> But farder still she gallopeth in hast.
> Each leafe that stirs in her doth feare procure,
> And maketh her affrighted, and agast:
> Each noise she heares, each shadow she doth see,
> She doth mistrust it should *Renaldo* be.
>
> Like to a fawne, or kid of bearded goate,
> That in the wood a tyger fierce espide,
> Killing her dame, and first to teare the throate,
> And then to feed vpon the hanch or side,
> Fearing lest she may light on such a lot,
> Doth seeke it selfe in thickest brackes to hide,
> And thinks each noise the wind or aire doth cause,
> It selfe in danger of the tygers clawes.
> (*Orlando Furioso*, 1. 32-34)[9]

Spenser handles the scene quite differently. Florimell is described in some detail; we are told that she is afraid, but everything in this description points to the effect she has on her observers.

> All as a blazing starre doth farre outcast
> His hearie beames, and flaming lockes dispred,
> At sight whereof the people stand aghast:
> But the sage wisard telles, as he has red,
> That it importunes death and dolefull drerihed.
> (3.1.16)

We know even less of Florimell's motivations than we do of Angelica's. At that point Spenser brings the "griesly Foster" out of the woods, and part of Florimell's motivations is revealed. We know only that she is a damsel in distress and that her flight is patterned on Ariosto's Angelica.

Guyon and Arthur ride off after her and Timias after the

---

[9] Harington, *Orlando Furioso*, 1591, sig. Aiij. Hereafter all quotations from this poem will be from this edition and will be cited in the text.

INTRODUCTION

Forester, the significance of which will be revealed in later cantos, although Spenser does not tell us so at this point. Only "faire *Britomart*, whose constant mind,/ Would not so lightly follow beauties chace,/ Ne reckt of Ladies Loue, did stay behind...." With the disappearance of the others the point of view changes. We cannot suppose that Spenser intends the reader to think ill of Arthur and Guyon. They have gone, and now we are focusing on Britomart, whose thoughts these are.[10] We are not to build up any kind of animosity between Britomart and her companions. The motivation attributed to Britomart is one way of emphasizing the fact that she is a woman, which is the subject Spenser is about to undertake.

This opening episode of Book III is typical of one style of allegorical narrative. The allegorical meaning is exactly the meaning presented by the narrative—no more, no less. We may say that two chivalrous knights attempt to rescue a beautiful woman in distress, but if we should proceed one step further and say that beauty pursued by lust must be rescued by magnificence and temperance, we leave out much of the pleasure of the narrative and dispel the air of mystery that Spenser is apparently using to arouse interest in his new narrative. We also raise questions that cannot be answered: why is it that chastity does not (or cannot) rescue beauty? Such a question is a dreadful burden for a poem to bear, since it takes us immediately out of the realm the poet is creating.

A more interesting and fertile clue to the meaning of this first episode is the fact that Florimell is patterned on Ariosto's proud, coy, flirtatious Angelica. With this perception another question arises: is Florimell to be a repetition of Ariosto's heroine? Once more we may take a hint from Harington's

[10] Although this interpretation explains the present situation, the figures in Spenser's poem are not characters in that they do not have continuous interior feelings, nor are they required to react to situations with psychological realism. See chapter I, where the problem is treated in more detail.

treatment of the allegory in the beginning of *Orlando*. Even with the more fully developed characterization of Ariosto at hand (and before him Boiardo) Harington is cautious about labelling Angelica: "*In the hard adventures of* Angelica, *we may note how perilous a thing beautie is if it be not especially garded with the grace of God, and with vertue of the mynde, being continually assayld with enemies spirituall and temporall. In* Orlandos *dreame we may see how vnquiet thoughtes are bred in the myndes of those that are geuen ouer to the passion of loue or ambicion or whatsoeuer else may be vnderstood by* Angelica."[11] The point is not that Angelica has no meaning, but that her meaning or meanings have not been specified at this point in the poem. The reader must be patient; he should not try to assign meanings to Florimell until the poem warrants it.

At the opposite extreme of Spenser's allegorical technique is the episode of Cambell and Triamond. Here Spenser loads his narrative with every indication that the episode should be read allegorically. At that point in Book IV where the futures of the major figures are darkened by the hellish power of Ate, Cambell and Cambina, Triamond and Canacee seem almost a pledge of Ate's defeat, for immediately after their appearance Spenser devotes the second half of canto 2 and all of canto 3 to the story of their initial conflict and eventual concord. He further separates this episode from the main narrative by beginning it with his famous invocation to Chaucer, whose unfinished tale he is apparently taking over as his own.[12] Most important are the names Agape, Priamond, Diamond, and Triamond, which clearly point at the concepts

[11] Harington, *Orlando Furioso*, 1591, sig. Fiij.
[12] In fact, he borrows the names Canacee and Cambalo (significantly changed to Cambell or Cambello), the magic ring, whose properties are reduced to the "power to staunch al wounds, that mortally did bleed," and the fact that Cambalo fights with brothers (their number increased from two to three). The rest of the tale is Spenser's, a fact unsurprising since the brevity of the Chaucerian original makes reconstruction impossible.

INTRODUCTION

they represent. (The tenor has been drawn over into the vehicle in what the rhetoricians would call a mixed allegory.)[13] Agape is, of course, the Greek term for Christian love; the names of her sons mean first, second, and third world. Any reading of Spenser—in particular, the *Fowre Hymnes*—will tell us that Love did, in fact, create the three worlds: terrestrial, celestial, and supercelestial. Spenser realized that the mysteries of Christianity could not be loosed on his Faeryland too freely, but here he is clearly demanding that the reader view this episode as a metaphysical conflict as well as a literal battle between some knights. This much of the meaning is clear, but how do the details fit together and what do the actions of these figures mean?

An important hint occurs in the original title of Book IV: "The Fovrth Booke of the Faerie Queene. *Containing* The Legend of Cambel and Telamond, or Of Friendship." Each of the other books follows the same pattern and includes the name of the titular hero or heroine. Unless we are to doubt the authenticity of these titles, we should be prepared to accept the episode of Cambell and Triamond as the major exemplum of friendship in Book IV. A further problem arises with the name Telamond. All the early editions read Telamond until the 1734 edition of Jortin, who emended this word to Triamond. It is a sensible emendation, but unnecessary. Spenser's etymologizing instincts would easily have led him to conflate the first syllables of the names of the three

---

[13] Puttenham's comment on the following lines will illustrate:

The cloudes of care haue coured al my coste,
The stormes of strife, do threaten to appeare;
The waues of woe, wherein my ship is toste.
Haue broke the banks, where lay my life so deere.
Chippes of ill chance, are fallen amidst my choise,
To marre the minde that ment for to reioyce.

"I call him not a full Allegorie, but mixt, bicause he discouers withall what the *cloud, storme, waue,* and the rest are, which in a full allegorie should not be discouered, but left at large to the readers iudgement and coniecture." (*The Arte of English Poesie*, ed. G. D. Willcock and A. Walker, Cambridge, 1936, p. 188.)

brothers into one word that might suggest their meaning. Such a word is the Greek *téleios*—perfect. Thus the title would run "Cambell and the Perfect World," which is consonant with the action of a story devoted to the miracle of perfect amity and concord achieved between enemies. The legend of Cambell and Telamond is in one allegorical sense a metaphysics of friendship and in another the symbolic statement of the metaphysics of *discordia concors,* as interpreted by Christian philosophers of the Middle Ages and the Renaissance. To see how Spenser's myth exemplifies the emergence of order from chaos and of friendship from enmity let us examine the action of the narrative, keeping in mind the kind of analysis that Harington gave to the Perseus myth.

At the beginning of the narrative Cambell sends out his challenge to those who desire his sister. We do not need to know what they represent specifically; he is a brave and temperate knight; she is a learned and chaste lady and a much sought prize. The challenge is accepted by the three brothers, who we learn have a strange fate. At this point it will be useful to recall two popular Renaissance symbols: (1) an emblem from Alciati, and (2) the nature of Demogorgon as popularized by Boccaccio.

(1) Spenser devotes three stanzas to the description of the three brothers, in each of which he emphasizes their triune nature. In 2.41 he explicitly states that they were "All three as one." Stanza 42 recapitulates this statement in an elaborate rhetorical pattern of repetition and inversion. The third stanza elaborates the initial statement:

> These three did loue each other dearely well,
>   And with so firme affection were allyde,
>   As if but one soule in them all did dwell,
>   Which did her powre into three parts diuyde;

The fortieth emblem in the expanded version of Alciati is called "Concordia insuperabilis" and pictures a man with

INTRODUCTION

three heads, six arms, and six legs. The quatrain explains this grotesque by saying that such concord as well as piety and love existed among three brothers that they could not be overcome and that they held kingdoms under the one name of Geryon. Despite the facts that Spenser concludes his stanza with a different simile and that Geryon appears in a much different context in Book V, Spenser's and Alciati's brothers do benefit from comparison. The Paris 1584 edition of Alciati

Alciati, *Emblemata*, Paris, 1608, sig. Qiiij.

comments: "De cecy nous apprenons que ceux qui sont de bon accord & vnanimes, se rendent inuincibles: lesquels estans separez & en discord, ou qui ne se veulent entendre ensemblément, se rendent du tout debiles, & aisez à surmounter."[14] This elaborate development of the essential unity of the brothers not only explains the relationship of the three worlds they represent, but it also heightens the dramatic impact of the story by suggesting their invincibility.

(2) Boccaccio follows the authority of the mysterious Theodontius in making Demogorgon "summum primumque

[14] Andrea Alciati, *Emblemata*, Paris, 1584, sig. G12ᵛ. See also Collucio Salutati, *De Laboribus Herculis*, ed. B. L. Ullman, 2 vols., Zurich, n.d., vol. 2, p. 378.

deorum gentilium," presumably a corruption of Plato's Demiurge. He is coeternal with Eternity and Chaos and the father of an innumerable brood including Discord, Pan, and the Fates. According to Boccaccio his name is Demogorgon in Greek and god of the earth in Latin: "For *demon* means god, as Leontius says, and *Gorgon* means earth. Or rather wisdom of the earth, since often *demon* means knowing or wisdom. Or, more pleasing to others, the terrible god, because it is written of the true God Who dwells in heaven: Holy and terrible is His name."[15] Thus two radically different interpretations could be given to the figure of Demogorgon: he could be (a) a variant on the name of Plato's Demiurge, that dark and mysterious creator of the universe and by analogy a name for the Christian God in His role as creator, or (b) an equally dark, mysterious, and idolatrous perverter of true worship, invoked by Faustus.[16] The latter interpretation is used by Spenser when Archimago invokes the spirits from hell (1.1.37).[17] Agape's trip to the Fates in the deep abyss of Demogorgon partakes of the hellish mystery and dread of this figure without being idolatrous blasphemy. It is rather an attempt on Spenser's part to foster an awed respect for those dark forces that constitute the material

[15] Boccaccio, *Genealogie*, vol. 1, pp. 14, 15 (Book 1, Prohemium). "Sonat igitur, ut reor, Demogorgon grece, terre deus latine. Nam demon deus, ut ait Leontius, Gorgon autem terra interpretatur. Seu potius sapientia terre, cum sepe demon sciens vel sapientia exponatur. Seu, ut magis placet aliis, deus terribilis, quod de vero Deo qui in celis habitat legitur: Sanctum et terribile nomen eius."

[16] The invocation to Demogorgon in act 1, scene 3, of Marlowe's *Dr. Faustus* probably is due to a comparable invocation in the *Thebaid* of Statius (4.512ff) in which Tiresias is too terrified to cry out the name of Demogorgon. Boccaccio quotes this passage. The most familiar parallel to this understanding of the heathen gods is the catalogue in *Paradise Lost*, I. 356ff.

[17] Spenser demonstrates his mythical eclecticism here because in 1.5.22 Duessa invokes Night as "most auncient Grandmother of all,/ More old than *Ioue*, whom thou at first didst breede,/ Or that great house of Gods celestiall,/ Which was begot in *Daemogorgons* hall. . . ." See Maurice Castelain, "Demogorgon ou le barbarisme déifié," *Bulletin de l'association Guillaume Budé*, 36 (July 1932), pp. 22-39.

INTRODUCTION

source of our being. Anything more than this would involve us in heresies too obvious to be endured.

The same may be said of the conception of Agape's sons. If we even begin to speculate on what the "noble youthly knight" represents or why Agape should be combing her golden locks by a crystal stream, we are not reading allegorically, and it is very possible that we are not even reading poetically. The extraordinary loveliness of the few stanzas describing the incident preserves the decorum of nymphs being taken by handsome young men and at the same time reinforces the basic theme of the episode as a whole. He "oppressed" her, and from the conflict of the oppression come "these louely babes, that prou'd three champions bold." If a poet chooses to write about the ineffable mysteries of universal creation, the figures in his myth had better be able to sustain themselves without the puppet-string of one-for-one equivalents, for there are none.

Agape's trip to the Fates belongs to the same world of romance as her conception. Part of the pleasure of this incident comes from the very fact that Spenser chooses a vehicle that reduces the scope of the tenor. The charming incongruity of the lovely nymph seeking out the ominous Fates for love of her children images the loving care of Agape in all its meanings, and her amazement at the shortness of the threads of their lives is a figure for the grief felt by all fathers and mothers at the discrepancy between the desired achievements of their creations and the actuality. Her humble yet shrewd petition to the three Fates assures her an ultimate victory over the forces of chaos and disorder. It begs for life in another form, and for more than this no Christian reader would inquire. The double vision of this enigmatic petition echoes the double vision of Spenser's "mixed allegory" without transgressing the limits of either tenor or vehicle. In view of the essential unity of the three brothers already stated in the poem Spenser probably knew that Agape might be comforted by the fact that the created universe "we may also call [One,] (sic) not onely because the three worlds doe proceede of one onely and selfe cause, and tend to the like end; or else because being duly tempered by numbers, they are ioyned together by an harmonious accord and affinity of nature, and by ordinary succession of degrees: but also because that that which is in all the three is likewise comprised in one of them, and that there is not one wherein all things, which are in the other three, do not remaine."[18] Thus Agape can leave the house of the Fates, as Spenser tells us, "with full contented mynd."

The third canto begins with two stanzas of Spenserian irony on the question: "O why doe wretched men so much desire, To draw their dayes vnto the vtmost date...?" The answer is implicit in the irony of the second stanza:

> Therefore this Fay I hold but fond and vaine,
>   The which in seeking for her children three
> Long life, thereby did more prolong their paine.
> Yet whilest they liued none did euer see
> More happie creatures, then they seem'd to bee,
> Nor more ennobled for their courtesie,
> That made them dearely lou'd of each degree;
> Ne more renowmed for their cheualrie,
> That made them dreaded much of all men farre and nie.
>
> (4.3.2)

The fond vanity of Agape finds ample compensation in the lives of her sons; the general misery of most lives is contradicted by the nobility and courtesy of the three brothers. The ironic apology is necessary because of Spenser's myth. By explicitly identifying his nymph with the concept she represents Spenser places a double burden on his myth, which he eases by ironies such as these stanzas and the fact that

---

[18] Pierre de la Primaudaye, *The French Academie*, p. 671. Also found in Pico, *Heptaplus*, loc. cit.

INTRODUCTION

after the initial act of naming Agape he always refers to her merely as "Fay."

The past history of his heroes explained, Spenser can give his full attention to the battle for Canacee, which is the most bloody in the poem, no doubt to suit the occasion, "the dreddest day that liuing wight Did euer see vpon this world to shine. . . ." The battle is meant to be exciting, and accordingly Spenser varies the description of each succeeding joust with epic similes and with ever increasingly hideous wounds. The air of unreality is maintained by the magical powers of Canacee's ring to restore Cambell and by the mysterious process of traduction that translates the soul of one brother into the next. This process requires some comment since its physiology is more complicated than the physiological architecture of Alma's castle. Priamond is struck such a blow that "His weasand pipe it through his gorget cleft," and his soul enters Diamond, "In whom he liu'd a new, of former life depriued" (4.3.12-13). Diamond is beheaded, and the spectators are amazed to see his trunk still standing. Except for the fact that his body had been dismembered his soul would have remained. As it is, the soul enters Triamond, filling him with "double life." The phrase is ambiguous, but from later events we must assume that the "double" refers to the dual soul of Priamond and Diamond, and thus Triamond's life is trebled. Two of these souls are lost in the ensuing joust, and the third is saved by the sudden appearance of Cambina.

It should be mentioned at this point that I am entirely conscious of the fact that we have not determined a single allegorical meaning for any event in the narrative so far. This is as it should be. The appearance and description of Cambina is the culmination of these most obscure battles, and although we may have inklings of what this or that detail means, we (and therefore the allegory) will be better served if we defer to the poet's story and wait until his meaning is fully declared in the figure of Cambina. She is not so much a character as an aggregate of iconographical details, all of which have long histories that enrich and consolidate the larger issues that Spenser's narrative is meant to suggest. Spenser's description of her and her chariot contrasts with the painter's use of iconographical details. A picture makes an immediate total impression, after which the viewer may pick out various attributes and (if he is lucky) may see how and why they relate to the central image. The verbal description can give no immediate total impression; it is a linear progression of details. The process is additive rather than total, and the difference between the two media will be apparent to those who have turned from the immediate impact of one of Ripa's images to his verbal description. The difference is primary and intellectual and should be observed whenever one is tempted to extol Spenser's pictorialism.[19] A picture is no doubt worth a thousand words—but only to the trained observer. The poet can bring into his conception of any figure any number of details that enrich his presentation but would obscure a picture.

So it is with Cambina. She arrives in a chariot drawn by two lions. In her right hand she holds a caduceus, and in her left a cup. So much the artist could give, and we would know (if we were trained to read the figure correctly) that this female figure was meant to represent Concord or Peace. Spenser's verbal description can go deeper.

The relation of the lions to Cambina recapitulates the basic theme of *discordia concors*. Through the power of Cambina these two most wild beasts of the wood have been made to "forget their former cruell mood" and call to mind the figures of Love and Hate held together by Concord at the entrance to the Temple of Venus in canto 10. It is obvious that these animals by their very presence in the narrative add to the air of wonder and mystery, but they also relate this

[19] A brilliant discussion of this problem may be found in Paul Alpers, "Narrative and Rhetoric in the *Faerie Queene*," SEL, 2 (1962), pp. 36, 41-42.

INTRODUCTION

Alciati, *Emblemata*, Augsburg, 1531, sig. A4ᵛ.

wondrous chariot to others of more venerable history. Alciati has an interesting emblem, entitled "Potentissimus affectus amor," which pictures a blind Cupid riding in a chariot drawn by two lions, to show that Love does indeed conquer all. The chariot of Cybele, Magna Mater, goddess of civilization, is drawn by two lions, who (we are told) are the transformed Atalanta and Hippomenes.[20] The three sets of lions exemplify

Alciati, *Emblemata*, Padua, 1661, sig. Ee5.

[20] The lions are mentioned in Ovid, *Fasti*, 4.215-218; Lucretius, *De rerum natura*, 2.600ff., Vincenzo Cartari, *Imagines Deorum*, Lyons, 1581,

24

Cartari, *Le Imagini* . . . , Venice, 1592, sig. X3^v.

an initial discord overcome by the figure whose chariot they draw. The relationship among the three is not that of source or of parallel. The fact that Alciati did invent his emblem and that Cybele's chariot is traditionally drawn by lions allows Spenser to use his lions to point us toward a context in which his Cambina benefits from our recollection of these other figures without any kind of explicit identification. She is not Love, and she is not Nature, but her function in the poem is amplified if we have these other figures in mind.

The lion-drawn chariot simply sets the stage for the other two attributes. The caduceus Spenser explicitly identifies as "the rod of peace." The entwined serpents, as Lotspeich points out, are suitably allegorized by Natalis Comes as *"concordiae securitatem."*[21] The cup is filled with nepenthe, "A drinck of souerayne grace," which has a history extending back to Homer.[22] In the fourth book of *The Odyssey* Helen gives nepenthe mixed with wine to drown cares and anger. Chapman refers to "Sacred Nepenthe, purgatiue of care." This is the usual way of treating the drink, but Spenser goes beyond this tropological sense:

> Few men, but such as sober are and sage,
> Are by the Gods to drinck thereof assynd;
> But such as drinck, eternall happinesse do fynd.
>
> (4.3.43)

Christian meanings begin to infiltrate this apparently pagan drug, especially when Spenser ends his description with an allusion to a similar magic potion in Ariosto:

---

see "Magna mater"; Cesare Ripa, *Iconologia*, Rome, 1603, see "carro della Terra." The story that the lions are the transformed Atalanta and Hippomenes is found in Ovid, *Metamorphoses*, 10.681-707. All these commentators emphasize the initial discord of the beasts overcome by the power of Cybele.

[21] H. G. Lotspeich, *Classical Mythology in the Poetry of Edmund Spenser*, Princeton, 1932, p. 44. See also Abraham Fraunce, *The third part of the Countess of Pembrokes Yuychurch*, London, 1592, sig. K4.

[22] Homer, *Odyssey*, 4.219-225; Milton, *Comus*, 675ff.; Chapman, *Ovid's Banquet of Sense*, stanza 10, line 1.

> Much more of price and of more gratious powre
> Is this, then that same water of Ardenne,
> The which *Rinaldo* drunck in happie howre,
> Described by that famous Tuscane penne:
> For that had might to change the hearts of men
> Fro loue to hate, a change of euill choise:
> But this doth hatred make in loue to brenne,
> And heauy heart with comfort doth reioyce.
>
> (4.3.45)

Once more Spenser overgoes Ariosto in turning a magic potion from merely tropological to metaphysical ends. Spenser's nepenthe drives deeper into the essential nature of man.

Cambina's attributes are the handles by which we catch her meaning, and if we now proceed to call her Concord, we do not mean to specify an abstraction. Just as the figure of the statue of Liberty calls forth all that we know and mean and feel by saying "American," so Cambina figures forth all the associated meanings of Cybele and Love driving their lions, of Mercury taming the "hellish fiends" with his caduceus, of Helen's and Ariosto's magic potions to purge care. She means the bond of friendship wrought from discord. She means the universal bond of harmony that sustained the world in which Spenser lived. She means the metaphysical mystery of love evolved from hate, and many other related concepts that we need not name because she contains them all in the essence of her being. The relationship of mother and daughter established in the poem between Agape and Cambina (4.3.40) suggests the deeper metaphysical grounds of her being. She is not to be understood merely tropologically. She is basically an abstraction, but we should remember that to name a *quidditas* was and is a more real activity of the human mind than to recreate a particular embodiment by enumerating particulars. Much of the work of modern criticism has been the naming of the essential quality of particularized beings in literature. We call it practical criticism; Spenser was writing practical poetry.

To complete his description of Cambina Spenser calls these attributes into action. The exhausted warriors, touched with the caduceus, spring back to life and drink from the offered cup of nepenthe.

> Of which so soone as they once tasted had,
> Wonder it is that sudden change to see:
> Instead of strokes, each other kissed glad,
> And louely haulst from feare of treason free,
> And plighted hands for euer friends to be   (4.3.49)

Alciati, *Emblemata*, Paris, 1584, sig. G10ᵛ.

The reconciliation is almost anticlimactic, but if we refer once more to Alciati, we shall see that Spenser is simply adding another emblem of his basic theme. Emblem XXXIX pictures two warriors shaking hands, and the title is appropriately "Concordia." One might also refer to the emblems called "fictus amicus" and "verus amicus."

The episode is simply an allegory of concord, but we should remember when we name the meaning of the episode that

FAERYLAND AS FICTION

Sambucus, *Emblemata*, Antwerp, 1564, sig. N3ᵛ.

it has taken all our literary skill and tact to discover Spenser's meaning, and that in naming the quality that Spenser is exemplifying we are not forgetting the means by which Spenser led us to his meaning. At this point we can once more enter the main stream of the narrative, knowing that we have been lulled into a knowledge and new awareness of the forces that will eventually triumph in Spenser's book of

Sambucus, *Emblemata*, Antwerp, 1564, sig. A8ᵛ.

friendship. "Allegory is a method of reading in which we are made to think about things we already know."[23] This is a more positive way of speaking about abstractions in our older literature.

We may now attempt to specify allegorical meanings for the various incidents in these cantos, but we shall still find that the essential toughness of the narrative will not allow us to make easy leaps between tenor and vehicle. Let us postulate that Cambell is man and that his name represents the warring elements of *bellum intestinum* and that Canacee represents those human elements that sustain man in his battle against himself and the world, whether we call this mind or soul or reason. The magic ring then would become the sustaining link between the two. Cambell's battle with the three brothers figures man's battle with the three worlds to find his place in the universe, to establish harmony in God's creation, and ultimately to achieve salvation.

But since in any metaphysics regulated by analogy and mathematical proportions, any triad may be the analogue of another, the three brothers could become the three worlds of man's soul, in which the defeat of Priamond and Diamond figure the defeat of the vegetative and sensitive souls and the eventual harmony of man with the angelic mind. (This would account for the death of the two brothers, which cannot be understood if we accept them merely as the three worlds.) Already we are getting far from Spenser's myth and the basic generosity of charity that urges one brother without his knowledge to give his life to another, but from our more simple tropological apprehension of Spenser's exemplum, we can begin to understand the difficulty and necessity of seeing this story as a "likely tale" of the workings of that mysterious process that brings concord out of discord.

My explication of the allegory in this episode is not meant

[23] Rosemond Tuve in the Christian Gauss Seminar, Princeton University, May 1959.

to be conclusive; indeed, *no explication can be conclusive* owing to the very nature of allegory. We began this examination of allegorical reading by suggesting that the entire narrative of an allegorical poem is the vehicle of a continued metaphor and that the tenor may be any concept or object outside the poem that conforms to the pattern or patterns inherent in the narrative. Such a definition of allegory extends the commonly accepted meaning of the term. We cannot restrict ourselves to a sterile hunt for one-for-one relationships. There is no single meaning, at least no single meaning to be stated apart from the experience of the poem. The heresy of paraphrase applies as much to allegory as to other forms of poetic expression. Nor should we complain about the blurring of large concepts. Allegory, as I read it, is not trying to present clear and distinct speculations about philosophical niceties. There is no single object to receive the entire energy of the vehicle; there are always complexes of large and simple ideas, which are illuminated and realigned. These allegorical meanings, when explicitly stated by critics, become a part of the history of the poem in the same way that the allegorical accretions to the Song of Songs belong to that poem. Allegorical poetry is in the best tradition of meditative poetry and finds its source in Biblical exegesis and its latest manifestation in Hopkins' theory of inscape and instress. We may learn from this comparison that the images of allegorical poetry are inexhaustible both in themselves and in the fact that the poet has received these images as a rich and varied vocabulary with a long and venerable history. The rest of this book will attempt to show the coherence of the narrative and images in the middle books of *The Faerie Queene* by examining this inherited vocabulary.

ii · THE NATURE OF FAERYLAND

At this point it may be useful to suggest the direction that this book is taking. Many readers may feel that the minute

INTRODUCTION

details I have suggested about reading the allegory are unnecessary. I have included them because it seems to me that the recent books and articles about Spenser do not share my view of the relation of narrative to allegory, and I would as soon have no reader be startled in the middle of the book with the realization that we have actually been travelling different routes through the poem. The problem of reading Spenser, however, is not the only difficulty besetting the critic who attempts to explicate separate books of the poem.

Each book of the poem has a life of its own, but it is also part of the total design of the poem as we have it today. Uniting all the books of the poem is a design, not previously noted, that provides the best introduction to a study of Books III and IV. It is all the more important because the major exposition of this design occurs not in Books III or IV but in Book II, where the major metaphor of the poem—Faeryland—is explained. With the major metaphor of the poem in mind the reader will be better able to decide about the value of my explication of individual episodes of Books III and IV.

The Faerie Queene is different from all other epics in that it exists in a world entirely of Spenser's creation. Homer, Virgil, Ariosto, and Tasso, whether they wrote of the mythical or historical past, "set" their epics in a known world, at least a world with recognizable dimensions and locations. When Ariosto sends Astolfo into the empyrean, or Virgil send Aeneas to the underworld, the reader remains secure in the knowledge that they will return. One may think of the worlds of Dante and Milton, but in this respect they have given but local habitation to names thoroughly familiar as Christian symbol. Nor can we say that Spenser's world is merely derived from the land of romance adventures, for the writer of romance is not concerned to maintain a complex relationship between the historical or geographical locale he may have chosen and the locale where his marvellous adventures occur. Spenser is concerned with just such a relationship. The degree of complexity is well illustrated by two brilliant passages from Coleridge:

"You will take especial note of the marvellous independence and true imaginative absence of all particular space or time in the Faery Queene. It is in the domains neither of history or geography; it is ignorant of all artificial boundary, all material obstacles; it is truly in land of Faery, that is, of mental space."[24]

In this land of "mental space" one senses an encompassing awareness that our daily experience has taken on the condition of dream or nightmare as we are impelled through adventure after adventure, intimate yet remote. But Coleridge continues in what seems to be a complete reversal of his position:

"In Spenser we see the brightest and purest form of that nationality which was so common a characteristic of our elder poets. . . . There is a great magic in national names. . . . No one of our poets has touched this string more exquisitely than Spenser; especially in his chronicle of the British Kings (B. II, c. 10), and the marriage of the Thames with the Medway (B. IV, c. 11), in both which passages the mere names constitute half the pleasure we receive."[25]

In reading Spenser one feels no sudden jarring shift from the land of "mental space" back to the real world of history and geography, from the green world of Faeryland to the red and white world of Tudor history; on the contrary one senses what C. S. Lewis has called "the seamless continuity of the whole."[26] So unobtrusively has the real world entered the world of Spenser's creation that the two are in danger of

[24] S. T. Coleridge, *Miscellaneous Criticism*, ed. T. M. Raysor, London, 1936, p. 36.
[25] *Ibid.*, pp. 37-38.
[26] Northrop Frye, *Anatomy of Criticism*, Princeton, 1957, p. 144.

INTRODUCTION

being confused, yet Faeryland is not merely a more remote dream version of England. The origins and destinies of both worlds are carefully distinguished in the poem.

The clearest exposition of the history of Faeryland occurs in Book II, canto 10, where Guyon and Arthur as their final illumination in the House of Alma read the history of their respective races, the chronicle of British kings and the "*Antiquitie* of *Faerie* lond." The history of Faeryland falls into three periods:

(1) the creation by Prometheus of Elfe and his finding Fay in the Garden of Adonis,

(2) the building of Cleopolis under the first seven emperors, followed by an interregnum of seven hundred princes,

(3) the reigns of Elficleos through Tanaquil, or Gloriana.

It is generally agreed that the third period is the Faeryland representation of the Tudor monarchy. About the first two periods there is general disagreement.[27] The usual assumption is that Elfe is the Faery equivalent of Adam and that the history of Faeryland runs parallel to the history of Britain. Hence Cleopolis must be just another name for London. Once this substitution is made, the Elfin chronicle becomes another version of the chronicle of British kings, translated and abridged; and the critical problem is to identify as many of the Elfin emperors as possible. But why should Spenser duplicate this material? And if he is duplicating, how does Faeryland differ from England?

Despite the clear parallel to the Genesis story Spenser's stanzas about the Promethean creation belong to another intellectual tradition. The Elfin chronicle relates

    how first *Prometheus* did create
 A man, of many partes from beasts deriued,

---

[27] See Isabel E. Rathborne, *The Meaning of Spenser's Fairyland*, New York, 1937, pp. 66ff. and *TLS*, 1948, 7 Feb., p. 79; 24 April, p. 233; 15 May, p. 275; 26 June, p. 359; 3 July, p. 373.

And then stole fire from heauen, to animate
His worke, for which he was by *Ioue* depriued
Of life him selfe, and hart-strings of an Ægle riued.

That man so made, he called *Elfe*, to weet
Quick, the first authour of all Elfin kind:
Who wandring through the world with wearie feet,
Did in the gardins of *Adonis* find
A goodly creature, whom he deemd in mind
To be no earthly wight, but either Spright,
Or Angell, th'authour of all woman kind;
Therefore a *Fay* he her according hight,
Of whom all *Faeryes* spring, and fetch their lignage right.
(2.10.70-71)

The stanzas, with their continual emphasis of run-on lines, reflect the importance of this creation, but the creation and animation of Elfe and the punishment of Prometheus are subordinated to the full stanza devoted to the wanderings of Elfe and the discovery of his Eve, who seems to have had no part in the Promethean creation. Elfe's inspiration at the sight of this woman recalls Arthur's vision of the Faery Queen. In fact, this stanza can be taken as an adumbration of Arthur's search for Gloriana and of the glory he will attain when his quest is completed.

Spenser's stanzas, I believe, are intended to refer to a late medieval tradition that interprets the Promethean creation as the beginning of human civilization.[28] The earliest reference to this tradition is apparently Petrus Comestor's statement that Prometheus "de rudibus doctos fecit." The idea is elaborated by Boccaccio in the *Genealogie*. Just as there is a natural man and a civil man, both inspired with a rational soul, so there are two Prometheuses. The first is God, Who

---

[28] Olga Raggio, "The Myth of Prometheus: Its survival and metamorphoses up to the eighteenth century," *JWCI*, 21(1958), pp. 44-62. I am indebted throughout my discussion of Prometheus to this excellent article.

made man from the slime of the earth. The second is the "doctus homo," who created natural man anew. "That which was made by nature both rude and ignorant was made civil, outstanding in the virtues and in the ways of knowledge so that it is patently obvious that nature produced the one and doctrine reformed the other."[29] There is a nice propriety in having the highest reaches of the House of Alma contain the history of the second creation, besieged as the House is by Maleger, the forces of corruption in natural man.

This idea of a second creation, a creation that leads men to a society centered around "the city," is elaborated in the stanzas immediately following the creation of Elfe. Four of the seven emperors are identified solely in terms of their contributions to the creation of Cleopolis.

> Of these a mightie people shortly grew,
>   And puissaunt kings, which all the world warrayd,
>   And to them selues all Nations did subdew:

---

[29] "Est enim homo naturalis, et est homo civilis, ambo tamen anima rationali viventes. Naturalis autem homo primus a deo ex limo terre creatus est, de quo et Ovidius et Claudianus intelligunt, esto non adeo religiose, ut christiani faciunt; et cum ex luto illum Prometheus iste primus formasset, insufflavit in eum animam viventem, quam ego rationalem intelligo, et cum hac sensitivam et vegetativam potentias, seu secundum quosdam animas; verum he naturam habuere corpoream, et nisi peccasset homo, fuissent eterne, sicuti et rationalis est, cui divina natura est. Hunc perfectum fuisse hominem circa quoscunque actus terreos credendum est; nec opinari debet quisquam opportunum illi fuisse ad eruditionem temporalium rerum Prometheum aliquem mortalem; verum qui a natura producta sunt, rudes et ignari veniunt, imo ni instruantur, lutei agrestes et belue. Circa quos secundus Prometheus insurgit, id est doctus homo, et eos tanquam lapideos suscipiens quasi de novo creet, docet et instruit, et demonstrationibus suis ex naturalibus hominibus civiles facit, moribus scientia et virtutibus insignes, adeo ut liquido pateat alios produxisse naturam, et alios reformasse doctrinam." *Genealogie*, ed. Romano, vol. 1, pp. 198-199. The distinction between the natural and the civil man is also related to the Prometheus myth by Charles de Bouelles, *Liber de Sapiente*, ed. R. Klibansky in Ernst Cassirer, *Individuum und Kosmos*, Leipzig, 1927, p. 320. Dr. Raggio remarks: "The idea of the *sapiens Prometheus* is found over and over again in the writers influenced by the Florentine Neoplatonists." *op. cit.*, p. 55.

> The first and eldest, which that scepter swayd,
> Was *Elfin*; him all *India* obayd,
> And all that now *America* men call:
> Next him was noble *Elfinan*, who layd
> *Cleopolis* foundation first of all:
> But *Elfiline* enclosd it with a golden wall.
>
> His sonne was *Elfinell*, who ouercame
> The wicked *Gobbelines* in bloudy field:
> But *Elfant* was of most renowmed fame,
> Who all of Christall did *Panthea* build:
> Then *Elfar*, who two brethren gyants kild,
> The one of which had two heads, th'other three:
> Then *Elfinor*, who was in Magick skild;
> He built by art vpon the glassy See
> A bridge of bras, whose sound heauens thunder seem'd
>   to bee.   (2.10.72-73)

The reigns of the first seven emperors as Spenser describes them are really the evolution of Cleopolis. If we regard Cleopolis as the ideal of "the city," and not simply as London, we shall see that it is the archetype of all cities, of Troy and Rome and London. The early history of Cleopolis is the story of every civilization, of man establishing himself in society. This history of Faeryland has caused difficulty for critics mainly because they want to make particular identifications of the Elfin emperors, and thus miss the main point. Elfinan, who laid the foundations, is Tros and Aeneas and Brutus and any other founder of a nation. Elfant is Romulus as well as Lud. These mythical rulers are particular embodiments of Spenser's archetypal Faery mythology. The details of the Elfin chronicle are confusing precisely because they were meant to convey the general idea of the evolution of "the city."[30]

---

[30] If Spenser had not known the economy of an audience that read allegorically, this brilliant cluster of meanings would have been impossible.

INTRODUCTION

This view of Cleopolis is supported by Spenser's strange description of the interregnum following the first seven emperors.

> He [Elfinor] left three sonnes, the which in order raynd,
> And all their Ofspring, in their dew descents,
> Euen seuen hundred Princes, which maintaynd
> With mightie deedes their sundry gouernments;
> That were too long their infinite contents
> Here to record, ne much materiall:
> Yet should they be most famous moniments,
> And braue ensample, both of martiall,
> And ciuill rule to kings and states imperiall. (2.10.74)

They present "ne much materiall" because the evolution of the ideal city was complete before their reigns. They are "most famous moniments, And braue ensample, both of martiall, And ciuill rule to kings and states imperiall," because they have attained in "their sundry gouernments" the ideal state of Cleopolis and are thus its true offspring, but the achievement of their civilizations did not surpass the originals on which they modelled themselves.

This brings up the problem of the inclusion of the Tudors. Faeryland has the permanence of the Platonic Idea world, as Josephine Waters Bennett has suggested, in that the highest ideal of civil life will always stand as an ideal for later civilizations.[31] Troy was such an ideal for Rome, and both are the ideal of London. But there is always the possibility of greater achievement. The ideal world of Faeryland, symbolized by Cleopolis, contains within it the seeds of unfulfilled potentiality. Faeryland is an expanding ideal, and thus the achievement of the Tudors, rightly or wrongly, represents for Spenser an expansion of the ideal of civil life.

The ideal of the civil life, as opposed to the ideal of the

---

[31] Josephine Waters Bennett, "Britain among the Fortunate Isles," *SP*, 53 (1956), p. 136.

contemplative life, is part of a shift in emphasis of the late Middle Ages and Renaissance, to which we can connect Spenser through Lodowick Bryskett's *A discourse of civill life*. Spenser as one of the dialoguists declines the honor of discoursing on the "Ethicke part of Morall Philosophie":

"For sure I am, that it is not vnknowne vnto you, that I haue already vndertaken a work tēding to the same effect, which is in *heroical verse*, vnder the title of a *Faerie Queene*, to represent all the moral vertues, assigning to euery vertue, a Knight to be the patron and defender of the same: in whose actions and feates of armes and chiualry, the operations of that vertue, whereof he is the protector, are to be expressed, and the vices & vnruly appetites that oppose themselues against the same, to be beatē downe & ouercome. Which work, as I haue already well entred into, if God shall please to spare me life that I may finish it according to my mind, your wish (*M. Bryskett*) will be in some sort accomplished, though perhaps not so effectually as you could desire."[32]

As a substitute Spenser suggests that Bryskett read from his translation of Giraldi Cinthio's *Tre Dialoghi della vita ciuile* both to edify his company and to show that his retirement from active life had not withdrawn him "from seruice of the State, to liue idle or wholy priuate to himselfe...."[33] Bryskett's translation leaves no doubt that he is opposed to a cloistered virtue:

"The end of man in this life, is happinesse or felicitie: ... because all vertuous actions are directed thereunto, and because for it chiefly man laboureth and trauelleth in this world. But for that this felicitie is found to be of two kinds, wherof one is called ciuill, and the other contemplatiue: you shall

---

[32] Lodowick Bryskett, *A Discovrse of civill life*, London, 1606, sig. E^v-E2.
[33] *Ibid.*, sig. E2^v.

INTRODUCTION

vnderstand that the ciuill felicitie is nothing else then a perfect operation of the mind, proceeding of excellent vertue in a perfect life; and is atchieued by the temper of reason, ruling the disordinate affects stirred vp in vs by the vnreasonable parts of the mind . . . and guiding vs by the meane of vertue to happy life."[34]

Bryskett's civil felicity is not merely a personal virtue, for "by the study of Morall Philosophie . . . not onely particular persons might in this life attaine to liue happily, but also purchase the same happines to their families, yea to whole Cities and Commonwealths."[35] Virtuous actions directed toward the bettering of society had always been a great good, but with the growth of nationalism in the sixteenth century civil virtue became more and more important and tended to realign the composition of the older Augustinian dualism as shown in Tasso's allegorization of Jerusalem: "*Ierusalem* the strong citie placed in a rough and hilly countrey, whereunto as to the last ende, are directed all the enterprises of the faithfull armie, doth here signifie the *Ciuill happines*, which may come to a Christian man . . . which is a good, verie difficult to attaine vnto, and situated vpon the top of the Alpine and wearisome hill of virtue; and vnto this are turned (as vnto the last marke) all the Actions of the politicke man."[36]

The implications of Tasso's interpretation are astonishing in view of earlier medieval interpretations of Augustine's two

---

[34] *Ibid.*, sig. F4ᵛ.

[35] *Ibid.*, sig. D4. An interesting variation on this theme applicable to Spenser can be found in Robert Ashley, *Of Honour*, ed. Virgil B. Heltzel, San Marino, Cal., 1947, p. 35: "For how shold freindshipp be exercised, liberalitie, equitie, iustice, magnanimitie, decencie, modestie, and the rest of the vertues which are conversant in common societie, or do any way concerne yt, be practized and putt in vre yf you deale altogether inwardly with yourself and do not thincke that the goodnes of your mind ought to be brought to light?"

[36] Torquato Tasso, *Godfrey of Bulloigne, or The Recouerie of Ierusalem. Done into English Heroicall verse, by Edward Fairefax, Gent.*, London, 1600, sig. A3.

cities, Babylon and Jerusalem.[37] Man must make of his earthly sojourn either a Babylon or a Jerusalem, but except for the dream of the Holy Roman Empire few thinkers expected an actual earthly Jerusalem. Nor did the metaphorical implications of Augustine's dualism require a third term, but in the sixteenth century we find a third term that complements but does not contradict Augustine. In Tasso the physical city is equated with an earthly ideal. The same impulse can be seen in Calvin's attempt to establish an earthly Jerusalem in Geneva. In Spenser, in Bryskett, in Tasso, in Calvin, we find the city of man in distinction, but not opposed, to the earthly and the heavenly cities. Tasso felt no contradiction in adding this third city, for he ends his allegory: "But for

[37] Rathborne, *The Meaning of Spenser's Fairyland*, pp. 6-61. Professor Rathborne's pioneering work needs to be supplemented by a complete historical study of this subject. The early medieval view is stated by Augustine, *De Civitate Dei*, xv.2. See the discussions of the problem of the third city by H. I. Marrou, "Civitas Dei, civitas terrena: num tertium quid?" *Texte und Untersuchungen zur Geschicte der Altchristlichen Literatur*, 64 (1957), pp. 342-350; F. Edward Crantz, "De civitate Dei,' xv.2, and Augustine's Idea of the Christian Society," *Speculum*, 25 (1950), pp. 215-225; Theodor E. Mommsen, "St. Augustine and the Christian Idea of Progress: The Background of *The City of God*," *Medieval and Renaissance Studies*, ed. Eugene Rice, Ithaca, 1959, pp. 265-298.

The possibility of supplementing Augustine's original plan are contained in Augustine himself. Since the two cities are primarily states of mind, Augustine is neutral about the part that civil society plays in man's journey to salvation. See *De Civitate Dei*, xv.4: "But the temporal, earthly city (temporal, for when it is condemned to perpetual pains it shall be no more a city) has all the good here upon earth, and therein takes that joy that such an object can afford. But because *it is not a good* that acquits the possessors of all troubles, therefore this city is divided in itself into wars, altercations, and appetites of bloody and deadly victories. . . . It desires an earthly peace, for very low ambitions, and seeks it by war, where if it subdue all resistance, it attains peace. . . . This peace they seek by laborious war, and obtain (they think) by a glorious victory. And when they conquer that had the right cause, who will not congratulate their victory, and be glad of their peace? Doubtless those are good, and God's good gifts. But if the things appertaining to that celestial and supernal city where the victory shall be everlasting, be neglected for those goods, and those goods desired as the only goods, or loved as if they were better than the other, misery must needs follow and increase that which is inherent before." The translation is that of John Healey, first published in 1610.

that this *Politike blessednes*, ought not to be the last marke of a Christian man, but he ought to looke more high, that is, to *Euerlasting felicitie*, ... the *Vnderstanding* being trauelled and wearied in ciuill actions ought in the ende to rest in deuotion and in the contemplation of the eternall blessednes of the other most happie and immortall life."[38] This final affirmation of the Christian ideal is in no sense a denial of earthly glory. Tasso's Jerusalem, like Spenser's Cleopolis, falls under the shadow of inadequacy only when compared to the brightness of the heavenly city.

> Till now, said then the knight [Red Cross], I weened well,
> That great *Cleopolis*, where I haue beene,
> In which that fairest *Faerie Queene* doth dwell,
> The fairest Citie was, that might be seene;
> And that bright towre all built of christall cleene,
> *Panthea*, seemd the brightest thing, that was:
> But now by proofe all otherwise I weene;

---

[38] Tasso, sig. A4ᵛ. The full extent of this shift can be seen by comparing an early medieval writer like Boethius to the passages quoted above. In Book I, Prose 4, of the *De consolatione philosophiae* Dame Philosophy instructs Boethius in the doctrines of Plato but reprimands him for expecting a reward for his virtuous service to the state. The later writers emphasize the reward of honor and glory. The shift from the early medieval view to the Quattrocento view in Florence has been studied by Hans Baron, who shows that in writers like Coluccio Salutati a new ideal of civil life was emerging. See especially *The Crisis of the Early Italian Renaissance*, 2 vols., Princeton, 1955. The same shift is treated by Eugene Rice, *The Renaissance Idea of Wisdom*, Cambridge, Mass., 1958, chapter 2, pp. 30-57. The development of this shift in England has not been studied, but Lodowick Bryskett after the passage quoted remarks that he has been reading the same ideas in Alexander Piccolomini, Cinthio, and Guazzo. Piccolomini's *Della institutione di tutta la vita dell 'uomo nato nobile et in città libera* was published in 1542. Although Piccolomini is not mentioned, the political and intellectual background for his ideas is partially studied in Nicolai Rubinstein, "Political Ideas in Sienese Art: the Frescoes by Ambrogio Lorenzetti and Taddeo di Bartolo in the Palazzo Pubblico," *JWCI*, 21 (1958), pp. 179-207. Guazzo's *Civil Conversations* was translated by George Pettie in 1581.

For this great Citie that does far surpas,
And this bright Angels towre quite dims that towre
    of glas.

Most trew; then said the holy aged man;
    Yet is *Cleopolis* for earthly frame,
The fairest peece, that eye beholden can:
And well beseemes all knights of noble name,
That couet in th'immortall booke of fame
To be eternized, that same to haunt,
And doen their seruice to that soueraigne Dame,
That glorie does to them for guerdon graunt:
For she is heauenly borne, and heauen may justly
    vaunt.   (1.10.58-59)

Faeryland is the best that earth offers, but in the Christian view it is only midway to the heavenly city. Nevertheless they are validly distinct realms and in Spenser's time did not present contradictory views of man.

We are now in a position to see why Spenser has Arthur read a different history. His is the chronicle of British kings and follows the pattern established by the Tudor historians.[39] The civilization originally started by Samothes,

---

[39] The division of history into periods was apparently adopted from the six divisions of universal history popular in Biblical commentaries. The divisions are from Adam to Noah, from Noah to Abraham, from Abraham to David, from David to the Captivity, from the Captivity to the Incarnation, from the Incarnation to the Day of Judgment. See Rathborne, *op.cit.*, p. 74, and Arnold Williams, *The Common Expositor*, Chapel Hill, 1948, p. 140. The slight variations in the chronology of the chroniclers should not prevent our seeing that there was essential agreement about the periods of universal history and about the place that Britain occupied in this scheme. For example William Slatyer's poem *The history of Great Britanie from the first peopling of this iland to this presant raigne of o^r hapy and peacefull monarke K. James*, London, 1621, or as the running title reads *Palae-Albion*, consists of ten "Odes," each one representing one phase of British history: *Samothes, Albion, Gigantes, Brutus, Mulmutius, Caesar, Hengistus, Swanus, Gulielmus,* and *Jacobus*. See also Thomas Heywood, *The Life of Merlin, sirnamed Ambrosius . . .* , London, 1641. Holinshed combines the first three of Slatyer's periods into the first book of his chronicle; Fabyan devotes one chapter to this time before Brute,

INTRODUCTION

sixth son of Japhet, son of Noah, is supplanted by that of Albion, son of Neptune, and destroyed by the anarchy of the Giants. The arrival of Brute, grandson of Aeneas, and his defeat of the Giants is the proper beginning of British history, linking the Britons (or Brutans) to the tradition of Troy. The line of Brutus extends to the reign of Gorboduc or Gorbogud (as Spenser calls him) and his sons Ferrex and Porrex. The fifth period extends from the reign of Mulmutius Donwallo to the conquest of Julius Caesar. The Roman period lasts until the reign of Hengistus and the Saxon heptarchy, which is supplanted by Swanus and the Danes, who in turn are supplanted by the Norman invaders of William the Conqueror, until finally the true British stock regains the ascendancy in the person of Henry Tudor.

The minute particularization of the history and the vigorous sweep of its narrative should not blind the reader to Spenser's intention:

> There chaunced to the Princes hand to rize,
> An auncient booke, hight *Briton moniments*,
> That of this lands first conquest did deuize,
> And old diuision into Regiments,
> Till it reduced was to one mans gouernments.
>
> (2.9.59)

---

and Grafton ignores it completely. Both Holinshed and Fabyan begin new sections in their chronicles with the reign of Mulmutius, and Fabyan agrees with Slatyer in setting the commencement of the Roman period in the time of Cassibelane. Holinshed places this same division in the reign of Cymbeline, no doubt influenced by the fact that Christ was born during his reign. Grafton, following closely the outline of Biblical history, begins his Pars septima here. See dumbshow, Act 5, *Gorboduc*. Fabyan divides this Roman period in half, ending the first half with King Lucius, the first Christian king, and the uprising of Bonduca, and the second with the reign of Constantine II. Holinshed makes the reign of Constantine II the beginning of the Saxon period. Both Fabyan and Holinshed end divisions of their chronicles with the death of Cadwallader. The time from William onwards, and the periods into which it is divided, is of course dependent on the date of composition of any particular chronicle. For discussions of Spenser's use of this chronicle material see Carrie Anna Harper, *Sources*

44

The theme of this history is the division and unification of the British kingdom, the countless defeats by foreign peoples, the eventual enrichment of the original stock, and the flowering of this Providential evolution in the Tudor monarchy. What we and Arthur read is the Tudor view of history, the progress and triumph of British nationalism in the full heat and patriotism of the late sixteenth century.

The chronicle of British kings, read by Arthur, and the Elfin chronicle, read by Guyon, are juxtaposed as contrasting histories. The British chronicle emphasizes the temporal succession of kings, the diversity of nations that have been grafted onto the original stock, and the continual division and unification of the kingdom. The Elfin chronicle emphasizes the atemporal succession of a unified stock that has never known division. The first is a history of an individual nation within the Providential scheme of Christian history. The second is the expanding cycle of human glory. The history of the Christian is his journey from the earthly to the heavenly city. The history of the Christian nation is part of that universal history that moves from Fall to Redemption to Apocalypse. Within this Providential history, both on the individual and the national levels, is the history of human glory—fallen man transforming his life into virtuous action. Christian history is fixed within the limits of Fall and Apocalypse. Human glory is always increasing, pushing hard against the consequences of that First Sin. Those who have pushed hardest and become ideals are the stuff of which Faeryland is made. Insofar as they have become ideals, Faeryland is outside space. Insofar as they are not related in temporal sequence, it is outside time. Insofar as they are from every age and nation, it is non-Christian. Faeryland is the ideal world of the highest, most virtuous *human* achievements. Faeryland is like Augustine's City of God in that

---

of the British Chronicle History in Spenser's Faerie Queene, Bryn Mawr, 1910, pp. 179-180, and Harry Berger, *The Allegorical Temper*, New Haven, 1957, p. 92.

INTRODUCTION

it exists morally as a state of being in man and metaphorically as a fictional world. It can be attained as a state of mind but not as a human society because the time was and is not ripe.

Spenser's apparent confusion of Britain and Faeryland is in reality a careful poetic discrimination. The poem is a fulfillment of the ideal of civil life that is to occur historically during the reign of the Tudors. From the point of view of the narrative Elizabeth is only a descendant of Britomart, still far off in the future. From the point of view of the poet Elizabeth is the fulfillment of the prophecy in the chronicle of British kings. The action of the poem is the evolution of the civil ideal and is conceived as a reciprocal interchange between England and Faeryland.

Spenser's statement in the Letter to Ralegh supports this distinction: "*In that Faery Queene I meane glory in my generall intention, but in my particular I conceiue the most excellent and glorious person of our soueraine the Queene, and her kingdome in Faery land.*"[40] Gloriana is the personification of glory, the abstract concept. Elizabeth is an embodiment of glory. Their relation is not directly to each other but through the abstract concept of glory. To prove further that a univocal relation does not exist between Spenser's two queens we need only consider Belphoebe. She is an allegorical representation of Elizabeth's state of virginity—a quality not emphasized in Gloriana—and in the poem she also represents the concept of virginity. Belphoebe *is* virginity and Gloriana *is* glory, while Elizabeth is both *virgin* and *glorious*. Elizabeth is both more and less than either Belphoebe or Gloriana. With this distinction in mind we may say that Elizabeth is to the embodiment of glory in a person what Gloriana is to the abstract concept. Elizabeth embodies glory in the real world as Gloriana does in Faeryland, both representing an ideal in their respective worlds. To this extent Gloriana is the analogical equivalent of Elizabeth, a relation-

[40] *Var.* 1.168.

ship that dictates Spenser's manipulation of the time and action of the poem.

The time is during Uther's reign; the action is in Faeryland. Gloriana is the center of the narrative, the pattern of which is circular, issuing from and returning to the Faerie Queen. The main narrative was to have been Arthur's quest for Gloriana and their eventual union. But how was Spenser to develop this quest and at the same time illustrate the *"twelve priuate morall vertues, as Aristotle hath deuised, the which is the purpose of these first twelue bookes"*?[41] The answer is found in the idea of tasks imposed by Gloriana on the other knights. Red Cross must free Una's parents, Guyon must destroy the Bower of Bliss, Arthegall must free Irena, and Calidore must chain the Blatant Beast. This accounts for the narratives in all but Books III and IV, and in these books we are faced not with a task but with another quest—that of Britomart for Arthegall, a situation that exactly reverses Arthur's quest for Gloriana. The main narrative of Books III and IV is the only one in *The Faerie Queene* that is neither initiated by Gloriana nor has her as its goal.

The parallelism between Arthur and Britomart is not accidental, for Spenser has carefully worked it into the time scheme of the narrative. In the earlier part of this chapter I treated the chronicle of British kings as if it were a continuous history from the beginnings to the reign of Elizabeth. In fact, the later part of the history is not read by Arthur but given as a prophecy to Britomart by Merlin (3.3.25-50). These two historical passages really form one continuous history, but since the time of the action is Uther's reign, the chronicle read by Arthur breaks off:

> After him *Vther*, which *Pendragon* hight,
> Succeding There abruptly it did end,
> Without full point, or other Cesure right. . . .
>
> (2.10.68)

[41] *Var.* 1.167-168.

INTRODUCTION

The division of the history into chronicle and prophecy and the parallelism between Arthur and Britomart is determined by the plan of *The Faerie Queene* and Spenser's conception of Arthur's role.

One might expect the prophecy to begin with the reign of Arthur, but this is not the case. Instead we find Arthegall, while Arthur is omitted entirely from Spenser's history. The fact that Arthegall is mentioned in the Tudor chronicles and etymologically means "equal to Arthur" probably suggested to Spenser the possibility of substituting him for Arthur.[42] This substitution avoided the necessity of introducing the feats of the historical Arthur, which Spenser had carefully shunned in depicting his hero, and yet allowed him to continue his history without a break. Britomart and Arthegall replace Arthur in Spenser's history; together they fill the gap created by Spenser's plan for his poem. Historically this solution does least violence to the chronicle material, since Conan, the son of Britomart and Arthegall, takes the crown away from his cousin Constantius, Arthur's successor. Poetically it provides a reversal of the quest motif, the woman seeking the man, and thereby gives greater scope to the narrative.

The substitution of Britomart and Arthegall for Arthur

[42] Arthegall is the brother of Cador, son of Gorlois, and therefore the half-brother of Arthur. Dr. Harper comments, p. 144: "These three stanzas [3.3.26-28] make the transition from romance to chronicle material. . . . Arthegall . . . stands in the same relation to Cador that Arthur does both in Hardyng and in the *Brut Tysilio*. Arthegall, like Arthur, fights against the pagan and is 'Too rathe cut off by practise criminal/ Of secret foes.' After a fashion, then, Arthegall takes Arthur's place in the chronicle." Professor Rathborne objects to this "mystical identification" of Arthur and Arthegall and suggests that Spenser intended to make Arthegall Arthur's successor. This would account for the changes in the characters of Conan and Constantine in Spenser's chronicle. Since this suggestion depends on Spenser's plans for his second poem, of which we know nothing, it seems to me a needless hypothesis. Dr. Harper's idea stays within the facts of the present and has nothing at all to do with "mystical identification." Rathborne, pp. 226-229.

does more, however, for the ultimate plan of the poem. The line established by them will last until

> eternall vnion shall be made
> Betweene the nations different afore,
> And sacred Peace shall louingly perswade
> The warlike minds, to learne her goodly lore,
> And ciuile armes to exercise no more:
> Then shall a royall virgin raine, which shall
> Stretch her white rod ouer the *Belgicke* shore,
> And the great Castle smite so sore with all,
> That it shall make him shake, and shortly learne to fall.

But yet the end is not.   (3.3.49-50)

The implication of later successors makes it clear that Elizabeth is being regarded merely as a descendant of Britomart, since she can exist only as prophecy in the action of the poem. By his elliptical treatment of Arthur, Spenser is able to imply a relationship between the historical Arthur and Elizabeth that he could not convey if either were present in the action as historical personages. The Arthur of *The Faerie Queene* exists only in his quest for Gloriana. Elizabeth exists ony as prophecy and in the archetype of her glory, Gloriana. But at that point (unrealized) when Arthur finds Gloriana, England and Faeryland, Elizabeth and Gloriana, become one: Spenser's treatment of Arthur is really a vehicle to unite the ideal British king and queen. In this sense Arthur's quest in Faeryland is an expedient to recast history. The introduction and recasting of the historical material at these points in the narrative show Spenser the epic poet manipulating history and his created world so that the reader will make the proper correlations between his heroes and heroines of history and Faeryland, all subsumed in the triumph of the Tudor Apocalypse.

But Arthur's quest is also related to Gloriana's tasks imposed on the knights of individual books, and this relationship poses the question of the ultimate significance of the narrative pattern of Spenser's poem. Morally Arthur is the virtue of magnificence, "the perfection of all the rest," and his quest for Gloriana becomes the exemplar of the perfection of the individual virtues demonstrated in the completed tasks. The command of glory sends forth each virtue to be perfected and awaits its return, and with their return magnificence shall be one with glory. In a world where holiness and temperance, courtesy and justice, are triumphant, virtue and reward are commensurate.

Thus the main narrative suggests a complexity of correspondences similar to the ancient four senses of allegory. Literally the marriage of Arthur and Gloriana would have been the union of a prince with his loved one after a number of marvellous adventures. Allegorically, by which the Old Law was interpreted in the light of the New, the marriage becomes the fulfillment of the old order of British kings in the new Tudor monarchy. Tropologically, or morally, it means the union of virtue with glory, or for Spenser's purpose, the completion of the perfect gentleman. Anagogically it means Apocalypse. This is the point where the two chronicles would have merged, where the distinctions between England and Faeryland, between the real and the ideal, have no meaning. Apocalypse means completion, the stasis of the completed quest, the return to God. In this sense Arthur's marriage with Gloriana is the unification of England and Faeryland, of Elizabeth and Gloriana. But the Apocalypse is rarely reached in poetry, and the true Apocalypse will make poetry meaningless. We can only speculate on how Spenser would have completed his poem or whether he saw that no poet can survive the crisis of completion.

Chapter One
The Image of Britomart

My Dear One is mine as mirrors are lonely,
And the high green hill sits always by the sea.
—AUDEN

We cannot love your love till she take on
Through you, the wonders of a paragon.
Sing her triumphant passage to our land,
The sun her footstool, the moon in her right hand....
Sing her descent on the exulting shore
To bless the vines and put an end to war.
—AUDEN

THE image of Britomart, presented to us in the third and fourth books of *The Faerie Queene*, is a more dramatic characterization than any other in the poem. We see her puzzled and disturbed in the first throes of love and comforted by the protective antics of Glauce. The whole flashback of the inception of the love is treated with extraordinary delicacy and homeliness. Similarly we are always totally unprepared for Britomart to tease Amoret at the beginning of Book IV after the harrowing experience of Busyrane's castle, nor are we prepared for her almost girlish nervousness when she recognizes the subdued Arthegall. But these details are part of the image of chastity. In Britomart Spenser was able to make his allegorical method subsume the smaller, more human details of psychological realism. As the ancestress of Elizabeth she embodies the conflicting claims of idealism and reality that the Queen herself embodied for Spenser the courtier.

Despite these touches of realism Britomart is not more

"real" than the other characters in the poem. To treat Britomart as if she were a character in a drama or a novel is to deny the psychological validity of the allegorical method, and no patient reader of Spenser will allow this. In the literature of psychological realism—let us say a novel by Virginia Woolf or D. H. Lawrence—something more is gleaned from the details, some new insight into the subtle shifts of personality, some further evidence of the kind of person we are reading about. Conditioned as we are by the novel, we might expect Spenser's details to suggest some shift from the psychology of the virgin to the psychology of the wife. This Spenser does not give us, for it is not the way of allegory. Surface realism is no indication of the symbolic significance of character or action in *The Faerie Queene*. We learn as much about Britomart as we need to know, but we shall never know her so well as we do Mrs. Dalloway. In fact, Britomart is hardly a character in our modern sense of that word; she is an image that Spenser uses to lead us to an increased awareness of the concept of chastity. The development of her character is not "dramatic" or "novelistic"; it is thematic and allegorical.

Britomart is Spenser's allegorical representation of love directed by the virtue of chastity. The stages in her quest for Arthegall are marked by those who accompany her. She sets out with Glauce her nurse, the figure of protection in childhood, who accompanies her until her trial in the House of Busyrane. This is the end of her preparation, and Glauce must be left outside the wall of flame while Britomart endures alone the trial of perverted love. The original ending of Book III made Britomart merely the champion of married love; the second installment carries the quest to its fulfillment, in which chastity is not only the champion of married love but also becomes married love. Britomart's companion until her encounter with Arthegall is Amoret; her companion after this encounter is Scudamour. From the point of view of the action Amoret's disappearance before the encounter is annoying, but it does allow the thematic development of Britomart's character. It would be untrue to say that this encounter is the symbolic analogue of a consummated marriage, but it does exchange the shadow with which Britomart started for the reality that she sought. In this sense the shift from Amoret to Scudamour symbolizes what she has gained from her encounter with Arthegall, a new and more complete realization of that love which is the moving spirit of her quest. This is the kind of development that Spenser gives to his image of Britomart; we look in vain for evidence to show this development "within" the character itself.

In the Introduction I tried to show how the range of English history was focused through the image of Britomart. In this chapter we shall explore how the image of Britomart defines the concept of chastity and how it extends our knowledge of this concept through Britomart's adventures at Castle Joyous, at the House of Busyrane, and in her confrontation with Arthegall.

i · BRITOMART AS CHASTITY

Although Britomart's name clearly suggests her function as the warrior maiden of Britain, it even more precisely symbolizes her function as the knight of chastity. Merritt Y. Hughes has pointed out that the source of the name is Virgil's *Ciris* and that Spenser has emphasized his source by making the dialogue between Britomart and Glauce in Book III, canto 2, little more than a translation of a similar dialogue in Virgil's poem.[1]

The *Ciris* is a poem about the passion of Scylla, daughter of King Nisus, who betrays her father's kingdom to obtain the

---

[1] Merritt Y. Hughes, "Virgil and Spenser," *Univ. Cal. Pub. in English*, vol. 2, no. 3, 1929, pp. 348-354. The parallels are *FQ*, 3.2.30, ll. 220-228; *ibid.*, 32, ll. 232-235; *ibid.*, 34, ll. 250-252; *ibid.*, 35-36, ll. 257-262; *ibid.*, 40-41, ll. 237-249; *ibid.*, 47, ll. 251-252; *ibid.*, 48, ll. 349-354; *ibid.*, 50-51, ll. 369-376.

love of Minos his enemy. The portion that Spenser imitated is the long discussion between Scylla and her nurse Carme, who tries to help Scylla in her unfortunate love. Carme already knows the power of Minos, for to escape the love of Minos her own virgin daughter Britomartis fled into the sea, for which act of heroic virtue she was rescued and made a goddess by Diana.

> ut quid ego amens
> te erepta, o Britomarti, mei spes una sepulchri,
> te, Britomarti, diem potui producere vitae?
> atque utinam celeri nec tantum grata Dianae
> venatus esses virgo sectata virorum,
> Gnosia nec Partho contendens spicula cornu
> Dictaeas ageres ad gramina nota capellas![2]

Carme's lament is undoubtedly the source of Spenser's name, but he has transferred the name of the chaste daughter to the passionate foster-child of Carme. Britomart then has the name of a dedicated virgin and the passion of a love-sick maiden who brings destruction to herself and to her kingdom.

The fusion of the two young women in Spenser's image of Britomart is more appropriate than might at first sight appear. Britomartis resists love; Scylla yields. They represent the two extremes of dedicated virginity and lust, extremes that lead to a god-like transmutation or to a debasement of humanity, bringing with it political as well as personal ruin. Spenser, like Virgil, sees love as a force that can destroy nations as well as individuals, and as a result his Britomart shares qualities with both Britomartis and Scylla. Her chastity is derived from Britomartis, but it is a chastity that springs from a love as passionate as Scylla's. Spenser makes it quite

---

[2] "Why have I, frenzied one, when thou, Britomartis, thou Britomartis, the sole hope of my tombe, wert torn from me—why have I been able to prolong my day of life? And would that thou, maiden so dear to fleet Diana, hadst neither pursued, a maiden, the hunt that belongs to men, nor, aiming Gnosian shafts from Parthian bow, hadst driven the Dictaean goats to their familiar meadows!" Virgil, *Ciris*, ll. 294-300.

clear that this kind of love is the foundation of both political and personal integrity: "such loue not lyke to lusts of baser kynd,/ the harder wonne, the firmer will abide" (*Am.*, vi). The element of restraint is always evident in Spenser's examples of the proper use of love. In chaste love the strength of the passion is moderated by the virtue of the loved one.

> You frame my thoughts, and fashion me within,
> you stop my toung, and teach my hart to speake,
> you calme the storme that passion did begin,
> strong thrugh your cause, but by your vertue weak.
>
> (*Am.*, viii)

But even in chaste love there must be an eventual surrender. Amoret, though reluctant, does leave the Temple of Venus, and Britomart is finally won by Arthegall. To surrender one's self to love is either to lose one's integrity or to transmute it into a higher unity. The legend of Britomart is an exemplum of this transmutation, not in the manner of Britomartis, but in the "famous Progeny" of her union with Arthegall.

Spenser images the eternal battle of pleasure and virtue, fought anew in every love, in the traditional Petrarchan metaphor of love as war. The metaphor is so common that it has almost ceased to be metaphorical. We may be describing the psychomachia of pleasure and virtue, the winning of a rose, a Game of Chess, the Rape of a Lock, or the Battle of the Sexes, but somehow the imagination of Western civilization images the relation of man and woman in terms of a game, a chase, or a battle, and for good reason. How else are the two to become one? For Spenser, as for many Elizabethans, the metaphor is grounded in a metaphysics of creation. Out of the discord of chaos came the concord of creation, out of the discord of the Fall came the concord of the Redemption, out of the discord of man's disordered passions comes the concord of love and propagation. We have already seen that Spenser allegorizes the *discordia concors* of the world in the story of Cambell and Triamond, and we shall see that all the good loves of Books III and IV emerge from an initial conflict of man with woman, woman with man. With the love that moves the sun and stars as example Spenser cannot view chaste love in any other way.

The theme of *discordia concors* is everywhere implicit in the image of Britomart. We see the ambiguity in her name. We see it in the Saxon armor that clothes this British maiden. We see it in the fact that Spenser reverses all the details taken from Arthurian romance. We see it as the major narrative episode in the middle books, where the culmination of Britomart's quest leads her to battle with the man she loves. We see it in the imagery used consistently to describe her.

The metaphor of love as war emphasizes the duality of man and woman as it emphasizes the element of restraint in a chaste love affair, but Spenser's image of love is more elemental, more unified and bears with it the stamp of its divine origins. To complement the metaphor of love as war and to symbolize the singular power of chastity as a positive force Spenser uses the image of light breaking through an obscuring veil.[3] At every point in the poem where Britomart removes her armor the effect of her beauty and chastity on her companions is described in images that make her virtue apparent to the reader as a visible force. In Castle Joyous Britomart lifts only the visor of her helmet,

> And so did let her goodly visage to appere.
>
> As when faire *Cynthia,* in darkesome night,
>   Is in a noyous cloud enueloped,
>   Where she may find the substaunce thin and light,
>   Breakes forth her siluer beames, and her bright hed
>   Discouers to the world discomfited;

[3] Britomart's removal of her helmet at 4.1 and 4.6 as a symbol of concord has been pointed out by Calvin Huckabay, "The Structure of Book IV of *The Faerie Queen,*" *Studia Neophilologica,* 27 (1955), pp. 56, 59, 63.

Of the poore traueller, that went astray,
With thousand blessings she is heried;
Such was the beautie and the shining ray,
With which faire *Britomart* gaue light vnto the day.
(3.1.42-43)

Again in canto 9 when she removes her helmet,

Her golden locks, that were in tramels gay
Vpbounden, did them selues adowne display,
And raught vnto her heeles; like sunny beames,
That in a cloud their light did long time stay,
Their vapour vaded, shew their golden gleames,
And through the persant aire shoote forth their azure streames. (3.9.20)

Likewise, in Book IV, canto 1, after defeating the "Younker" she enters the castle, removes her helmet and is compared to

the shining skie in summers night,
What time the dayes with scorching heat abound,
Is creasted all with lines of firie light,
That it prodigious seemes in common peoples sight.
(4.1.13)

At the climax of her encounter with Arthegall, her "ventail" has been "shared away":

With that her angels face, vnseene afore,
Like to the ruddie morne appeard in sight,
Deawed with siluer drops, through sweating sore,
But somewhat redder, then beseem'd aright,
Through toylesome heate and labour of her weary fight.
(4.6.19)

In each instance the comparison is based on light breaking through an obscuring veil. The image is appropriate on these occasions when Britomart reveals herself—light, goodness, beauty, truth breaking through darkness, evil, ugliness, or falsity,[4] but in particular these similes symbolize the force of her chastity. Neither the image nor its consistent use is of especial novelty to readers brought up on the analysis of image patterns, but a word of caution should be spoken at this point about Spenser's use of consistent image patterns.

Modern criticism generally teaches that the coherence of an image pattern is part of the formal structure of the poem, and very often the shorter forms of poetry do conform to this criterion. We may even find the criterion met in such long poems as *Paradise Lost*, where the enormously rich image patterns are part of the formal structure, but the modern teaching falls short of the mark when we read the great invocation to light at the beginning of *Paradise Lost*, III. It does form part of the pattern of light and dark imagery, it is consistent; but here Milton is not simply using images, he is invoking the source of the image. He has pushed us past the confines of verbal coherence, in which images of light and dark are part of a verbal pattern, and is asking us to pass from the sign to the thing signified. If this were not the case, the invocation would be pointless.

Spenser has been criticized for his failure to form coherent image patterns, but the fact that he does not conform to modern usage in this matter is not a sign that he has failed but that he is making his images do something else. The point is all the more important when we do find him using consistent image patterns as in the similes describing Britomart, for I think that Spenser was not intending us to read them primarily as part of the formal structure of his poem. These similes bear more resemblance to Milton's images in his invocation to light. Their primary allegiance is not to the verbal pattern of which they are a part but to the fundamental energy of which they are a sign. They have the startling sim-

[4] Similes of light occur at 3.1.43, 3.3.20, 3.4.13, 3.9.20, 3.11.25, 4.1.13, 4.4.47, 4.6.19. The comparison is not always so simple as those quoted. It becomes clear that the veil as well as the light can be part of the description, e.g., 3.4.13 and 4.4.47.

plicity of such lines as Nashe's "Brightness falls from the air" and Lovelace's "But shake your head and scatter day." No amount of verbal analysis will *elucidate* these images so much as the immediate human response to that "something far more deeply interfused" investing the images themselves. Similarly Spenser's images ask us to turn from epistemology to ontology to find our criterion for judging their goodness.[5] In these similes Spenser is invoking another realm of being to invest his image of chastity with analogical significance. They do not depend for their validity on what Rosemond Tuve calls the criterion of sensuous vividness; they are patently artificial. Rather the image of Britomart as Spenser's image of chastity attracts to it that image of light which best characterizes its inner qualities and for the Neoplatonist best symbolizes its ultimate source. The primal nature of these similes rather than their exfoliation in the verbal pattern of the poem is more characteristic of Spenser: significant intensity rather than formalistic extension.

Thus the Temple of Isis episode in Book V identifies Britomart and Arthegall with Isis and Osiris. Earlier in the canto we learned that "*Isis* doth the Moone portend; Like as *Osyris* signifies the Sunne. For that they both like race in equall iustice runne" (5.7.4). This is the imagistic core (to expropriate Professor Lewis' term) of the light imagery associated with Britomart. It is not so much a culmination as an intensification of that imagery which has been generally used to describe her. Reading through the poem, one finds that the identification presented in this episode has been anticipated. Arthegall first appears to Britomart in Venus's mirror "as *Phoebus* face out of the east . . ." (3.2.24). Glauce explains to Merlin, "Now haue three Moones with borrow'd brothers light, Thrice shined faire, and thrice seem'd dim and wan," since a "sore euill" took hold on Britomart (3.3.16). Brito-

[5] It seems to me significant that Spenser separates the images from an intimate metaphoric connection with his narrative by isolating them in epic similes.

THE IMAGE OF BRITOMART

mart, as she listens blushing to the prophecy of Merlin, is described "As faire Aurora rising hastily . . ." (3.3.20), and it is from a window "that opened West, Towards which coast her loue his way addrest" (5.6.7) that she sees Talus approaching to tell her of Arthegall's subjection by Radigund.

It would be unfair to call these occurrences of light imagery an image pattern. To do so is to attribute to Spenser aims he either did not foresee or carried off rather badly. He is not trying to make the kind of coherent pattern of sun and moon images that we find in *Henry the Fourth, Part I*, but neither is he trying to obliterate all trace of associations that, consciously or unconsciously, he is moving toward in the Temple of Isis episode. Part of Spenser's pictorialism is due to the fact that he restrains his descriptive talents until he reaches a place where he can utterly concentrate and intensify those images that he might have been weaving into the texture of his narrative. Much of the power of the great set pieces comes from this intensification of the imagery into great, simple iconographic symbols.

Nevertheless Spenser uses again and again the sequence of time as a symbol and organizing force; the calendar device in *The Shepheardes Calendar*, the movement from morning to night in *Epithalamion*, the faint pattern of the church year in *Amoretti*, and the cycle of the months in the *Mutabilitie Cantos*—all these emphasize the profoundly simple devices that Spenser used to obtain some of his most brilliant effects. To see in the descriptions of Britomart and Arthegall a submerged metaphor of the journey of the sun from east to west, to see in Britomart a light, at first obscured by a veil, progressively realizing itself, occasionally breaking through the veil as beauty or the power of chastity, until the moment of revelation occurs, when she and Arthegall meet and recognize, when her quest is completed—to see this is only to enrich the poem, to give due praise to Britomart and Arthegall as the founders of the line that was to produce Elizabeth,

>   Goddesse heauenly bright,
> Mirrour of grace and Maiestie diuine,
> Great Lady of the greatest Isle, whose light
> Like *Phoebus* lampe throughout the world doth
>   shine. . . . (1.Pr.4)

But images of light are not the only means that Spenser uses to create his image of Britomart. Spenser's chronicle of British kings in Book II stresses the importance of racial conflicts later resolved by national unification. This *discordia concors* works not only in the total plan of the poem, as discussed in the Introduction, but also in the details Spenser employs to create Britomart, his invented British queen. Immediately after Merlin's prophecy Glauce the old nurse suggests the "bold deuise" of setting out on their quest disguised as knights. The time is very carefully specified.

> Ye see that good king *Vther* now doth make
> Strong warre vpon the Paynim brethren, hight
> *Octa* and *Oza*, whom he lately brake
> Beside *Cayr Verolame*, in victorious fight,
> That now all *Britanie* doth burne in armes bright.
>   (3.3.52)

This was no ordinary battle but the great victory of Uther over the Saxons. This battle and Uther's affair with Igerne are often the only details given in the chronicler's accounts. The time is particularly appropriate in light of the Saxon's eventual victory as foretold in Merlin's prophecy, but Spenser carefully shows that this later British defeat is only a necessary stage in the unification of Briton and Saxon. Glauce reminds Britomart of the armor of a Saxon virgin warrior that now hangs in her father's chapel.

> Ah read, (quoth *Britomart*) how is she hight?
> Faire *Angela* (quoth she) men do her call,
> No whit lesse faire, then terrible in fight:

> She hath the leading of a Martiall
> And mighty people, dreaded more then all
> The other *Saxons*, which do for her sake
> And loue, themselues of her name *Angles* call.
> Therefore faire Infant her ensample make
> Vnto thy selfe, and equall courage to thee take.
>
> (3.3.56)

Angel, Angle, England—we are reminded of the Pope's pun on first seeing the fair Angles. The names themselves suggest the unity Britomart's offspring will create from the diversity of Saxon and Briton. The armor of this Saxon warrior, the best example of her people, becomes the protection of Britomart in her search for Arthegall and a symbol of the eventual unity of the best of Saxon and Britain in that greater warrior and queen, Elizabeth. It is in this armor that we first see Britomart in the opening episode of Book III, as she rides along with Arthur, Guyon, and their squires.

The moral implications of both the light imagery and the armor are brought to bear on Britomart's role in British history in Book III, canto 9, where she hears Paridell's story of the fall of Troy. The whole Malbecco episode provides a fit background for a retelling of the Troy story, since it is itself a reenactment. The interplay of the themes of love perverted and society destroyed depends for its success on the correspondence between the love of individuals and the welfare of the body politic. Britomart, whose progeny will create a new Troy, is receiving a negative exemplum of the government of self and state. It is particularly appropriate for Paridell to tell of Troy, for he is about to take another Helen from another Menelaus. Paridell's story is a version slanted to suit his personality. To him Troy is now "but an idle name," which is in entire accord with the *ubi sunt* motif of Troy moralized, but Paridell sees in the fall of Troy not an exemplum of human misgovernment but a "direfull destinie" from "angry Gods and cruell skye." Paridell's blindness is shown in his description of Paris:

> Most famous Worthy of the world, by whome
> That warre was kindled, which did *Troy* inflame,
> And stately towres of *Ilion* whilome
> Brought vnto baleful ruine. . . .   (3.9.34)

Just as Paris and Helen are unaware of the claims of the body politic, Paridell is unaware of their moral responsibility in causing the ruin he so lightly describes. Paridell then identifies himself as the descendant of Paris and Oenone. She, deserted, named her son Parius.

> Who, after *Greekes* did *Priams* realme destroy,
> Gathred the *Troian* reliques sau'd from flame,
> And with them sayling thence, to th'Isle of *Paros* came.
>
> That was by him cald *Paros*, which before
> Hight *Nausa*, there he many years did raine,
> And built *Nausicle* by the *Pontick* shore,
> The which he dying left next in remaine
> To *Paridas* his sonne.   (3.9.36-37)

Parius, the son of Paris's true marriage, sets off like the other Trojan exiles to establish a new city. Upton was unable to find Nausa among the names given to Paros and conjectured that the myth of Paros and Parius was Spenser's own. This is very probably true. The Greek word *nausa* means ship. In this city founded by Paris's son we are to see the countless voyages clustered around the Troy story—the ship that bore Paris from Oenone to Helen, the ship that bore Paris and Helen to Troy, the ships of the Greeks, the ships of the wandering Ulysses and the Trojans in exile. These are the ships of discord and the ships that will bring the concord of new cities from the fall of Troy.

THE IMAGE OF BRITOMART

> From whom I *Paridell* by kin descend;
> But for faire Ladies loue, and glories gaine,
> My natiue soile haue left, my dayes to spend
> In sewing deeds of armes, my liues and labours end.
>
> (3.9.37)

But Paridell's departure from Paros is another sign of his inheritance from Paris: the ability to ignore the higher allegiance to one's country in favor of a personal passion. He like Britomart is on a quest, indeed, a quest of love, but his aim is a succession of Helens and the purpose of his deeds of arms is personal glory, not the furtherance of civil life. His quest becomes the inversion of Britomart's quest for Arthegall, as we can see from her response to his story.

> She was empassiond at that piteous act,
> With zelous enuy of Greekes cruell fact,
> Against that nation, from whose race of old
> She heard, that she was lineally extract:
> For Noble *Britons* sprong from *Troians* bold,
> And *Troynouant* was built of old *Troyes* ashes cold.
>
> (3.9.38)

Opposed to his selfish view of Troy as "but an idle name" Britomart thinks of the famous town "in one sad night consumd,"

> What stony hart, that heares thy haplesse fate,
> Is not empierst with deepe compassiowne,
> And makes ensample of mans wretched state,
> That floures so fresh at morne, and fades at euening late?   (3.9.39)

Troy as example of the mutability of this life has moved Britomart, "For nothing may impresse so deare constraint, As countries cause, and commune foes disdayne." In asking him to turn back his course to the story of Aeneas, Britomart, probably unaware, is asking for the story of the Trojan who gave up love for the higher destiny of founding the second Troy. But even here Paridell's personality intervenes. Significantly his story does not mention Dido, the one episode in Aeneas's life that repudiates Paridell's wantonness. Paridell brings his story to the time of Romulus's founding of Rome.

> There there (said *Britomart*) a fresh appeard
> The glory of the later world to spring,
> And *Troy* againe out of her dust was reard,
> To sit in second seat of soueraigne king,
> Of all the world vnder her gouerning.
> But a third kingdome yet is to arise,
> Out of the *Troians* scattered of-spring,
> That in all glory an great enterprise,
> Both first and second *Troy* shall dare to equalise.
>
> It *Troynouant* is hight, that with the waues
> Of wealthy *Thamis* washed is along,
> Vpon whose stubborne neck, whereat he raues
> With roring rage, and sore him selfe does throng,
> That all men feare to tempt his billowes strong,
> She fastned hath her foot, which standes so hy,
> That it a wonder of the world is song
> In forreine landes, and all which passen by,
> Beholding it from far, do thinke it threates the skye.
>
> (3.9.44-45)

Britomart is aware of the past as it is relived in the present, and her praise of the third Troy provokes Paridell to recall the story "whilome I heard tell From aged *Mnemon*; for my wits bene light." His tale is that of Brute's journey to Britain and his founding of Troynouant,

> so heard I say
> Old *Mnemon.* Therefore Sir, I greet you well

THE IMAGE OF BRITOMART

> Your countrey kin, and you entirely pray
> Of pardon for the strife, which late befell
> Betwixt vs both vnknowne. So ended *Paridell*.
>
> (3.9.51)

The encounter of these two descendants of Troy presents the basic problem facing Britomart as progenitrix of Troynovant and as knight of chastity. The history that Paridell relates is at times distorted by his own selfish interests. His forgetfulness and omissions reveal to the reader his essential lack of understanding of his lineage. His apology and lip service at the end of his tale refer to his overthrow by Britomart outside the wall of the little Troy represented by Malbecco's castle. Despite the apparent amity Britomart will ride off in the morning, and Troy will fall again. Unlike their prototypes the easy love of Paridell and Hellenore will not destroy any state but the inverted world of Malbecco. Of this fall Britomart need not know. Her love is to be hard won. As with Rome and Troynovant it is to be a concord won from discord, climaxed in the fight between Arthegall and Britomart in Book IV, canto 6, and reinforced throughout the poem by the Virgilian source of her name, by the lineage of her armor, and by the light imagery consistently used to describe her.

ii · THE QUEST DEFINED

Many critics have complained that the adventures of Britomart do not constitute the major narrative of Book III, and it is true that she appears only at the beginning and at the end.[6] Nevertheless her adventures in Book III and her confrontation with Arthegall in the central canto of Book IV suggest that Spenser viewed them as a kind of structural principle in the legends of chastity and friendship. Part of the difficulty stems from the erroneous expectation that Books

---

[6] See Bennett, *Evolution*, pp. 138, 143, and *Var.*, 3.310-329.

III and IV will present us with a straightforward romance in which we shall see the consecutive adventures of the hero accomplish his quest. Another part of the difficulty comes from the equally erroneous assumption that the figure of chastity will be presented to us solely in the person of Britomart. Spenser's conception of chastity is more complex; it includes the chastity of Belphoebe and Timias, of Amoret and Scudamour, and of Florimell and Marinell. Only when we understand the relationship of these adventures to those of Britomart—that is, only when we understand the structures of Books III and IV and why Spenser followed one episode with another—will we begin to understand the complexity of the legends of chastity and friendship. As an approach to this understanding let us examine the three major adventures of Britomart in these books to see whether they do not, in fact, constitute a continuous narrative of love directed by chastity and whether they also do not present a vantage point from which to view the other adventures of these books as integrated parts of the legends of chastity and friendship.

(a) Castle Joyous

The general significance of Castle Joyous is readily apparent. It is a place of unchastity, symbolized by its mistress Malecasta, whose name literally means "badly chaste." Her castle is defended by six knights, whose names symbolize the kind of unchaste love that exists in the castle: Gardante, Parlante, Jocante, Basciante, Bacchante, and Noctante. These knights have been explained as "an amatory progression" and "a ladder of lechery," but one should be more precise, for nothing ever actually happens in Castle Joyous.[7] Its essence

---

[7] Allan H. Gilbert, "The Ladder of Lechery, *The Faerie Queene*, III, i, 45," *MLN*, 56 (1941), pp. 594-597; James Hutton, "Spenser and the 'Cinq Points en Amours,'" *MLN*, 57 (1942), pp. 657-661. Hutton's disagreement with Gilbert about the ultimate source of this ladder seems beside the point, since all the examples cited in both articles point to a

is that it provides the occasions for lechery. The knights represent those common social occasions, which may lead to lechery—the glances, the pretty speeches and jokes, the chance kiss, the party and late nights. To suppose for one minute that Spenser's Noctante is a euphemism is to forget his complete frankness where sex is concerned. Castle Joyous is a world where love is a game. The inhabitants indulge in love as play, and accordingly they are not mature knights and ladies, but

> all was full of Damzels, and of Squires,
> Dauncing and reueling both day and night,
> And swimming deepe in sensuall desires,
> And *Cupid* still emongst them kindled lustfull fires
>
> (3.1.39)

C. S. Lewis has caught the particular tone of Castle Joyous when he describes the tapestries of Venus and Adonis which adorn its walls as "a picture not of 'lust in action' but of lust suspended—lust turning into what would now be called *skeptophilia.*"[8]

Lust of the eyes is the particular vice of Castle Joyous, and the tapestry of Venus and Adonis is its appropriate emblem:

> And whilest he bath'd, with her two crafty spyes
> She secretly would search each daintie lim. . . .
>
> (3.1.36)

The vice of skeptophilia is precisely what Spenser emphasizes in describing Malecasta:

> She seemd a woman of great bountihed,
> And of rare beautie, sauing that askaunce

---

common source in classical or early Christian literature. Hutton's attempt to restrict this idea to Provençal poetry neglects the most common feature of medieval love poetry in which the lover is always struck in the eyes by the darts of Cupid (cf. Chaucer, *The Knight's Tale*, ll. 1070ff.).

[8] C. S. Lewis, *The Allegory of Love*, Oxford, 1936, p. 332.

> Her wanton eyes, ill signes of womanhed,
> Did roll too lightly, and too often glaunce,
> Without regard of grace, or comely amenaunce.
>
> (3.1.41)

Spenser leaves the reader in no doubt about his opinion of Malecasta and her lascivious glances:

> Nought so of loue this looser Dame did skill,
> But as a coale to kindle fleshly flame,
> Giuing the bridle to her wanton will,
> And treading vnder foote her honest name:
> Such loue is hate, and such desire is shame.
>
> (3.1.50)

What appears obvious to Spenser and to the reader is not understood by Britomart. Her reaction to Malecasta and Castle Joyous is indicative of her state of innocent inexperience:

> All were faire knights, and goodly well beseene,
> But to faire *Britomart* they all but shadows beene.
>
> (3.1.45)

They are shadows in the same sense that Arthegall is but "th'only shade and semblant of a knight" (3.2.38); she has no real experience of them. Similarly she is incapable of seeing through Malecasta's designs and reads them in the light of her own love.

> But the chaste damzell, that had neuer priefe
> Of such malengine and fine forgerie,
> Did easily beleeue her strong extremitie.
>
> Full easie was for her to haue beliefe,
> Who by self-feeling of her feeble sexe,
> And by long triall of the inward griefe,
> Wherewith imperious loue her hart did vexe,
> Could iudge what paines do louing harts perplexe.

> Who meanes no guile, beguiled soonest shall,
> And to faire semblaunce doth light faith annexe;
> The bird, that knowes not the false fowlers call,
> Into his hidden net full easily doth fall.   (3.1.53-54)

Although she considers Malecasta's love "too light, to wooe a wandring guest," her natural charity prevents her from rebuking Malecasta, "Which she misconstruing, thereby esteemed That from like inward fire that outward smoke had steemd" (3.1.55). The consequence is Malecasta's attempt to seduce Britomart, leading to the scuffle in which Britomart receives a slight wound from Gardante.

This wound is important because it is Britomart's initiation into the realities of love. The knights, whom she saw only as shadows at Malecasta's feast, have the power to hurt. In any attempt to make love a game we may forget that the rules must be obeyed by all the players, if the game is to be a success. Britomart does not know the rules. When this happens, the makebelieve world suddenly becomes real, and we are left with the spectacle of Adonis dying in the arms of Venus or of Britomart wounded. With the wound comes a realization that love is something other than an interior passion. Her encounter at Castle Joyous forces her to an awareness of love in others and of herself as a love object.

The wound also represents the everpresent dangers of maintaining chastity unimpaired in the active life. Britomart has merely "countenanced" the world of unchastity, but this nevertheless puts her temporarily in the power of Gardante. Britomart is the cause of the difficulty. Her sympathy for Malecasta's situation has led her to be evasive in her responses; at least her glances can be misinterpreted by Malecasta. Or perhaps Spenser is telling us that Britomart has partially succumbed to the beauty of Castle Joyous and thus deserves this slight wound. His psychology of love will permit both interpretations, for the power of beauty to draw the eyes is the basis of both lewd and chaste love. Beauty cannot be avoided, and Castle Joyous as the ordinary social world is deliberately set up to trap the eye, to dispel the tedium of a leisurely existence. This is the meaning of Malecasta's trial of every passer-by, that continual impingement on the senses of the material world asserting itself to be the only reality worthy of our consideration.

After Britomart leaves Castle Joyous, she gives way to a momentary despair, in which she complains about the troubles of her quest,

> The whiles that loue it steres, and fortune rowes;
> Loue my lewd Pilot hath a restlesse mind
> And fortune Boteswaine no assuraunce knowes,
> But saile withouten starres, gainst tide and wind:
> How can they other do, sith both are bold and blind?
> (3.4.9)

The despair is occasioned by the young girl's first encounter with love and her reaction against it. Almost immediately the opposite danger to her chastity appears—Marinell, the selfish knight afraid to love. Marinell means several things in the poem, but Britomart's overthrow of him means that she has overcome the temptation to withdraw into herself. The wound she inflicts on Marinell could be given only after her encounter with Gardante, at that time when she learns that love is not contained solely in the mind or in the image of a mirror. After her first vision of Arthegall she wonders whether she is more foolish than

> *Cephisus* foolish child,
> Who hauing vewed in a fountaine shere
> His face, was with the loue thereof beguild;
> I fonder loue a shade, the bodie farre exild.
> (3.2.44)

The danger to Britomart at this point is the erotic delusion of Narcissus, which the Renaissance recognized as self-love.

In escaping Castle Joyous she overcomes another form of self-love—self-gratification. Her overthrow of Marinell is an escape from the opposite tendency—self-denial.

(b) *The House of Busyrane*

The pattern of encounter and despair is reversed in the closing episode of Book III when Britomart comes upon Scudamour despairing of Amoret's rescue from the power of Busyrane. There are a number of parallels in these two episodes that point up their differences—Gardante and his brothers outside Castle Joyous as opposed to the wall of flame, the tapestries within each castle, the two night adventures. Castle Joyous represents love as play; the house of Busyrane is love as destruction. Comparison is difficult, however, not only because the poetry in the Busyrane episode is so much better but also because the allegorical situation is more complex and subtle.

The position of this episode at the end of Book III suggests that it is analogous to Red Cross's battle with the dragon and Guyon's destruction of the Bower of Bliss as the climactic actions of Books I and II. It has already been suggested that the house of Busyrane represents the trial of Britomart's chastity and her knighthood. Literally it offers no difficulties; it is the romance motif of the distressed maiden's rescue from the evil magician, and so it is described at the end of the Garden of Adonis canto. Venus brought Amoret forth to the world,

> To be th'ensample of true loue alone,
> And Lodestarre of all chaste affectione,
> To all faire Ladies, that doe liue on ground.
> To Faery court she came, where many one
> Admyred her goodly haueour, and found
> His feeble hart wide launched with loues cruell wound.

> But she to none of them her loue did cast,
> Saue to the noble knight Sir *Scudamore*,
> To whom her louing hart she linked fast
> In faithful loue, t'abide for euermore,
> And for his dearest sake endured sore,
> Sore trouble of an hainous enimy;
> Who her would forced haue to haue forlore
> Her former loue, and stedfast loialty,
> As ye may elsewhere read that ruefull history.
>
> (3.6.52-53)

Since Britomart represents chastity, Busyrane is generally interpreted as lust, but here we run into difficulties.[9] The episode is extremely problematical, but let us for the moment concentrate on the situation before the arrival of Britomart.

At the beginning of Book IV Spenser tells us the circumstances of Amoret's abduction. We are told that Busyrane brings a mask to the wedding feast, that it is the same mask we have just seen in canto 12 *through the eyes of Britomart*, and that by its power Amoret has been "conveyed quite away to liuing wight vnknowen." The initial impact of the mask in canto 12 is one of horror and evil, ill-suited for a wedding feast, but we should remember that it *was* presented at the wedding. This apparent contradiction can be reconciled by examining the mask outside the context of canto 12. We shall see that its power lies in the essential ambiguity of its figures, an ambiguity that allows three interpretations, that of the wedding guests, that of Amoret, and finally that of Britomart, which is the one we accept as we read the mask in canto 12.

The mask is presented by Ease, who is followed by six couples: Fancy and Desyre, Doubt and Daunger, Feare and

---

[9] Much of the subtlety of the allegorical method has been obscured by too much concern with tropological interpretations. There is no reason to believe that either Amoret or Britomart must have experienced lust to be in the power of Busyrane—unless one is reading the allegory as psychological realism. See the discussion of this point in Alpers, "Narrative and Rhetoric in the *Faerie Queene*," SEL, 2 (1962), pp. 41ff.

Hope, Dissemblance and Suspect, Grief and Fury, Displeasure and Pleasance. Amoret is led in between Cruelty and Despight, who carry her heart in a silver basin. Riding in triumph, Cupid lifts his blindfold to behold his latest conquest, and the mask ends with Reproach, Repentance, and Shame, followed by a confused mob of allegorical figures.

We may not immediately be struck by the appropriateness of these figures for a wedding mask, but we should see that Ease is a brother to that charmer Ydelnesse in Chaucer's *Romaunt of the Rose*,[10] and as presenter of the mask he introduces us to a world we have all seen under a different light—the world of Renaissance love psychology. This is love as mock war, the battlefield of the conventional sonneteer. Ease, the traditional figure of gay and irresponsible love, presents a progressive allegory of a courtship that might have been taken from any sonnet sequence; the twelve figures that follow Ease are sonnet metaphors come to life. Furthermore Cupid and the first six couples are almost duplicated in a similar wedding mask performed in Beaumont and Fletcher's *A Wife for a Moneth* of 1624.

>   Cupid *descends, the Graces sitting by him,*
> Cupid *being bound the Graces unbind him, he speaks.*

CUP. Unbind me, my delight, this night is mine,
  Now let me look upon what Stars here shine,
  Let me behold the beauties, then clap high,
  My cullor'd wings, proud of my Deity;
  I am satisfied, bind me again, and fast,
  My angry Bow will make too great a wast
  Of beauty else, now call my Maskers in,
  Call with a Song, and let the sports begin;
  Call all my servants the effects of love,
  And to a measure let them nobly move.

---

[10] Chaucer, *The Romaunt of the Rose*, Fragment A, ll. 531-584, *Works*, ed. F. N. Robinson, Cambridge, Mass., 1957.

Come you servants of proud love,
    Come away:
Fairly, nobly, gently move.
Too long, too long you make us stay;
Fancy, Desire, Delight, Hope, Fear,
Distrust and Jealousie, be you too here;
Consuming Care, and raging Ire,
And Poverty in poor attire,
March fairly in, and last Despair;
Now full Musick strike the Air.

Enter the Maskers, Fancy, Desire, Delight, Hope, Fear, Distrust, Jealousie, Care, Ire, Despair, they dance, after which Cupid *speaks.*

CUP. Away, I have done, the day begins to light,
    Lovers, you know your fate, good night, good night.
       Cupid *and the Graces ascend in the Chariot.*[11]

The context of this mask is the bold bawdry of the courtiers and country wenches who have come to see the wedding solemnities. Their knowing and amusing antics remind us that Beaumont and Fletcher's wedding mask is just another manifestation of Cupid the boy archer surveying his latest conquest.

The second half of Spenser's mask, which introduces Amoret between Cruelty and Despight, can also be interpreted in the light of sonnet metaphors. Cruelty is a personification of the metaphor of the cruel mistress or cruel love so common in the sonnets, and similarly Despight is derived from the medieval "despitous" lady. Amoret's main tormentors are those very qualities which have preserved her chastity during her courtship, and she is being punished for her long resistance to the power of love. Amoret, her heart

---

[11] Beaumont and Fletcher, *A Wife for a Moneth, Works*, ed. Arnold Glover and A. R. Waller, 10 vols., Cambridge, 1905-1912, vol. 5, pp. 25-26.

"drawne forth" and "transfixed with a deadly dart," is followed by Cupid, riding on a lion and brandishing his dreadful darts. Behind him come Reproach, Repentance, and Shame,

> And after them a rude confused rout
> Of persons flockt, whose names is hard to read:
> Emongst them was sterne *Strife*, and *Anger* stout,
> Vnquiet *Care*, and fond *Vnthriftihead*,
> Lewd *Losse of Time*, and *Sorrow* seeming dead,
> Inconstant *Chaunge*, and false *Disloyaltie*,
> Consuming *Riotise*, and guilty *Dread*
> Of heauenly vengeance, faint *Infirmitie*,
> Vile *Pouertie*, and lastly *Death* with infamie.
>
> (3.12.25)

Even the bloody details of Amoret's predicament and the figure of Cupid can be viewed as dramatic presentations of common sonnet metaphors. In the context of the wedding feast Cupid is exhibiting not evil but the pride of the conqueror surveying his latest conquest. Reproach, Repentance, and Shame are exactly those qualities which would trouble the lady for her cruel treatment of the lover, and it should be remembered that ignominious death is always the threat to the scornful lady.

The mask that the wedding guests see is the mask of the triumph of love, in which Amoret, the prize, is about to surrender to her victor knight. It is performed in a spirit of jovial festivity, but it presents a view of love that considers only the male's trial in "winning" his lady. This is not the mask that Amoret sees.

Walking among the maskers at the wedding feast, she sees, not the personification of the sonneteers' psychology, but the vengeance of male sexuality on the chastely reticent female. The figures of Cruelty and Despight become for her physical torments of sexual love; the triumphant Cupid is not the allegorical representation of a playful metaphor but a promise of sadism. Her share in this triumph of love can only be reproach, repentance, and shame, the price of her surrender. This means the loss of a fastidious integrity, replaced by strife, sorrow, care, and "lastly Death with infamie." The dreary assortment of ills that follow Cupid corresponds precisely with the Christian interpretation of adulterous love. These are the effects of love outside Christian marriage, but presumably the marriage of Amoret and Scudamour is a Christian marriage. Amoret makes no distinction between them; for her there is only the horror and enslavement of physical surrender. Scudamour is not mentioned in the description of the wedding feast, and he does not appear at all in the House of Busyrane except as an abstract masculinity. The mask that takes place at the House of Busyrane is Amoret's interpretation of the wedding mask. The guests see one side of the ambiguity inherent in the mask; Amoret sees the other.

The proof of this reading lies in the ambiguity of Spenser's presentation, which begins in the last line of the description of the wedding feast. Busyrane conveys Amoret "quite away to liuing wight vnknowen" (4.1.3). This line can be interpreted in two ways. It can mean (1) that Busyrane took Amoret away to a place not known to anyone at the feast, or (2) that Busyrane took her away without being noticed by anyone at the feast. Now the first interpretation is ruled out because Scudamour does know where she is imprisoned. The second interpretation works in two ways. For the narrative it means that unnoticed Amoret has been carried to the House of Busyrane. Allegorically it means that Busyrane has got possession of Amoret's mind. Thus the House of Busyrane is presented as if it were an objectification of Amoret's fear of sexual love in marriage.[12]

[12] This theory is supported by Scudamour's statement that nothing can rescue Amoret "Out of her thraldome and continuall feare." (3.11.16).

If the description of the wedding feast is a clue to the significance of the House of Busyrane as the female fear of sexual love, the description of the mask itself embodies the double vision of love suggested. The maskers come out in pairs, "enranged orderly." They are dressed and act appropriately for the qualities they represent; Spenser is quite explicit in his description. The picture they present is the joys and pains of love. Then Crueltie and Despight enter with Amoret. We are given a picture of Amoret and the triumphant Cupid, and here the description stops. Of Crueltie, Despight, Repentance, Reproach, and Shame, and the other maskers we have no idea. We are told where they come in the mask, but we do not know how they looked. This seems to me purposeful.

The first six couples present the progress of an allegorical courtship in terms of medieval and Renaissance love psychology. The first hint of any ambiguity occurs in Daunger. Instead of the usual defensive figure (4.10.17) we see an active figure with a net and rusty knife (3.12.11), whose name, as C. S. Lewis suggests, is probably nearer to our modern word *danger*.[13] From this point on, Spenser's descriptions are both sonnet conventions and visions of the horrors of love, depending on whether we read them from the man's or woman's point of view. For example, Feare and Hope are the two figures following Daunger. Feare may be either the man protecting himself from his lady's disdain or the lady protecting herself from the figure of Daunger which has preceded. Hope with its holy water sprinkler is to the man his hope of obtaining his lady's "blessing and grace" and to the

[13] In his study of the word *daunger* C. S. Lewis discusses the two senses inherent in the medieval usage, the one leading to the modern word synonymous with *peril*, the other being the obsolete sense of "refusal, or difficult granting of love." Lewis concludes that, although both senses are implicit in the word, Spenser is working with the modern sense in the mask and the obsolete sense in the Temple of Venus. (C. S. Lewis, *The Allegory of Love*, pp. 364-366.)

woman the hope of protection from a Power outside herself. Similarly the other figures, although traditional, betray signs of hypocrisy, jealous voyeurism, masochism, sadism, and finally helplessness in the face of superior power.

At the point of Amoret's entry the description stops. Spenser has set up his ambiguous mask in the description of the first twelve figures, in which the sonnet conventions are predominantly stressed through the use of iconographical details. For the rest of the mask the normal denotations of the names are predominant. The sonnet convention carries over, but we are forced more and more to see these figures as the names they represent in normal usage. The transition is remarkably effective since by the time Spenser describes Amoret's wounded heart, the reader is hardly aware that he has read the same lover's curse in sonnet after sonnet.

This double meaning in the figures of the mask is more than hinted at in the strange way Spenser concludes his account.

> There were full many moe like maladies,
> Whose names and natures I note readen well;
> So many moe, as there be phantasies
> In wauering wemens wit, that none can tell,
> Or paines in loue, or punishments in hell;
> All which disguized marcht in masking wise....
>
> (3.12.26)

Is Spenser not suggesting that the particular tone of terror that these figures present in canto 12 are the fantasies of one wavering woman's wit? But we need only look carefully at their names and attributes to see that the wedding guests could, and did, interpret them differently. The ambiguity of the figures in this allegorical courtship is the charm by which Busyrane gets possession of Amoret's mind. Who then is Busyrane?

A moment's consideration reveals that, although the episode may be clearly remembered, Busyrane cannot be recalled. The reason for this is simply that Spenser does not characterize him as he does almost every other important figure in the poem. He is called the "vile Enchantour" in abducting Amoret, and Scudamour merely names him "Busirane with wicked hand" (3.12.10) and even when Britomart comes upon him, we are told only,

> And her before the vile Enchaunter sate,
> Figuring straunge characters of his art,
> With liuing bloud he those characters wrate,
> Dreadfully dropping from her dying hart,
> *Seeming* transfixed with a cruell dart,
> And all perforce to make her him to loue.
>
> (3.12.31)   (Italics mine)

The general assumption that Busyrane represents merely lust is usually accompanied by the tacit assumption that he is trying to possess her, but this need not be the case.[14] First, Busyrane does not appear in the mask and, second, Spenser represents this kind of lust in Book IV, canto 7, where Amoret is rescued from rape by the fortunate appearance of Belphoebe and Timias. Third, the brief passage in which we see Amoret in Busyrane's power does not reflect the nature of lust in action.

Busyrane is trying to transfer Amoret's love for Scudamour to himself by charms, but the conventional romance structure of this episode should not blind us to its real meaning. He is literally trying to kill Amoret. His love is not sexual but destructive—destructive of the will to love within Amoret herself. Amoret is afraid of the physical surrender which her marriage to Scudamour must entail. The wedding mask crystallizes this fear, and she turns from a joyful acceptance

---

[14] See *Var.*, 1.441; 3.303, 320, 326, 354, 373; 8.446. Spenser makes a similar statement in the Letter to Ralegh, but see my Conclusion where the relation of Letter to poem is discussed.

to a cold rejection of the claims of the physical. This is why Busyrane is the great enemy to chastity; he represents a negative force of which chastity is the positive ideal. He represents the negation of chastity, and this for Spenser did not mean lust.

Although Spenser gives no iconographical details to identify his Busyrane, we may learn much from the etymology of his name. Warton suggested long ago that Busyrane is derived from Busiris, "The king of Egypt, famous for his cruelty and inhospitality."[15] Warton, I believe, is correct. The history of Busiris is too complicated to relate. It must suffice to say that Busiris originally was the location of the chief tomb of Osiris, and that in later writers Busiris became the king of the place where Osiris was killed. The complicated traditions agree that Busiris is a location or an agent of sacrificial destruction and is associated with the sacrifice of Osiris.[16] The connection may seem remote, but we must recall the identification of Britomart and Arthegall with Isis and Osiris in Book V and remember that Britomart triumphs over Busyrane before she encounters Arthegall. Even more important is Ovid's retelling of the Busiris legend in the first book of the *Ars Amatoria.* This relates Busiris to the qualities I have been trying to establish as the traits of Busyrane:

"If you are wise, cheat women only, and avoid trouble; keep faith save for this one deceitfulness. Deceive the deceivers; they are mostly an unrighteous sort; let them fall

---

[15] *Var.*, 3.287.
[16] See Sir Ernest A. T. Wallis Budge, *Osiris and the Egyptian Resurrection*, 2 vols., London, 1911. Chapter I gives a summary of the ancient writers who deal with this story, including Plutarch, Diodorus Siculus, Apollodorus, Isocrates, Herodotus, and Ovid. See also Heywood's dumbshow in *The Brazen Age, Dramatic Works of Thomas Heywood*, ed. John Pearson, 6 vols., London, 1874, vol. 3, p. 183; Ralegh, *The History of the World*, London, 1614, sig. S2ᵛ; *Paradise Lost*, I. 307, and Isabel Rathborne, *The Meaning of Spenser's Fairyland*, pp. 86-90. Professor Rosemond Tuve has kindly pointed out to me the significant appearance of Busiris in Christine de Pisan, *The Epistle of Othea to Hector*, ed. James D. Gordon, Philadelphia, 1942, pp. 68-69.

into the snare which they have laid. Egypt is said to have lacked the rains that bless its fields, and to have been parched for nine years, when Thrasius approached Busiris, and showed that Jove could be propitiated by the outpoured blood of a stranger. To him said Busiris, 'Thou shalt be Jove's first victim, and as a stranger give water unto Egypt.' Phalaris too roasted in his fierce bull the limbs of Perillus, its maker first made trial of his ill-omened work. Both were just; for there is no juster law than that contrivers of death should perish by their own contrivances. Therefore, that perjuries may rightly cheat the perjured, let the woman feel the smart of a wound she first inflicted."[17]

Ovid's ironic advice to his hypothetical lover throws a new light on the Busiris legend and brings us back to Warton's suggested etymology. These lines betray an attitude toward love and women; it is the same attitude that underlies the conceit of love as war, and it is of particular interest that the well-known Ovidian treatise should link this attitude with the figure of Busiris. Here, it would appear, is the nexus between the conventional figure of Busiris and Spenser's Busyrane; here is the deceit, the sadism, and the destruction, which we associate with Amoret's plight.

But there are further possibilities in Busyrane's name, possibilities that suggest the sixteenth century usage of the word *abuse* as imposture, ill-usage, delusion. For example, Sidney's sentence from the *Arcadia* quoted in the OED is entirely appropriate: "Was it not enough for him to have deceived me, and through the deceit abused me, and after the abuse forsaken me?" or we might use the obsolete form *abusion*, which the OED defines as "perversion of the truth, deceit, deception, imposture," giving as an example Spenser's lines, "Foolish delights and fond Abusions, Which do that sence besiege with fond illusions." All of these meanings are

[17] Ovid, *Ars Amatoria*, Book I. 643-658.

implicit in the etymology of Busyrane—the illusion, the deceit, the sadism, the destruction.

What then does this make of Busyrane? Is he not the abuse of marriage just as his house is the objectification of Amoret's fears of marriage? He is the abuse of marriage because his mask of Cupid presents an image of marriage as a sacrifice just as Busiris was a place of sacrifice. He is an abuse of marriage because the mind he possesses cannot distinguish between the act of marriage and adulterous love. He is an abuse of marriage because the falsity of his view of love can lead only to lust or death. His power is derived from the *abusion* of the mind in distorting the image of love. The meaning he presents to the wedding guests is trivial, at the most, lust; the meaning he presents to Amoret is the sacrifice of personal integrity. Lust is the least complex of his perversions; he is the image of love distorted in the mind, distorted by lascivious anticipation or horrified withdrawal. He becomes the denial of the unity of body and soul in true love. And in all these respects he is the chief adversary of Britomart as the knight of chastity. Britomart's response to the mask and to Busyrane is that of the intelligent moral reader, who can detect the difference between true and false love.

This interpretation of Busyrane and his power over Amoret explains why Scudamour cannot rescue her. Amoret's fears are based on moral and physical grounds. Scudamour can dispel neither. Unwillingly he is the cause of these fears, and any attempt on his part to dispel them would be self-defeating since it would mean her eventual surrender, the basis of her fears. Britomart, on the other hand, can attack these fears on both the moral and physical grounds. As a woman she understands Amoret's attitude toward the physical side of love, and as the exemplar of chastity she is able to make the moral distinction between marriage and adulterous love. Her entry through the wall of flame gives her an intimate knowledge of the House of Busyrane, and her understanding finally allows her to release Amoret from her fears.

Britomart's adventure in the House of Busyrane takes her through three rooms, in each of which she learns something about the transforming power of love. The first two rooms contain images of love, which constitute the foundation of the attitude toward love presented in the mask of Cupid. They represent the psychological suppositions of Amoret's attitude toward love and lead easily to the more horrible interpretation of Busyrane's mask.

The first room contains tapestries depicting the transformations of love.

> And in those Tapets weren fashioned
> Many faire pourtraicts, and many a faire feate,
> And all of loue, and all of lusty-hed,
> As seemed by their semblaunt did entreat;
> And eke all *Cupids* warres they did repeate,
> And cruell battels, which he whilome fought
> Gainst all the Gods, to make his empire great;
> Besides the huge massacres, which he wrought
> On mighty kings and kesars, into thraldome brought.
>
> (3.11.29)

The description of these tapestries is one of Spenser's greatest poetic achievements; his mastery of the stanza never once falters. This passage has been quoted out of context so often that its function in the House of Busyrane may be overlooked. Its main purpose, however, is its depiction of the gods' debasing themselves in pursuit of love. Jove appears in all his animal metamorphoses, ravishing his mortal loves. The pull of the verse is overwhelming, showing the ease and attraction of sin, but we should not ignore the fact that it is a picture of love as bestiality. The description of Apollo's love illustrates another aspect of debasement. Apollo, the god of light, destroys his mortal loves—Daphne, Hyacinth, and Coronis; they are all transformed into flowers. And so it is with Neptune and Saturn and Mars and Venus and even Cupid himself. The love of a god and a mortal brings debasement for the god and possible destruction for the mortal. Cupid's victory over the gods is perhaps the original triumph of love.

> Whiles thus on earth great *Ioue* these pageaunts playd,
> The winged boy did thrust into his throne,
> And scoffing, thus vnto his mother sayd,
> Lo now the heauens obey to me alone,
> And take me for their *Ioue*, whiles *Ioue* to earth is gone.
> (3.11.35)

The second room contains transformations of another sort. The "monstrous formes" and "wilde Antics" of mighty Conquerours and Captaines strong" display their captivity to Cupid in the pure gold walls. In contrast to the bestial transformations of the first room these conquerors conquered represent the effects of love as destruction not only of personal but also of political power. The scenes, although Spenser does not describe them, probably illustrate the philosophy of "the world well lost." The images of love in both rooms share a common element in depicting love from the male point of view. With the possible exception of Venus all the images are of man transformed and the effect of this transformation on the woman. There are no Medeas or Pasiphaes. Both rooms present a challenge to Britomart.

> The warlike Mayde beholding earnestly
> The goodly ordinance of this rich place,
> Did greatly wonder, ne could satisfie
> Her greedy eyes with gazing a long space,
> But more she meruaild that no footings trace,
> Nor wight appear'd, but wastefull emptinesse,
> And solemne silence ouer all that place:

> Straunge thing it seem'd, that none was to possesse
> So rich purueyance, ne them keepe with carefulnesse.
>
> And as she lookt about, she did behold,
>   How ouer that same dore was likewise writ,
>   *Be bold, be bold,* and euery where *Be bold,*
>   That much she muz'd, yet could not construe it
>   By any ridling skill, or commune wit.
> At last she spyde at that roomes vpper end,
>   Another yron dore, on which was writ,
>   *Be not too bold*; whereto though she did bend
> Her earnest mind, yet wist not what it might intend.
>
> (3.11.53-54)

Britomart is alone and cannot understand either the import of these images of love or their costly art in the absence of any human artificer or owner. The House of Busyrane to Britomart is but "wastefull emptinesse."

As if to tease her to a half-answer the gnomic commands present their own challenge, for these words are nothing more than the ironic commands of Busyrane. The first two rooms image the boldness of love: desire, pursuit, and victory. And yet in every case the victory goes not to the pursuer but to Cupid. Over the entrance to the third room is the contradictory command "Be not too bold," the most ironic of all. It applies to all those who think they understand the mask of Cupid. To those who see it as the wedding guests, it is a warning that the final triumph will be Cupid's. To the true lovers of this world it is a warning that the course of true love never did run smooth—even within the sanctity of marriage. It stands as a cynical introduction to the plight of Amoret.

With this preparation Britomart enters the third room. Alone Britomart is exposed to the terrors of night and "hideous storm," which precede the mask. After describing the storm and earthquake Spenser introduces the presenter of his mask with a simile:

> And forth issewd, as on the ready flore
> Of some Theatre, a graue personage,
> That in his hand a branch of laurell bore,
> With comely haueour and count'nance sage,
> Yclad in costly garments, fit for tragicke Stage.
> (3.12.3)

This tragic figure is none other than Ease, the traditional figure of amatory delight. The theatre simile is not only appropriate to introduce the mask; it also imposes a further unreality on the action of the mask—the tragic unreality of Amoret's mind. The ambiguity imposed by the simile is Spenser's way of telling the reader that Britomart is seeing the mask in a manner different from the wedding guests and Amoret, and therefore will be able to resolve the basic ambiguity of the mask itself. This is made clear by Britomart's reaction at the close of the mask. She runs up to the door through which it has disappeared, but "it vaine she thought with rigorous vprore, For to efforce, when charmes had closed it afore" (3.12.27). And we are reassured as she enters the inner room on the next night that we are seeing "Bold *Britomart*, . . . Neither of idle shewes, nor of false charmes aghast" (3.12.29). Without describing the process by which Britomart comes to this knowledge Spenser informs us that she has seen the mask as an idle show, the product of a false charm; and it may be significant that this resolution comes from "Bold *Britomart*": the boldness of love conquered by the boldness of chastity. Only at this point do we catch a glimpse of the offender Busyrane, when his charm has been detected. Only at this point can he be defeated. Spenser, perhaps wisely, does not tell us what his charm was, yet from this encounter Britomart and Amoret learn the dangers that Busyrane represents, and Britomart can bind him with the same chain that had imprisoned Amoret. We never learn what happens to Busyrane as Britomart leads Amoret to freedom, but there is no need to know. He is no longer of any importance, and like his castle disappears from the poem and the consciousness of the reader. As in Petrarch, the triumph of Cupid is succeeded by the triumph of chastity, but Spenser saw that even this triumph might prove empty and thrusts his heroine into new situations in the legend of friendship.

(c) *Britomart and Arthegall*

Just as the chance encounter with Florimell initiates the action of Book III the various encounters with Ate in canto 1 initiate the action of Book IV, establishing an atmosphere of discord that prevails unchecked for the first six cantos. Ate's power reaches a climax in cantos 4 and 5 at Satyrane's tournament and the contest for Florimell's girdle, but the forces of discord that she has set in motion are finally defeated in canto 9 with the help of Arthur. In this chapter we shall concern ourselves only with the effect of Ate on Britomart and Arthegall together. Having sustained her trial at the House of Busyrane and revealed herself to Amoret, Britomart renews her quest for Arthegall and meets first of all Ate and her company of evil companions. The encounter is slight, but it provides Ate with the opportunity of turning Scudamour against Britomart. The next time that we see Britomart is at the tournament of Satyrane, where after her sudden appearance she overthrows Arthegall and wins the day for the knights of Maidenhead. Thus through the power of Ate Britomart has made two enemies, who have vowed revenge and do not know that she is a woman. This is the situation at the beginning of canto 6.

The narrative action of this episode offers no difficulties; the problem for the critic is the significance of details. The first of these details is Arthegall's appearance. He has disguised himself for his part in the tournament. No longer is he clad in the armor of Achilles (3.2.25); he now appears as the "salvage knight."

> Till that there entred on the other side,
> A straunger knight, from whence no man could reed,
> In quyent disguise, full hard to be descride.
> For all his armour was like saluage weed,
> With woody mosse bedight, and all his steed
> With oaken leaues attrapt, that seemed fit
> For saluage wight, and thereto well agreed
> His word, which on his ragged shield was writ,
> *Saluagesse sans finesse*, shewing secret wit. (4.4.39)

The secret wit behind this disguise is never revealed, but one suspects that Arthegall's assumption of this role owes something to the fact that the tournament is Satyrane's, who has played the part of the natural man every time he appears in the poem. For our purposes in this chapter it will be enough to comment on the appropriateness of this disguise to the meeting of Britomart and Arthegall. The motto means literally "savagery without finish." Arthegall is an incomplete man; we learn for the first time that he has disdained "womans hand" and been "rebellious vnto loue" (4.6.31). The new disguise symbolizes what he is before he falls in love with Britomart. Love brings completion and fulfillment to Arthegall as well as to Britomart. She is the tempering that his sternness requires.

The fight itself is less important than the symbols Spenser uses to suggest the significance of the encounter. Scudamour is immediately overthrown, and Arthegall as his second takes up the fight. The match is equal. He is unhorsed. She is unhorsed. He is wounded, and finally her "ventayle" is "shard away."

> With that her angels face, vnseene afore,
> Like to the ruddie morne appeard in sight,

Deawed with siluer drops, through sweating sore,
 But somewhat redder, then beseem'd aright,
Through toylesome heate and labour of her weary fight.

And round about the same, her yellow heare
 Hauing through stirring loosd their wonted band,
 Like to a golden border did appeare,
 Framed in goldsmithes forge with cunning hand:
 Yet goldsmithes cunning could not vnderstand
 To frame such subtile wire, so shinie cleare.
 For it did glister like the golden sand,
 The which *Pactolus* with his waters shere,
Throwes forth vpon the riuage round about him nere.
                                        (4.6.19-20)

The light imagery of the first stanza clearly relates this passage to the similes describing Britomart discussed earlier. The "angels face" may be read as simple hyperbole, but there are other phrases that suggest a more precise significance. When commenting on the cruelty of the fight, Spenser writes of Arthegall attempting "To spoyle so goodly workmanship of nature, The maker selfe resembling in her feature" (4.6.17), and later he calls Britomart "so diuine a beauties excellence," "That peerelesse paterne of Dame natures pride, And heauenly image of perfection . . ." (4.6.21,24). These phrases, too, may be read as hyperbole, but the confrontation of Britomart and Arthegall takes on more meaning if we view these phrases as references to the concept of the *imago Dei* as it was understood in the Renaissance.

Arnold Williams in his informative book about Renaissance commentaries on Genesis discusses the variety of interpretations of the concept. The source is, of course, "And God said, Let us make man in our image, after our likeness . . ." (Genesis 1:26). Some commentators tried to differentiate between *image* and *likeness*; for example, *image* referred to natural gifts while *likeness* referred to supernatural gifts like justice, sanctity, and innocence, or image referred only to the Son and *likeness* to other men. Most of the commentators, however, assumed that the words were synonymous and constituted a unity, which they called the "image" of God in man. Every faculty of man was suggested by some commentator or other as this image, but two explanations were especially favored. The image consisted of man's domination of the earth, only partial since the Fall, or it consisted in the image of the Trinity that man's reason represents. As there are three Persons in one God, so there are three faculties in one reason: memory, will, and understanding.

"Reason was certainly the chief seat of the image. By reason man touches the supreme grade of being, that of the angels and God. The soul, which is partially synonymous with reason, is also a part of the image. Besides, there is an image in nature, signified by those manifold gifts of mind which everyone has noticed, and also an image in grace and righteousness, lost by Adam and regained in Christ. Man's domination over the animals is a sign of the image, being one of the similarities between his position on the earth and God's in the universe. The trinity of three faculties in his mind is certainly a demonstration of the image. In fact, the signs and manifestations of the image of God, even in fallen man, are almost infinite in number."[18]

[18] Arnold Williams, *The Common Expositor*, p. 74. The entire discussion of the various explanations is useful. Williams points out that the Renaissance commentators differed from the psychologists in making the memory a faculty of reason and not of the senses. This may have some bearing on the function of memory in the House of Alma and on the tale of Troy told by Paridell in 3.9. Paridell has forgotten some of the details but recalls that old Mnemon has told him about them, when he is reminded by Britomart. If Spenser is using this tradition, Paridell's failure of memory is another sign of his irrational and sinful life. Memory as part of the reason would affect one's conception of history, significantly connecting the moral acts of the individual to the Providential scheme of history expressed in the chronicle of British kings and the prophecy of Merlin.

Williams' summary of the commentators is supported by an equally explicit passage from de la Primaudaye: " . . . it is a common vse in schooles to teach, that man is a little world, and that within him the body is composed of the elements, the reasonable soule is celestiall, the vegetable power common to men and plants, the sense common to bruit beastes, the reason participated to Angels: and finally the image of God is therein seene and considered."[19]

Both are appropriate as a gloss on Britomart at the moment of her revelation. Britomart's face is described as an angel's; she is said to resemble God, and at the moment of revelation she is dominating Arthegall, the savage man.

But it is important to note that Spenser does not specify in what sense Britomart exemplifies the image of God; we are given a series of similes, comprised mainly of images of light and gold. However, the concept is explicitly linked to themes more characteristic of Spenser in several of his *Amoretti*:

> The glorious image of the makers beautie,
>   My souerayne saynt, the Idoll of my thought,
>   dare not henceforth aboue the bounds of dewtie,
>   t'accuse of pride, or rashly blame for ought.
> For being as she is diuinely wrought,
>   and of the brood of Angels heuenly borne:
>   and with the crew of blessed Saynts vpbrought,
>   each of which did her with theyr guifts adorne;
> The bud of ioy, the blossome of the morne,
>   the beame of light, whom mortal eyes admyre:
>   what reason is it then but she should scorne
>   base things that to her loue too bold aspire?
> Such heauenly formes ought rather worshipt be,
>   then dare be lou'd by men of meane degree.
>
> (sonnet 61)

---

[19] De la Primaudaye, *The French Academie*, p. 672.

THE IMAGE OF BRITOMART

One feels much more comfortable about the image of God when it is restated as radiant beauty, but some may still feel that the image as used here is the exaggeration peculiar to the sonnet. That the image is intended seriously we may gather from Sonnet 79, where Spenser warns his lady that all beauty will decay,

> but onely that is permanent and free
> from frayle corruption, that doth flesh ensew.
> That is true beautie: that doth argue you
> to be diuine and borne of heauenly seed:
> deriu'd from that fayre Spirit, from whom al true
> and perfect beauty did at first proceed.

Here Spenser explicitly relates beauty to that source which I have already suggested was the ultimate tenor of the images used to describe Britomart.

The problem of describing moral beauty is one that every artist must face, and the solution that springs immediately to mind is the metaphorical use of physical beauty. In a poetic that is based on analogy, where reality is described in terms of appearance, the poet must imply that the appearance and the reality are one, that the appearance is not merely a mask hiding something quite different from itself. The image that best represents the continuity of appearance and reality is the image of the light of reality shining through the fabric of appearance, and this image of light is supposed to call to the reader's mind the ultimate source of light and beauty.

Spenser is not advocating a theory of immanent deity in describing Britomart, but he does not let us forget that the image of God, if it is to shine at all, must shine through the flesh. Therefore, Britomart appears "like to the ruddie morne ... Deawed with siluer drops" from "sweating sore" and seems "somewhat redder ... Through toylesome heate and labour of her weary fight." Her yellow hair appears like a border of gold framing her face, but in its disorder it is a nature that surpasses the art of the goldsmith. Even the Pactolus reference in all its artificiality suggests the living, flowing quality that Spenser is trying to describe. The perfection he sees in Britomart is both moral and physical, and his mingling of art and nature, of human and divine, at the moment of her recognition is meant to convey this two-fold meaning.

The effect of Britomart's radiant beauty subdues Arthegall, who "fell humbly downe vpon his knee, And of his wonder made religion . . ." (4.6.22); and even Scudamour "blest himselfe, as one sore terrifide, And turning his feare to faint deuotion, Did worship her as some celestiall vision" (4.6.24). The effect is that of a religious conversion or revelation, and I believe that Spenser intends us to see that the inception of love is such a revelation, dazzling and illuminating, relating the beings involved to a more primary Love that we may merely signify through images of light.

As if to counteract the awesome aspects of the situation Spenser presents Britomart's reaction to the sight of Arthegall as the eternal female, somewhat confused, somewhat dissembling.

> Therewith her wrathfull courage gan appall,
>   And haughtie spirits meekely to adaw,
>   That her enhaunced hand she downe can soft withdraw.
>
> Yet she it forst to haue againe vpheld,
>   As fayning choler, which was turn'd to cold:
>   But euer when his visage she beheld,
>   Her hand fell downe, and would no longer hold
>   The wrathfull weapon gainst his countnance bold. . . .
>
> Soone as she heard the name of *Artegall*,
>   Her hart did leape, and all her hart-strings tremble,
>   For sudden ioy, and secret feare withall,
>   And all her vitall powres with motion nimble,

THE IMAGE OF BRITOMART

> To succour it, themselves gan there assemble,
> That by the swift recourse of flushing blood
> Right plaine appeard, though she it would dissemble,
> And fayned still her former angry mood,
> Thinking to hide the depth by troubling of the flood.
> (4.6.26,27,29)

Out of the distraught passions of Britomart and Arthegall, out of the discord prompted by Ate comes the concord of love. Out of the knowledge gained by overcoming Gardante and Busyrane Britomart's radiant chastity is prepared for the transmutation that her confrontation with Arthegall represents. Her quest has been accomplished, and in its accomplishment Spenser has revealed as much of his image of chastity as he saw fit. I stated at the beginning of this chapter that the adventures of Britomart define Spenser's conception of chastity, and so they do. Having experienced the powerful narrative and symbolism of these episodes, we cannot return to the simple equation that Britomart is chastity without realizing that our conception of chastity has been refined and deepened. We will not be able to write out a precise definition, nor should we want to. The definition of chastity is inextricably bound up with Britomart and her adventures. She does not ride through the poem with a signboard labelled "Chastity" around her neck, and the reader who saddles her with such a burden will find that he is almost invariably restricting the meaning of the adventures and of the conception that Spenser is trying to present. We may say that Britomart presents chastity as we meet it in our ordinary experience, but this will not exhaust the possibilities inherent in his conception. To see the other facets of chastity we must turn to the other heroines of these books.

Chapter Two
Belphoebe and Amoret

> They looked with such eagerness at Venus Naturalis because they had caught a glimpse of her inaccessible twin sister.
>
> —KENNETH CLARK, *The Nude*

THE problem of characterization discussed in the preceding chapter is intensified in turning to the figures of Belphoebe and Amoret. Unlike Britomart they display none of the traits associated with psychological realism. We never see the working of their minds or the motivations for their actions. They are presented in a series of adventures in which their emblematic natures constitute as much of the meaning of the episodes as the development of the action. Belphoebe and Amoret are archetypes or universals. They enjoy a status in the poem that Britomart never attains. They belong to the world of Faeryland and depend more than does Britomart on their status as conceptions realized in the poem. Again it will not be enough to call them virginity and married love, although we may so designate them, if we know where such labelling is leading us. Spenser is very careful to supply the reader with symbol so that we need not rely on our own ideas of what virginity or married love should or should not be. He does this mainly through the literary archetypes with which his figures are associated and through the series of adventures in which they participate. Belphoebe is defined primarily through the archetype and Amoret through the adventures. Let us begin with Belphoebe's first appearance in the poem, outside the proper limits of this book but definitively important in establishing what she is.

BELPHOEBE AND AMORET

i · BELPHOEBE AND THE THREE QUEENS

Belphoebe appears three times in *The Faerie Queene*, and on each of these occasions it is apparent that Spenser is defining her character and actions through the archetype of Diana the huntress and more particularly through reminiscences of this archetype as described by previous poets—Virgil, Ariosto, and Tasso.[1] Beyond the archetype of Diana is the person of Elizabeth, whom Spenser tells us Belphoebe represents: *"In that Faery Queene I meane glory in my generall intention, but in my particular I conceiue the most excellent and glorious person of our soueraine the Queene, and her kingdome in Faery land. And yet in some places els, I doe otherwise shadow her. For considering she beareth two persons, the one of a most royall Queene or Empresse, the other of a most vertuous and beautifull Lady, this latter part in some places I doe express in Belphoebe, fashioning her name according to your owne excellent conceipt of Cynthia, (Phoebe and Cynthia being both names of Diana.)"*[2]

We learn two facts from this passage: (1) Belphoebe represents Elizabeth as a private person and not the public queen; (2) Belphoebe as a character mediates between Elizabeth the private person and the Diana archetype. Any interpretation of Belphoebe must account for both these guiding principles of her characterization. Belphoebe is not a particularized portrait of Elizabeth but an idealization of those traits that characterized her private life, namely her virginity and hence her virtue and her beauty. This view is consistent with the Diana archetype and with any hopes of flattering Elizabeth. One cannot interpret the allegory simply by substituting "Elizabeth" every time the name "Belphoebe"

---

[1] *FQ*, 2.3.20ff.; 3.5.27ff.; 3.6; 4.7.23ff.; 4.8.1ff.; and a reference to Belphoebe and Timias, 6.5.12. The references to Virgil are *Aeneid*, 1.314-328, 498-499, to Ariosto, *Orlando Furioso*, 7.11ff., to Tasso, *Rinaldo*, 1.53-57. See *Var.*, 2.211-221.
[2] *Var.*, 1.168.

occurs. The result is inevitably confusion and disappointment.[3] This view of Spenser, wildly juggling an outmoded form of literary expression in order to keep the old queen happy while at the same time slyly criticizing her, is too absurd for comment, yet it is so commonly held that one wonders why so few have failed to realize its complete inconsistency with the epic plan of *The Faerie Queene* and the epic seriousness of its author. Nor should we go to the other extreme of reading Belphoebe where the details used to amplify the archetypal image are read as if they gave life to the image rather than taking their significance from the large and simple archetype.[4]

This is obvious as soon as one turns to Belphoebe's first appearance in the poem, Book II, canto 3. The canto is a deviation from the main narrative of Guyon's task. Braggadocchio has just stolen Guyon's horse, and the whole canto is an attempt to show the significance of this action. During the course of the canto Braggadocchio and his henchman Trompart meet two beings of an order other than their own: Archimago and Belphoebe. Since the reader is well aware of Archimago as a massive evil from Book I, there is no need for Spenser to amplify his appearance further. Archimago disappears almost as quickly as he appeared, but the intrusion of the archenemy of truth and the symbol of hypocrisy suitably darkens Spenser's pair of culprits. We cannot again accept these two would-be knights as simple comic interpolations. Their action is a travesty of all the values of knightly chivalry, and Spenser intends the reader to feel the inane evil of their action by confronting them with another force, opposed to Archimago and equally powerful. The "well consorted paire" hear a blast from a horn that "made the forrest ring, as it would riue in twaine," and Braggadocchio hides himself in some nearby bushes.

[3] See *Var.*, 4.205-207.
[4] See Harry Berger, Jr., *The Allegorical Temper*, pp. 120-160.

BELPHOEBE AND AMORET

> Eftsoone there stepped forth
> A goodly Ladie clad in hunters weed,
> That seemd to be a woman of great worth,
> And by her stately portance, borne of heauenly birth.
>
> (2.3.21)

The ten stanzas of description that follow amplify the image of Belphoebe as a fitting opposite to Archimago and leave no doubt that the tone of the episode has changed from irony to worshipful awe. To make sure that the reader will not miss the special nature of this encounter Spenser echoes the famous meeting of Aeneas and Venus in the first book of the *Aeneid*. He had already alluded to this same passage when praising Elizabeth in the April eclogue, but here he ends his description of Belphoebe by adding a simile that Virgil uses to describe the first appearance of Dido:[5]

> Such as *Diana* by the sandie shore
>   Of swift *Eurotas*, or on *Cynthus* greene,
> Where all the Nymphes haue her vnwares forlore,
>   Wandreth alone with bow and arrowes keene,
>   To seeke her game: Or as that famous Queene
> Of *Amazons*, whom *Pyrrhus* did destroy,
>   The day that first of *Priame* she was seene,
>   Did shew her selfe in great triumphant ioy,
> To succour the weake state of sad afflicted *Troy*.
>
> (2.3.31)

Professor Hughes has pointed out the incongruity of using the Dido simile to describe Belphoebe, but there is the common denominator of the Diana archetype to link them, and

---

[5] See the emblem at the end of the eclogue and E. K.'s gloss. Professor Hughes points out that the Virgilian phrase "O quam te memorem virgo" is used also by Marlowe, Tasso, and Petrarch. Hughes, *Virgil and Spenser*, pp. 294 and 359-364.

it may be that Spenser is purposely bringing in political allusion at this point.[6]

Dido, it must be remembered, has a public and a private character as much as Elizabeth: she is both Queen of Carthage and a woman. It is in the first of these capacities that she appears to Aeneas. All around her are the signs of her powerful kingdom, but as Aeneas approaches the temple he discovers that it depicts the fall of Troy and the deaths of Hector and Penthesilea. If, as Upton suggested, Braggadocchio and Trompart are meant to portray the Duc d'Alençon and his agent Simier, Spenser may be presenting the queen with an image of her own potential downfall.[7] Although these implications of the passage may have been subjects of interest in 1590, we cannot prove that they are in the poem, nor do they illuminate the primary issue of the episode.

Spenser's description of Belphoebe's first appearance is both a parody of a famous Virgilian passage and at the same time a manifestation of her essential quality. As Belphoebe assumes the characteristics of Virgil's Venus, Braggadocchio and Trompart assume the nature of the other two characters. They are parodies of Aeneas and Achates, the *pius* founder of Second Troy and his faithful companion. At their moment of revelation when Belphoebe speaks of true honor, Braggadocchio's response is an attempt to rape her, but Belphoebe turns and flees. The scene is provocative and symbolically defines Belphoebe's character, if we keep in mind the allegorical interpretations of Virgil's Venus. The ambivalence of Virgil's presentation of Venus as Diana, that strange juxtaposition of normally conflicting tendencies, is repeated and elaborated in Spenser's later descriptions of Belphoebe. The combination of Venus-beauty and Diana-chastity, which confounded Braggadocchio, is present in Belphoebe's later ap-

[6] Merritt Y. Hughes, "Virgilian Allegory and *The Faerie Queene*," *PMLA*, 44 (1929), pp. 696-697.
[7] *Var.*, 2.206.

pearances and helps to specify the particular kind of Diana figure she is meant to figure forth as well as her relation to Elizabeth.

ii · THE TWO VENUSES

Professor Hughes has demonstrated that Renaissance allegorists interpreted Virgil's Venus as "contemplation" and "divinely revealed truth," thus relating Belphoebe to the Heavenly Venus of the Neoplatonists.[8] If Belphoebe represented the Heavenly Venus in her first and most completely iconic manifestation, it is more than likely that she will also represent this figure in her later appearances. This is the interpretation proposed by Professor Lemmi.[9] His analysis begins with the Neoplatonic theory of the two Venuses developed by Ficino: "There are, then, two Venuses: one is that intelligence which we have identified with the Angelic Mind, the other is the power of generation attributed to the Soul of the World. Both are accompanied by Love, through which the first contemplates the Beauty of God, and the second creates divine beauty in earthly forms."

These two Venuses are also by analogy functions of man's soul: "The soul of man has two powers: that of knowing and that of generating. These powers are two Venuses in it, and they are accompanied by two Loves. When the beauty of the body appears before our eyes, our mind, which is in us the first Venus loves and worships it as an image of the beauty of God; our generative powers, which are in us the second Venus, desire to generate a form similar to it. Love, then, is in both these powers. In the first it is a desire to contemplate beauty; in the second, to generate it. The one love and the other are virtuous. Each follows a divine image."[10]

---

[8] Hughes, *Virgil and Spenser*, p. 362.

[9] Charles W. Lemmi, "Britomart: the Embodiment of True Love," *SP*, 31 (1934), pp. 133-139.

[10] Lemmi, p. 134. Lemmi's translation of Ficino, *Sopra lo Amore*, ed. G. Rensi, Lanciano, Carabba, 1914, II, 7, 36.

Lemmi asserts that Britomart corresponds to the Earthly Venus, the *vis generandi*, and, following the suggestion of Professor Hughes, that Belphoebe corresponds to the Heavenly Venus, "spiritual detachment or chastity." The importance of this theory of the two Venuses cannot be doubted in light of more recent research, but Lemmi's identification of Britomart and Belphoebe with these two Venuses is an error of judgment, which leaves Amoret unexplained. She is "just a maiden. As we read the story of her marriage and notice how greatly the whole episode is indebted to the *Romance of the Rose*, the thing dawns on us. Amoret and Scudamour are the oldest and yet the freshest and newest types in the world. They are the lovers, just as their names tell us."[11]

Lemmi has forgotten one important point—Amoret and Belphoebe are twins; it is unlikely that Spenser intended one twin to represent a heavenly power and the other merely a human lover. Although he is correct in calling Amoret and Scudamour the lovers in this world, the implication that they represent merely the human aspects of love is belied by Spenser's treatment of them. Neither Amoret nor Belphoebe reveals those strange quirks of human personality observable in Britomart. On the contrary, their miraculous birth in Faeryland as opposed to Britomart's origins in Wales suggests that they are less "realistic," more allegorical than Britomart. These details imply that they represent complementary aspects of one large concept that will include the chaste virginity of Belphoebe and the chaste love of Amoret. Such a double concept is Ficino's theory of the two Venuses. Simply by reversing the roles Lemmi assigned to Amoret and Britomart, a plausible relationship can be established among the three heroines. Belphoebe is the Heavenly Venus, eschewing earthly love; Amoret is the Earthly Venus, beset

---

[11] Lemmi, p. 138.

by all the dangers love is heir to. Britomart is the human embodiment of both types, passing from the virginity of youth to the chaste married love of maturity.

Still the identification of Belphoebe and Amoret can be made more precise, if no less broad: virginity and marriage; and this distinction brings us closer to our subject of chastity. "Chastity is the beauty of the soule and purity of life, which refuseth the corrupt pleasures of the flesh, and is onely possessed of those who keepe their bodies cleane and vndefiled; and it consisteth eyther in sincere virginity, or in faithful matrimony."[12] This is the particular aspect of the two Venuses that Spenser chooses to portray in Belphoebe and Amoret. Their allegorical personalities are specifically Christian virginity and Christian marriage. The imagery, iconography, and structural patterns of the episodes in which they appear reinforce the complementary nature of their roles in the poem.

This is not to say that at every moment in the poem they fully exemplify these concepts. They are figures in a narrative and are subject to the tugs and pulls of story-telling. Nevertheless they conform to the figures of mythological narratives, which Professor Tuve remarks "contract into metaphors, stand still and become emblems, and deepen into symbols. . . ."[13] Each time that Belphoebe and Amoret appear in the poem their conceptual status stands ready to clarify their ambiguous adventures.

iii · THE BIRTH

Canto 6 has been justly celebrated as one of the high points of *The Faerie Queene*; unfortunately the critics have dealt almost exclusively with the latter part of the canto, omitting

---

[12] Bodenham, *Wits Commonwealth*, London, 1655, p. 228, quoted in Bruser, p. 162.
[13] Rosemond Tuve, *Images and Themes in Five Poems by Milton*, Cambridge, Mass., 1957, p. 12.

the miraculous birth of Amoret and Belphoebe and the encounter of Venus and Diana.[14] While it is true that the description of the Garden of Adonis is extremely important as an expression of Spenser's ideas of love and creation—as its central position in Book III indicates—nevertheless its main purpose in the poem is to illuminate the structure of the book and the natures of Belphoebe and Amoret. When seen in this light, the Garden of Adonis becomes one part of three that Spenser devotes to the explanation of the roles of Belphoebe and Amoret in Books III and IV.

The first ten stanzas, describing the miraculous conception and birth of Belphoebe and Amoret, are introduced by Spenser rather boldly questioning Belphoebe as symbol. How is it, he asks, that the "saluage forests" have nurtured a lady of such perfections so far away from "The great schoolmistresse of all curtesy"—the Court. This question had also occurred to Braggadocchio: "But what art thou, O Ladie, which doest raunge In this wilde forrest, where no pleasure is, And doest not it for ioyous court exchaunge, Emongst thine equall peres, where happie blis And all delight does raigne, much more then this? . . . The wood is fit for beasts, the court is fit for thee" (2.3.39). The answer that Belphoebe gives Braggadocchio is her famous speech on honor, "In woods, in waues, in warres she wonts to dwell. . . ." Spenser never answers this question explicitly, but leads the reader on to the description of her birth, which should alert the reader to the significance of the occasion.

> Her berth was of the wombe of Morning dew,
>   And her conception of the ioyous Prime,
>   And all her whole creation did her shew

---

[14] See *Var.*, 3.340-352 and Brents Stirling, "Spenser's 'Platonic' Garden," and J. W. Bennett, "Reply: On Methods of Literary Interpretation," *JEGP*, 41 (1942), pp. 482-489.

BELPHOEBE AND AMORET

Pure and vnspotted from all loathly crime,
That is ingenerate in fleshly slime.

(3.6.3)

Upton has noted that the first line is almost a literal translation of the Prayer Book version of Psalm 110:3: "The dew of thy birth is of the womb of the morning."[15] Coverdale's translation differs markedly from the Vulgate and the later Douay and King James translations. The Vulgate reads simply "ex utero ante luciferum genui te." It was used as the communion versicle of the midnight Mass of Christmas, and the whole psalm was retained in the Evensong service for Christmas in the Anglican rite. It was generally accepted that verse 3 referred to the begetting or Incarnation of Christ[16] and by extension to the development of His Church.[17]

---

[15] *Var.*, 3.249. This psalm is 109 in the Vulgate or Douay. Coverdale's version of this verse was used in the Great Bible of 1537 and the Bishops' Bible of 1588.

[16] See Augustine, *Enarratio in Psalmum cix*, PL, 37.1459 and *Glossa ordinaria*, PL, 113.1030-1031. Since the verse was used as the communion versicle in the midnight Mass for Christmas, it was also applied to the nativity of Christ and to Mary. See St. Bernard, "Sermon for the Feast of the Nativity of the Blessed Virgin Mary." He says of the text "A spirit before our face is Christ the Lord; under His shadow we shall live among the Gentiles" (Jer. Lam., 4.20) "'Among the Gentiles,' yes, but not among the blessed angels: for there we shall live no longer under His shadow, but in the full splendor of His divine glory. 'In the splendours of the saints, from the womb before the day-star I begot thee' (Ps. cix.3): but these, as you know, are the words of the Heavenly Father addressed to His only begotten Son. It was under the shadow, not in the splendour, that the same Son was brought forth by His Mother, yet under no other shadow than that wherewith the Most High overshadowed her (Luke i.35)." (*St. Bernard's Sermons for the Seasons and Principal Festivals of the Year*, 3 vols., Westminster, Md., 1950, vol. 3, p. 282.) The Begetting of Christ is shown in the Utrecht Psalter, fol. 64^v and in the Canterbury Psalter, fol. 199^v. The illuminated initial of Bodleian, Douce 366, fol. 147^v shows Christ seated beside God the Father in similar poses. The initial of British Museum, Add. 38116 shows the Coronation of the Virgin. See also *Beatty Collection, Catalogue of Western Manuscripts*, vol. 2, 1930, pl. 128b.

[17] The Psalter of 1532 (*STC* 2364) says of this psalm: "A prophecy

That Spenser used this verse in full knowledge of its implications cannot be doubted in the light of his insistence on the miraculous nature of Belphoebe's and Amoret's conception and birth. Belphoebe's "whole creation did her shew Pure and vnspotted from all loathly crime, That is ingenerate in fleshly slime" (3.6.3); she and Amoret "not as other wemens commune brood, . . . were enwombed in the sacred throne Of her chaste bodie, nor with commune food, As other wemens babes, they sucked vitall blood. But wondrously they were begot, and bred Through influence of th'heauens fruitfull ray . . ." (3.6.5-6). The story of Chrysogonee's conception by the sun leads to the equally miraculous account of her labor: "Vnwares she them conceiu'd, vnwares she bore: She bore withouten paine, that she conceiued Withouten pleasure . . ." (3.6.27). It is hardly necessary to realize that Chrysogonee's name means "golden birth" and that she is the daughter of Amphisa, "of double nature," to see that Spenser is insisting that this miraculous birth is an analogue to the Incarnation. The reason is neither idly hyperbolic nor blasphemous; it is, I believe, Spenser's way of suggesting the true genealogy of Christian virginity and marriage.

---

of the birth of cryste/ and of his kingdom both here in his chirche/ and also in heuen" (fol. 175ᵛ). Luther calls it "a peculiar and glorious prophecy concerning the kingdom of Christ" (*A Manual of the Book of Psalms* . . . , trans. Rev. Henry Cole, London, 1837, p. 297). Calvin's version of this verse as translated by Arthur Golding, 1571, reads: "Thy people *shall come* vvith vviling oblations in the day of *the mustering of* thine armie, in beautie of holynesse: the deavv of thy youth *shall come* vnto the out of thy vvomb from the morning." Calvin's interpretation is that the verse refers to God's nurture of His people and the growth of His church (*The Psalmes of Dauid and others. With M. Iohn Calvins Commentaries*, London, 1571, sigs. Rrr 4ᵛ and Rrr 6). Similar interpretations may be found in the Psalter of 1530 (*STC* 2370) and in the Genevan Bible, 1560. See also Robert Abbot, *The Exaltation of the Kingdome and Priesthood of Christ. In Certaine Sermons Vpon 110 Psalme* . . . , London, 1601.

Immediately following the image of the rose, near the end of canto 5, another version of Belphoebe's creation is given.

> Eternall God in his almighty powre,
>   To make ensample of his heauenly grace,
>   In Paradize whilome did plant this flowre;
>   Whence he it fetcht out of her natiue place,
>   And did in stocke of earthly flesh enrace,
>   That mortall men her glory should admire:
>   In gentle Ladies brest, and bounteous race
> Of woman kind it fairest flowre doth spire,
> And beareth fruit of honour and all chast desire.
> (3.5.52)

Belphoebe's creation is here treated like that of a Platonic Idea, the embodiment of which on earth acts as example of its special virtue to man. Even here parallels to the Incarnation are evident, but the stanza is important because it tells us that the myth of Chrysogonee is the story of the incarnation of virtues already existent in Spenser's Platonic heaven and that they are related to the supernatural order of grace. It has been suggested that this twin birth represents the emergence of the Christian ideals of virginity and marriage and that the adventures of Belphoebe and Amoret exemplify the life of Christian virginity and Christian marriage. If this contention is correct, the details of the myth should lend themselves easily to an allegorical interpretation of the emergence of these ideals in the world.

This is Spenser's first analogy to his myth of Chrysogonee, what may be called the analogy from religion. A second analogy—the analogy from nature—immediately follows the myth.

> Miraculous may seeme to him, that reades
>   So straunge ensample of conception;
>   But reason teacheth that the fruitfull seades

> Of all things liuing, through impression
> Of the sunbeames in moyst complexion,
> Do life conceiue and quickned are by kynd:
> So after *Nilus* invndation,
> Infinite shapes of creatures men do fynd,
> Informed in the mud, on which the Sunne hath shynd.
>
> Great father he of generation
> Is rightly cald, th'author of life and light;
> And his faire sister for creation
> Ministreth matter fit, which tempred right
> With heate and humour, breedes the liuing wight.
> So sprong these twinnes in wombe of *Chrysogone* . . .
>
> (3.6.8-9)

Between these two analogies—the one from the order of grace, the other from the order of nature—is the meaning of Spenser's myth, and this meaning should harmonize with both analogies.

The point at which the analogies meet reveals the reason that Spenser employed religious imagery to explain his myth. The analogy from grace relates that God "did in stocke of earthly flesh enrace" the soul or "idea" of Belphoebe, and this is the same act that the analogy from nature describes as the conception of "the fruitfull seades Of all things liuing, through impression Of the sunbeames in moyst complexion;" but as C. S. Lewis reminds us, the sun is a symbol of God for Spenser. The Chrysogonee myth, then, is the act of embodiment of the Platonic Idea, which had already existed in Paradise. The religious analogy tells us that this birth is somehow different from ordinary reproduction; the natural analogy tells us that this conception is not contrary to nature. The paradox thus created must be described in terms available to a Christian reader, and those terms can be approximated only by comparison with the Incarnation.

The result of this conception is the sinless birth of Belphoebe and Amoret, symbolized by Chrysogonee's painless labor, a direct contradiction of God's curse on Eve. Here the Incarnational imagery ceases with no indication of the reason why it was used at all. The miraculous birth is just the first stage in Spenser's definition of Belphoebe and Amoret, for immediately after their birth they are discovered by Venus and Diana in search of the lost Cupid.

Strangely enough in a poem so indebted to classical mythology this is the only time outside the *Mutabilitie Cantos* and canto 12 of Book IV that any of the major Olympian deities appears as a character; they are encountered as statues in temples, as figures in processions, and in numerous allusions and similes, but this is the only time that they are part of the narrative action. It is more than a charming interlude, for Spenser's representation of Venus and Diana will throw light on the conceptual status of Amoret and Belphoebe, their foster children.

The critic who has made the most pertinent comments on this passage of canto 6 is C. S. Lewis. They deserve to be quoted in full:

"The first important event in the life of these twins was their adoption by Venus and Diana: Diana the goddess of virginity, and Venus from whose house 'all the world derives the glorious features of beautie.' Now the circumstances which led up to this adoption are related in one of the most medieval passages in the whole *Faerie Queen*—a *débat* between Venus and Diana; but this *débat* has two remarkable features. In the first place, the Venus who takes part in it is a Venus severed from Cupid, and Cupid, as we have already seen, is associated with courtly love. I say 'associated' because we are dealing with what was merely a feeling in Spenser's mind, not a piece of intellectual and historical knowledge, as it is to us. There is therefore no consistent and conscious identification of Cupid with courtly love, but Cupid tends to appear in one kind of context and to be absent from another kind. And when he does appear in contexts approved by our domestic poet, he usually appears with some kind of reservation. He is allowed into the Garden of Adonis on condition of his 'laying his sad dartes asyde': in the Temple of Venus it is only his younger brothers who flutter round the neck of the goddess. We are therefore fully justified in stressing the fact that Venus finds Amoret only because she has lost Cupid, and finally adopts Amoret *instead of* Cupid. The other important novelty is that this *débat* ends with a reconciliation; Spenser is claiming to have settled the old quarrel between Venus and Diana, and that after a singularly frank statement of the claims of each."[18]

Basically Professor Lewis's interpretation is sound, but it requires amplification and correction. Venus's search for Cupid (stanzas 11-17) is modeled after Moschus's idyl *Eros Drapetes*, the Fugitive Love, a poem of immense popularity during the Renaissance.[19] The motif of Venus searching for her lost son would have been recognized, and Professor Lewis is "fully justified" in asserting that Cupid is finally replaced by Amoret. He is wrong, however, in finding Cupid "associated with courtly love." This is neither the time nor the place to discuss the controversial subject of "courtly love," its origins or existence, but it must be observed that Venus's search does not restrict her to those places where only "courtly love" could exist. By Professor Lewis's definition "courtly love" is "love of a highly specialized sort, whose characteristics may be enumerated as Humility, Courtesy, Adultery, and the Religion of Love. . . . It is possible only to those

---

[18] Lewis, *Allegory of Love*, pp. 342-343.
[19] See J. Douglas Bruce, "Spenser's *Faerie Queene*, Book III, canto VI, St. 11ff., and Moschus's Idyl, "Love the Runaway," *MLN*, 27 (1912), pp. 183-185; James Hutton, "The First Idyl of Moschus in Imitations to the Year 1800," *AJP*, 49 (1928), pp. 105-136; Joseph G. Fucilla, "Additions to 'The First Idyl of Moschus in Imitations to the Year 1800,'" *AJP*, 50 (1929), pp. 190-193; "Materials for the History of a Popular Classical Theme," *CP*, 26 (1931), pp. 135-152.

who are, in the old sense of the word, polite. It thus becomes, from one point of view the flower, from another the seed, of all those noble usages which distinguish the gentle from the vilein; only the courteous can love, but it is love that makes them courteous."[20] But Venus searches not only the Court but the "Citties" (where Cupid is called "the disturber of all ciuill life"), "rurall cottages," and "gentle shepheard swaynes." Even with the idealization of the pastoral life this Cupid represents a broader concept of love than Professor Lewis's "courtly love" will allow. This Cupid represents the kind of love that Amoret sees in the tapestries at the House of Busyrane. It is courtly only in the sense that it venerates a "love that reaches but to dust," and this is a human frailty not restricted to any particular time or place, as Spenser's stanzas are intended to show.

The last place that Venus looks for Cupid is "the wastefull woods," "the secret haunts of *Dianes* company." Venus's separation from Cupid does indicate a divorce from the more lascivious love with whom she is usually identified; similarly the Diana whom she discovers is separated from her usual attributes. Her bow and quiver are hung on a tree, her buskins unlaced, and "Her golden lockes, that late in tresses bright Embreaded were for hindring of her haste, Now loose about her shoulders hong vndight...." She is naked and bathing, and Venus's sudden appearance, as Upton pointed out, is an imitation of the Diana and Actaeon story as told by Ovid.[21]

The story of Actaeon was one of the more popular myths in the English Renaissance.[22] It appears in the emblem books,

---

[20] Lewis, *Allegory of Love*, p. 2.   [21] *Var.*, 3.253.
[22] See, for example, the emblems in Alciati, Paris, 1561, pp. 61-62, Johannes Sambucus, *Emblemata*, Antwerp, 1564, p. 128, and Geoffrey Whitney, *Choice of Emblems*, London, 1586, p. 15. Douglas Bush points out Marlowe's use of the Diana and Actaeon myth in making Gaveston plan to win over the king with Italian masks, naked pages, and Diana and Actaeon (*Mythology and the Renaissance Tradition*, Minneapolis, 1932, p. 80). The nature of the allusion makes it clear that Marlowe was referring to a popular subject. Feuillerat describes a mask of Diana and

BELPHOEBE AND AMORET

in pageants, and in countless poetic conceits. The most usual interpretation of this myth is that Diana represents beauty and Actaeon's hounds his passions.[23] There was, however, considerable range to the possibilities. The author of the *Ovide Moralisé* interprets Diana as the Trinity and Actaeon as Christ,[24] and Abraham Fraunce offers three alternate interpretations.

"Actaeon *fed and maintained a number of idle and vnthankefull persons, noted by his doggs. Others expounde it thus: we ought not to be ouer curious and inquisitiue in spying and prying into those matters, which be aboue our reache, least we be rewarded as* Actaeon *was*. Ouid 2. de tristib.

Inscius Actaeon vidit sine veste dianam:
Praeda fuit canibus non minus ille suis.

Actaeon at court (*Documents of the Revells Office*, pp. 30-32, 33, 34, 35, 36, 38, 39, 43). Stranger still is the appearance of Diana and Actaeon in a May Games procession in company with such traditional figures as Robin Hood, St. George, and Noah (Charles J. Sisson, *Lost Plays of Shakespeare's Age*, Cambridge, 1936, pp. 156-185). Sisson's discovery of the description of the May Games procession at Wells in 1559 is the only available information on the contents of these games, but a possible reference to the tradition occurs in Robert Cox's interlude of Diana and Actaeon (1665-1666?) in which Actaeon, a country bumpkin, who wants very much to be in love, sets off for a May dance and comes upon Diana, dances with her, is warned not to do it again, unintentionally appears where she is bathing and is killed (*The Wits, or Sport upon Sport*, ed. John James Elson, Ithaca, 1932, pp. 415-421). The myth was also apparently popular as decoration on wedding chests. See Paul Schubring, *Cassoni*, Leipzig, 1915, Plates 3, 15, and 34. Chance references are to be found in *Gorgeous Gallery*, ed. Hyder Rollins, Cambridge, Mass., 1926, p. 52; Clement Robinson, *Handfull of Pleasant Delights*, ed. Rollins, Cambridge, Mass., 1924, p. 25; Francis Meres, *Palladis Tamia*, London, 1598, p. 105^v; Jonson, *Cynthia's Revels*, 1.1.91ff. A fascinating interpretation of the myth in Sidney is Walter Davis's "Actaeon in Arcadia," *SEL*, 2 (1962), pp. 95-110.

[23] See Bush, p. 71, for citations. A good example of this psychological interpretation is Pietro Bembo, *Gli Asolani*, trans. Rudolph B. Gottfried, Bloomington, Ind., 1954, pp. 104-105: "For through believing that he was in love while he met his lady only in imagination, he has become a solitary stag whom, like Actaeon, his hounded thoughts have pitifully torn. . . ."

[24] Jean Seznec, *The Survival of the Pagan Gods*, trans. Barbara F. Sessions, New York, 1953, p. 93.

Scilicet in superis, etiam fortuna luenda est,
Nec veniam laeso numine casus habet.

"Or lastly, thus, a wiseman ought to refraine his eyes, from beholding sensible and corporall bewty, figured by Diana: *least as* Actaeon *was devoured of his owne doggs, so he be distracted and torne in peeces with his owne affections, and perturbations."*[25]

Generally speaking, then, the interpretations of the myth make Diana a type of inviolable chastity, beauty, or knowledge and Actaeon a type of the rash intruder who suddenly comes to lust, to love, or to knowledge.

The situation in Spenser is analogous. Venus, whose province is usually the passions, comes upon Diana, but the revelation brings not death but reconciliation. The meeting of virginity and love repeats the paradox of the miraculous birth, and their reconciliation is achieved only after "a singularly frank statement of the claims of each." Diana's attitude is that of one who sees Venus as an opponent, but Venus makes the first rational plea for peaceful co-existence (3.6.22). The theoretical equality of these two "sisters" does not conciliate Diana; the very idea of having Cupid among her nymphs is an insult, which brings retaliation in the form of a slighting reference to Venus's adulterous affair with Mars and the threat of "emasculation" for Cupid. Spenser does not present the argument that finally wins Diana, but it is the result of Venus's "sugred words and gentle blandishment" (3.6.25). This reconciliation brings them almost immediately to "that same shadie couert, whereas lay Faire *Crysogone* . . . Who in her sleepe . . . Vnwares had borne two babes, as faire as springing day."

Vnwares she them conceiu'd, vnwares she bore:
She bore withouten paine, that she conceiued

[25] Fraunce, *The third part of the Countesse of Pembrokes Yuychurch,* sig. M.

Withouten pleasure: ne her need implore
Lucinaes aide: which when they both perceiued,
They were through wonder nigh of sense bereaued,
And gazing each on other, nought bespake:

(3.6.26-27)

The final reconciliation of Venus and Diana comes at this point when Chrysogonee, the maiden-mother, and her two babies are revealed. At this point Chrysogonee fades out of the poem, but the image of this maiden-mother and Spenser's insistent use of Incarnational imagery should warn the reader that the significance of the scene must not be overlooked.

Professor Lewis makes the scene a symbol of the shift from "courtly love" to Christian marriage and accounts for it "as a feeling in Spenser's mind, not a piece of intellectual and historical knowledge, as it is to us." This explanation is inadequate because it does not offer any reason for Diana's and Belphoebe's roles; opportunistically seizing this passage for the development of his thesis, he is forced into an historical apology. This need not be the case. There were in the sixteenth century events which were for Spenser, as they are for us, pieces of "intellectual and historical knowledge," which will explain the reconciliation more satisfactorily. These events were responsible for the revaluation of virginity and marriage as Christian ideals.

In England this revaluation was in part an outgrowth of the disgust with the monastic life and the question of clerical celibacy and in part due to the new ideal of civil life as opposed to the older ideal of the life of contemplation; all these factors tended to displace the medieval opinion of virginity as the Christian ideal. Yet to say that virginity as an ideal was replaced by marriage is to falsify the situation, for the disgust with virginity was not disgust with the ideal but with the practice of this ideal. Bishop Jewel's reply to Harding is instructive:

"No, M. Harding, chastity is no ill thing: it is the special gift of God. But an unclean and a filthy life under colour of a 'vow,' or the name of 'chastity,' is a wicked thing before God.

"To be short, the resolution hereof is this: *Better it is to marry, than to swelter inwardly with filthy affections*. St. Paul saith: 'I would wish all men to be as I am myself. But every man hath his gift:' one of *chastity*, and another of *marriage*. Though chastity be a singular gift of God, yet is it not good for him, that hath not the gift of chastity. . . .

"Single life for many causes is the best: I grant. Yet is it not best for everybody: but only for him that hath the gift of chastity, and can with quiet mind and upright conscience live single. Otherwise matrimony is much better. And therefore God hath left us indifferently free to both: that whomsoever cannot use the one, may choose the other."[26]

Chastity does not consist of a human vow but is a gift of God. Bishop Jewel is attacking the practice of virginity but at no point does he supplant the ideal itself by marriage.

Is it not probable that a controversy on such a basic issue should be reflected in Spenser's poem? The figures of Belphoebe and Amoret reflect the two alternatives of virginity and marriage, and Belphoebe, by Spenser's statement, is a representation of the virginity of the Queen. She is the first born, and her virginity can justifiably be called a gift of God. They are found by Venus and Diana, who represent the older view in which marriage is opposed to virginity, in which the Actaeon of passion may seldom enter into the mysteries of virginity. Their perennial debate is resolved by the sight of Chrysogonee, the maiden-mother, whom Spenser invests with the attributes of the Holy Maiden-Mother—a symbol of the

[26] John Jewel, "Defense of the Apology of the Church of England," *Works*, ed. R. W. Jelf, 8 vols., Oxford, 1848, vol. 4, pp. 566, 595, 605. See also vol. 4, p. 598. For further references see Elkin C. Wilson, *England's Eliza*, Cambridge, Mass., 1939, p. 207n.

essential equality of these two estates as a way to God and of the essential unity of these two estates as modes of existence. To leave no doubt about their equality and unity Spenser leads the reader on to the Garden of Adonis, that great philosophic poem of praise of life and generation, which is the ultimate answer to those who would make virginity the absolute human ideal.

iv · AMORET'S EDUCATION

Unlike Belphoebe the image of Amoret does not declare itself through familiar archetypes. We see her enfolded by a series of encounters that define her position in the poem. She is brought to the Garden of Adonis as an infant but at some point goes to the Temple of Venus, where she is found and won by Scudamour. On her wedding day she is captured by Busyrane in whose power she remains until rescued by Britomart. The original ending of Book III reunited her with Scudamour, but with the addition of Books IV-VI Spenser rejected the reunion in order to make Amoret the pawn in further adventures, most notably in the Cave of Lust. She is rescued by Belphoebe, succoured by Arthur, and finally wanders out of the poem. At no point in this series of encounters is she a character in the modern sense of that word. We learn about her only through the context in which we find her. The Garden and the Temple explain Amoret as well as themselves. We learn about Amoret in the House of Busyrane only because Britomart and the reader understand the significance of the House and its ambiguous pageantry. The House is, as I have already suggested, an objectification of her fears but only insofar as she partakes of the universal malady represented by Busyrane and his House. We should not read the episode solely as the particular malady of Amoret. Similarly her encounter with Lust need not be understood as a lapse in her own behavior. Amoret's actions in the poem do not involve behavior. As a character she is indeterminate. As an image her encounters exemplify the education of woman for her role in society. Amoret moves from the idyllic, natural innocence of the Garden of Adonis to the Temple of Venus, where (as C. S. Lewis has pointed out) ". . . all that nature did omit, Art playing second natures part, suppleyed it." Her last two encounters reverse her progress from nature to art. The House of Busyrane presents a perverted image of the art represented by the Temple of Venus as the Cave of Lust presents its perversion of nature in its subterranean gloom and in the figure of Lust. We never see the reunion of Amoret and Scudamour, but we are given the whole story of her education in the Garden and in the Temple, although we never see Amoret *at* school. Busyrane and Lust represent the everpresent dangers to those educated by nature and by art. It is just as well that Amoret disappears from the poem, for the companions of Busyrane and Lust are numberless and merely bring us closer to our own harassments and away from Spenser's bright vision of Garden and Temple, the archetypes of nature and art.

(a) *The Garden of Adonis*

The Garden of Adonis section of canto 6 has been treated at length as an expression of Spenser's "philosophy."[27] Every inch of the episode has been analyzed, both background and foreground. Analogues and sources have been sifted on the episode so that it is all but impossible to read it as part of the poem. Undoubtedly it is meant to stand out as a great set piece, but Spenser (I am sure) did not expect his readers to isolate it from the context in which it has been carefully placed.

[27] See especially Appendix III, *Var.*, 3.340-352 and T. P. Harrison, Jr., "Divinity in Spenser's Garden of Adonis," *TSE* (1939), pp. 48-73; J. W. Bennett, *JEGP*, 41 (1942), pp. 53-78; Brents Stirling, *JEGP*, 41 (1942), pp. 482-486; J. W. Bennett, *JEGP*, 41 (1942), pp. 486-489; A. S. P. Woodhouse, "The Argument of Milton's 'Comus,'" *UTQ*, 11 (1941), pp. 67ff.

The major question of published criticism has been the nature of Venus and Adonis and the "location" of the garden, but no critic has thought to question why Amoret is introduced into the scheme of this miraculous garden. The basic questions of poetic structure and logic have been overlooked in order to plaster the relics of the poem over the walls of the temple of source studies. Not that the study of sources is incompatible with poetic studies; the problem here is that the background looms too large and clear.

I shall not be so ungenerous nor so uneconomical as to attempt to answer those critics whose work has helped me to see what I do understand of the episode, but I shall attempt to pierce through their mass of evidence to answer three questions. The Garden of Adonis is accepted as a myth of generation. What generation does it describe? Why is Amoret introduced? How does the episode fulfill the requirements of allegory suggested in this book?

The basic problem demonstrated by all the critics is the impossibility of pinning any poet, whose very wrigglings are the manifestation of his life as a poet, to a philosophy. No one (to my knowledge) has ever thought to berate Dante for his un-Thomistic moments, although they are there, yet Spenser has been beaten consistently for his inconsistency as a Platonist and an Ovidian. The delicacy with which Milton, Spenser's greatest descendant, threads his way between conflicting cosmologies in his poem is a source of wonder and praise (probably because we know what each cosmology means for us), but Spenser's no less skillful maneuvers bring forth not understanding but criticism. The failure of illumination is due not to Spenser's ineptitude as thinker or as poet but to what Eliot has pointed out as an incomplete participation in the poetic world presented to us, a matter vastly different from belief or disbelief in any philosophic system or even from knowledge of it.

The world of the Garden of Adonis is not primarily pictorial. It does not serve the same function as the House of Alma or the Temple of Venus, where some attempt is made to create in words the sense of spatial relationships. Stanzas 29 through 42 give us little that is visual. We may see a double-walled garden whose gate is guarded by an old man. Within the garden we may see the "thousand thousand naked babes" and the figure of Time "with his flaggy wings," but the rest of the detail is defined either ambiguously or negatively. For example, Spenser's garden does *not* need a gardener nor a river nor clouds; it contains "Infinite shapes" and "vncouth formes." Most of the detail of this section lead the reader away from a precise visualization of the scene toward the concepts that the garden represents. In the Garden of Adonis Spenser is faced with a problem similar to Milton's in depicting Hell. Both are realized as actual places and as spiritual conditions. Both senses of these worlds are necessary to any comprehension of the poets' intentions.

Spenser's solution to this problem can be seen in the very first stanza of description: Venus brings Amoret

> to her ioyous Paradize,
> Where most she wonnes, when she on earth does dwel.
> So faire a place, as Nature can deuize:
> Whether in *Paphos*, or *Cytheron* hill,
> Or it in *Gnidus* be, I wote not well;
> But well I wote by tryall, that this same
> All other pleasant places doth excell,
> And called is by her lost louers name,
> The *Gardin of Adonis*, farre renowmd by fame.
>
> (3.6.29)

This paradise is Venus's favorite *earthly* haunt, but Spenser does not know where it is except *by tryall*, a paradox that sets up both senses of his world, a paradox that he immediately ignores by calling it as fair a place as nature can devise and naming it the Garden of Adonis.

In short, Spenser has experienced the Garden of Adonis yet does not know where it is. His evasive tactics are purposeful. Contemporary references to gardens of Adonis prove beyond any doubt that the phrase was used colloquially to represent any place of unusually rapid fertility.[28] Fast growing plants in small pots were often referred to as gardens of Adonis. Spenser simply appropriated the name for his own uses. His myth is meant to symbolize creation and fertility in all its aspects. Thus the complicated arguments of Professors Bennett and Stirling about the location of the garden are beside the point. The garden is the world because the world is engaged in the act of creation described in the poem. The garden is a Platonic realm too because Platonic forms are engaged in the process of creation. The garden is the womb of every mother and is the growth of every living thing. It is everywhere and nowhere *in particular*. Spenser's myth is not difficult unless we try to restrict its meaning to one particular kind of creation.

Problems arise when we try to visualize the place. For example, if the garden *is* the world and not some otherworldly Platonic realm, where do the "men" pass to when they leave old Genius's gate?

> He letteth in, he letteth out to wend,
>   All that to come into the world desire;
>   A thousand thousand naked babes attend
>   About him day and night, which doe require,
>   That he with fleshly weedes would them attire:

[28] Studies of gardens of Adonis are found in Giraldi, cols. 411-413, and Natalis Comes, *Mythologiae*, Lyons, 1602, sigs. Hhh8ᵛ-Iii. Chance references occur in Erasmus, *Praise of Folly*, ed. Hoyt H. Hudson, Princeton, 1941, pp. 12-13, Jonson, *Cynthia's Reuells*, ed. Herford and Simpson, vol. 4, p. 175: "I pray thee, light hony-bee, remember thou art not in *Adonis* garden, but in Cynthias presence, where thornes lie in garrison about the roses"; Shakespeare, *I Henry VI*, 1.6.6ff.: "Thy promises are like Adonis' gardens, That one day bloom'd, and fruitful were the next." The new Arden edition of this play gives valuable further references.

Such as him list, such as eternall fate
Ordained hath, he clothes with sinfull mire,
And sendeth forth to liue in mortall state,
Till they againe returne backe by the hinder gate.
(3.6.32)

The problem here is not one of poetic ineptitude but of a modern failure to hold several possible meanings or referents in mind at the same time. Spenser's poetic tactics in depicting the garden can be duplicated in the visual arts. One of Holbein's woodcuts, used as a title-border for several important books printed at Basle in the first quarter of the sixteenth century, shows a walled garden presided over by Genius, who stands at a gate in the bottom of the picture (see frontispiece).[29] Outside the gate and clustered around the lower wall are many naked babies, apparently trying to gain entry into the world represented by the garden. Logically these babies should not yet be babies, but the exigencies of representation necessitate depicting them in a form that the viewer will understand; hence they are represented as naked babies. Within the garden as through a maze we see a progress of allegorical figures depicting the virtues and vices, and at the top of the picture is a female figure called "Felicitas." The figures surrounding her make it clear that this is heavenly felicity, and we are faced with the incongruity of Genius presiding over a garden that includes an area of experience that does not rightly belong there. Holbein was illustrating the progress of human life. He and the publishers of the books using his woodcut were apparently unbothered by the incongruities of space, time, and logic plaguing his picture. No one, I think, would ask where the babies were coming from nor whether Holbein believed in a state of preexistence. The viewer accepts

[29] Raimond Van Marle, *Iconographie de l'art profane au Moyen-âge et à la renaissance* ... , 2 vols., La Haye, 1931-32, vol. 2, p. 157 (fig. 182) states that the woodcut was used as a title-border for Cebes, *Tabula*, Cracow, 1519; Erasmus, *New Testament*, Basle, 1522; Strabo, *Geography*, Basle, 1523.

the world presented to him and wanders through it without asking embarrassing questions about the shortness of the road leading from earth to heaven. Holbein was not doing a road map; space and time hardly enter the picture. We will understand it if we understand the assumptions underlying its art, and these assumptions concern man's metaphysical ends just as Spenser's do.

Spenser's "babies" are sent forth into the "world" just as Holbein's enter his garden: because this is the only way to pull together the disparate meanings of the myth. We as readers must be willing to let up on some of the meanings when these meanings do not fit the poetic narrative. Thus we can accept the Garden of Adonis as the womb of any mother just so long as we do not wonder how this can be when Spenser tells us that the babes return through another gate when their life is done: Spenser has moved on to another facet of his myth. Time can exist in a garden representing the world as we know it, but "continuall spring, and harvest there Continuall" cannot. But the contradictory statements can and do exist in a garden that represents the world *and* a mythical realm representing universal fertility. Such a reading of the Garden of Adonis obviates the problems of precise meanings of form and substance and other troublesome questions such as how is Adonis to be "Transformed oft, and chaunged diuerslie" by a boar that is "emprisoned for ay."[30]

The reader's progress through Spenser's garden leads him finally to the mount in its center where the various meanings of his myth are represented by the hierarchy of figures he describes. The hierarchy consists of three pairs of figures: Venus and Adonis, Cupid and Psyche, and finally Pleasure and Amoret. The earlier passages describing the garden show

[30] Spenser does not develop the seasonal aspects of his myth because they would restrict the larger, cosmic meanings his myth encompasses. To demonstrate the "eterne in mutabilitie" principle would utterly destroy the static timelessness he is at pains to produce.

conclusively that Spenser viewed creation as a union of form and matter, and he explicitly calls Adonis "the Father of all formes." We might reasonably expect Venus to be matter, and many critics do make this assumption. Professor Bennett dissents on the grounds that Venus cannot be matter because she is the goddess of beauty and no Neoplatonist would allow matter to be the basis of beauty. Her objection is nice, but it does not take into account the other side of Christian Neoplatonism, which perceived the goodness of material creation.[81] Venus is the matter by which God brought forth the goodness of His creation and hence is entirely acceptable even to Neoplatonists. Through the union of Venus (matter) and Adonis (form) Spenser begins his myth of generation. But Spenser's myth goes beyond this initial stage of creation and includes two other pairs, to explain which we must turn from Spenser's basic myth of generation to his mythology of generation.

Spenser mentions the Garden of Adonis on two other occasions, in both of which the mythoolgy differs from that of canto 6.[82] The difference is only apparent, for the same myth of generation is common to all three. A comparison of the three versions provides a basis for interpreting the functions of Cupid, Psyche, and Pleasure in canto 6. In *Colin Clout*, the only occasion on which Spenser alludes to the garden outside the *Faerie Queene*, he describes the birth of Cupid:

> For him the greatest of the Gods we deeme,
> Borne without Syre or couples of one kynd,
> For *Venus* selfe doth soly couples seeme,
> Both male and female, through c'ommixture ioynd.
> So pure and spotlesse *Cupid* forth she brought,
> And in the gardens of *Adonis* nurst:

[81] Erwin Panofsky, *Studies in Iconology*, New York, 1939, pp. 134-135.
[82] The other occasion in *The Faerie Queene* is at the beginning of the Elfin Chronicle, where Spenser relates the twofold creation of Elfe by Prometheus and Elfe's discovery of Faye in the Garden of Adonis (2.10.70-71). See Introduction.

> Where growing, he his owne perfection wrought,
> And shortly was of all the Gods the first.   (799-806)

A few lines later Colin describes in greater detail Cupid's creation.

> For long before the world he was y'bore
> And bred aboue in *Venus* bosome deare:
> For by his powre the world was made of yore,
> And all that therein wondrous doth appeare. . . .
> Then first gan heauen out of darknesse dread
> For to appeare, and brought forth chearfull day:
> Next gan the earth to shew her naked head,
> Out of deep waters which her drownd alway.
> And shortly after euerie liuing wight,
> Crept forth like wormes out of her slimie nature,
> Soone as on them the Suns life giuing light,
> Had powred kindly heat and formall feature. . . .
>   (839ff., 855ff.)

These two passages from *Colin Clout* should be compared to the myth of creation in the *Hymne of Love* (lines 50ff.) where Cupid, "Begot of Plentie and of Penurie," again is said to create the world.[33]

The parallelism of the *Fowre Hymnes* indicates that Venus and Cupid of the first hymn are parallels to the Father and the Son in the third, and more than that, it indicates that these hymns explain the same creation from a classical and an explicitly Christian point of view respectively. The Omnipotence of God the Father is compared to a hermaphroditic Venus, who begets Love, who in turn creates and moves the world. This is the cosmic myth of the primal creation. As

---

[33] It has never been suggested, but is there any reason for not interpreting Plenty and Penurie as principles within Venus herself? This explanation of this puzzling passage, which otherwise gives Cupid three parents, is consistent with the passage from *Colin Clout* where Venus contains both male and female and where the reconciliation of opposites is the chief characteristic of Cupid.

such it fits into the Neoplatonic scheme of the four hierarchies of the universe: the Cosmic Mind, the Cosmic Soul, the Realm of Nature, and the Realm of Matter. Venus, or Cosmic Mind here, begets Cupid, or Cosmic Soul, who inspirits the lifeless and formless Realm of Matter to create the Realm of Nature. This Venus is Venus Urania, the daughter of Uranus. She has no mother, which means that she belongs entirely to the immaterial realm since the word *mater* was associated with the world *materia*.[34] Neoplatonic theology postulated a God that contained but was not contained by nature, and Venus Urania, or Cosmic Mind, was the first principle of nature but still under the power of God. In the first hymn Spenser takes this Venus as his first principle, tacitly assuming her subservience to God, while in the third hymn he describes the orthodox Christian view of creation with God as the First Principle.

What happens in the Garden of Adonis passage is that the same myth is transferred from the description of the primal or universal creation to the continuing process of natural generation, from the realm of Venus Urania to the realm of Venus Pandemos, the *vis generandi*, which we have already associated with Amoret. Furthermore, the details of the myth are increased. The Venus and Cupid of the first hymn become Venus-Adonis and Cupid-Psyche in the garden. It is easy enough to see that the hermaphroditic Venus discussed in *Colin Clout* becomes Venus *and* Adonis, but why introduce Psyche? Now Psyche, even by modern standards of etymology, means the soul, and the learned reader of Spenser would have seen not only this but also that Spenser's Psyche was the Psyche of Apuleius's *The Golden Ass*, which was interpreted in the Renaissance as a Christian allegory of the soul. Spenser gives the bare outline of the story as told by

---

[34] Panofsky, *Studies in Iconology*, pp. 134-142. Professor Kristeller criticizes Panofsky for calling the Neoplatonic scheme he outlines Ficinian rather than Plotinian, but his objections do not interfere with my use of the scheme.

Apuleius, but it is clear that no other legend was intended. Martianus Capella, the pseudo-Fulgentius, and Boccaccio have elaborate commentaries on the tale of Apuleius, and all agree that Psyche is the rational soul.[35] Discussing Psyche's two elder sisters, whom he calls the Flesh and Free-Will, Martianus says that Psyche must be the youngest because it is known that the body is made first and then the soul is added.[36] This appears to be the reason that Psyche is introduced into the garden. Venus and Adonis figure forth the union of form and matter, the most general kind of generation in the Realm of Nature, common to animate and inanimate nature alike. Contrary to the opinion of A. S. P. Woodhouse, Cupid and Psyche do not represent "the same spirit and principle [as Venus and Adonis] in their specifically human application, which is marriage. . . ."[37] They represent that further creation, without which generation is incomplete, the emergence of the soul, the living principle, and thus Cupid and Psyche represent the next, more specific stage in generation—the creation of the soul through the action of Love. In the garden they are united and have a child, Pleasure. The mythographers interpret Apuleius's Pleasure as "timeless beatitude,"[38] the pleasure of the soul united to Love, but she also clearly may mean in this context the chaste joy of the soul generating itself again and—most important—sexual delight.

Into this hierarchy Spenser introduces Amoret, who represents the most specific aspect of generation—Christian marriage, which willingly and in knowledge brings human gen-

[35] See Don Cameron Allen, "On Spenser's 'Muiopotmos,'" *SP*, 53 (1956), pp. 146-149, for an admirable summary of the history of this legend as it came to the Renaissance.

[36] Allen, p. 146; see also Arnold Williams, *The Common Expositor*, pp. 76ff.

[37] A. S. P. Woodhouse, "The Argument of Milton's 'Comus,'" p. 69. Only in the most strictly Christian sense are Cupid and Psyche "human"—that is, when the soul and Love are one, but this is not what Woodhouse intends.

[38] Allen, p. 148.

eration into the cyclical process of God's Providence. Amoret's presence in the garden typifies the Christian woman as the embodiment of the Earthly Venus, bringing to fulfillment the whole process of generation and at the same time transfiguring it. "It is not good, that man should be alone. And therefore determined he with himselfe to make an helpe and comfort vnto man. In the which proces we perceiue all ready, where holy wedlock was instituted, namely in the paradise and garden of pleasure: yea and when it was ordained euen in the beginning of the world, before the fal of man in al prosperity."[39]

Amoret's presence in the garden completes Spenser's hierarchy of generation and presents a view of marriage that integrates the joys of human sexuality into the cosmic scheme of generation. My reading of the Garden of Adonis resembles closely the Neoplatonic hierarchy of Giulio Romano's program for the Sala di Psiche in the Palazzo del Te at Mantua.[40] Two walls of the room are decorated with a painting of the wedding feast, crowded with woodland deities and strange animals. Above these in a series of lunettes and octagons that cover the four walls and ceiling are depicted the love of Psyche for Cupid and her trials in winning her love. In the very center of the ceiling is the actual wedding of Cupid and Psyche. They stretch their hands across the heads of the observers standing on the level of the earthly marriage feast. Above the lovers are the figures of the gods bestowing their blessing on the couple, and beyond the gods the painting recedes to infinity and intense light. The room is constructed as a Neoplatonic ascent in which the marriage of Cupid and Psyche, purified by her labors, symbolizes all marriages of

---

[39] Heinrich Bullinger, *The Christian state of Matrimony*, trans. Miles Coverdale, London, 1575, fol. 1ᵛ.

[40] Frederick Hartt, *Giulio Romano*, 2 vols., New Haven, 1958, pp. 126-140. Hartt's explanation of the Sala di Psiche is interesting as an indication of the lengths to which the Renaissance mind could make a myth serve personal, artistic, and cosmic ends all at the same time.

earth and heaven and bestows its own blessing on the viewers standing below. Spenser's hierarchy performs a similar function because Amoret is not only part of the fixed hierarchy of generation but a figure in the action of the poem and carries the lesson of the garden into the poem as a whole.

The reader may well wonder just how this glorification of marriage answers the question posed by Spenser at the beginning of the canto. In a sense devoting the second half of the canto to Amoret is a tribute to Belphoebe. The historical context and presumably Spenser's own predilections made a glorification of marriage an essential part of developing the figure of Amoret, while the polar extremes of the figure of Belphoebe—the Diana archetype and Elizabeth—made a similar glorification of virginity unnecessary. The natures that Amoret and Belphoebe figure forth also indicated the structure of the canto. Amoret must be educated in the garden and later in the Temple of Venus for her role as wife and great lady, as we all must be educated for roles in society. Belphoebe, however, requires no education; her virginity, as a gift of God, is complete and self-sufficient. Her nature has no need for civil life; her teachers are an old Nymph to teach her the ways of solitude and the forest to teach the "life exempt from public haunt"—in itself a fitting compliment for the Queen.

(b) *The Temple of Venus*

The oblique definition of Amoret provided by the Garden of Adonis becomes even more oblique in the Temple of Venus episode. Unlike the other cantos of instruction and vision, Book IV, canto 10, is not the direct experience of character and reader but the flashback narrative of Scudamour's winning Amoret, told by Scudamour himself.[41] It is both a jus-

---

[41] The cantos of instruction and vision are the House of Holinesse, Alma's Castle, the Temple of Venus, the Court of Mercilla, and Mount Acidale. Spenser's intentions in these cantos are discussed in the Conclusion.

tification of Scudamour's innocence in Amoret's imprisonment by Busyrane and an emblematic exemplum of the theme of *discordia concors* in a courtship. The canto should not be read as an indictment of Scudamour's too eager masculinity.[42] It has little of the verbal intensity of the Busyrane cantos, but the heavily Petrarchan diction suggests a comparison to

[42] The nature of the characters in *The Faerie Queene* generally precludes psychologizing. Scudamour's moral fault of jealousy is provoked by Ate, and his responsibility for the act is somewhat lessened by the evil origin. I am not trying to take an heretical stand on the matter of moral responsibility, but nothing in the diction blames him for his moral deviation; if anything, he is to be pitied. The issue of psychologizing is the basis of Professor A. Kent Hieatt's disagreement with my interpretation of Amoret at the House of Busyrane (*PMLA*, 78 [1962], pp. 509-510). He assumes that I am blaming Amoret for her false fears. Spenser places the blame on Busyrane, and so do I. My suggestion that the mask of Cupid is presented from the point of view of Amoret's fears is not intended to mean that Busyrane is merely a figment of Amoret's imagination. He is a universal that the occasion of Amoret's and Scudamour's wedding allows Spenser to bring into his poem *before we learn about the occasion*. Spenser devotes no time to an explanation of why Amoret is in this situation and never alludes to the culpability of either Amoret and Scudamour. Hieatt's suggestion that Scudamour is to blame because of his aggressive mastery of Amoret is not an answer to my position, nor is it the most fruitful way of viewing Scudamour's action at the Temple of Venus. He cites the garden and the temple as emblems of the proper harmony that should exist between man and wife, but, as I point out above, the details of the temple exemplify the theme of *discordia concors* and Scudamour's initial conflict with Amoret is intended to continue this theme. Scudamour's *keckheit* is not culpable but absolutely requisite for his task. Concord grows only out of discord. Hieatt suggests that the repetition of the word *bold* is meant to recall the boldness of Britomart at the House of Busyrane. I wish I had. I do not agree, however, that this verbal pattern is to be used as a moral weapon against Scudamour. The Temple of Venus is not a manual of wooing; it is a vision of the relation of the sexes (as well as other hierarchical relationships) in which man *by nature* is the aggressor and must win the woman. The question of morality is important in the episode, but it is not simply a question of Scudamour's morality. How much boldness is necessary to win, not frighten or capture, a woman in order to produce human love? I do not want to restrict the question that the episode poses for the reader to Scudamour alone. The Temple of Venus is about love and chastity. Spenser presents the episode through the agency of Scudamour and with extraordinary vividness, but these two facts should not deter us from reading the episode *spiritually* as well as *morally*. To make it merely a moral explanation of Scudamour's behavior, a psychological interpretation, precludes those larger issues of Love that are the ground of its being.

Amoret's Petrarchan experience at the House of Busyrane, a comparison that further emphasizes the delusive qualities of that experience.

The first three stanzas of the canto set the Petrarchan tone by invoking the old dram of honey and pound of gall metaphor: love is more trouble than joy. Scudamour's heart is "launcht" with "deadly wound." His love, like all loves, is a "martyrdome vnmeet." But Scudamour's is not the conventional love lament:

> And yet such grace is giuen them [lovers] from aboue,
> That all the cares and euill which they meet,
> May nought at all their setled mindes remoue,
> But seeme gainst common sence to them most sweet. . . .
>
> (4.10.2)

The language is fitting not to maintain and to elaborate the contraries of Petrarchan love but to explain the difficulty of maintaining the decorum of courtship, of balancing the claims of natural desire and social propriety. The language and attitudes throughout the canto are Petrarchan, but behind these conventions is that grace that reconciles the antithetical posturing of love in its social aspects. Spenser symbolizes this grace in the figures of Concord and the hermaphroditic Venus, both of whom reiterate the basic theme of Book IV.

The island stronghold of the Temple of Venus is a different facet of Venus's power. In the Garden of Adonis she was represented primarily as generation, and appropriately the garden was filled with "babies." Here she is presented as human love, and hence the garden is subordinated to the temple, art supplying "all that nature did omit." Here the emphasis is on that anterior power that leads one human being to another, and appropriately there are no "babies" but "thousand payres of louers walkt, Praysing their god, and yeelding him great thankes, Ne euer ought but of their true loues talkt . . ." (4.10.25). More particularly the emphasis is on love in society. To differentiate this facet of Venus's power from the generation of the garden Spenser provides two sorts of lovers: the sexual lovers who "did sport Their spotlesse pleasures" and famous pairs of friends: Hercules and Hylas, Jonathan and David, Theseus and Pirithous, Pylades and Orestes, Titus and Gesippus, and Damon and Pythias. Spenser is equating chaste male friendship and sexual love so that the reader may see that the bond linking man and woman and man and man is the same. The desire of the former leads to the Garden of Adonis; the desire of the latter leads to "Braue thoughts and noble deedes." Wisely Spenser refrains from naming any pairs of male and female lovers and thereby emphasizes the non-sexual aspects of the Temple of Venus. To be sure, they are there, but they are to be subordinated to the non-physical aspects of love, to love as it appears in society. Scudamour sees that both sorts of lovers are "free from feare and gealosye" and concludes, comparing his lot to theirs: "Much dearer be the things, which come through hard distresse." With this exemplary preparation he comes to Dame Concord, who is portress of the temple.

Concord is described as a concept quite distinct from Venus: "She is the nourse of pleasure and delight, And vnto *Venus* grace the gate doth open right" (4.10.35). On either side stand two armed young men, Love and Hate, half brothers, whom Concord forces to join hands. Owing to this act she is commonly known as the mother of Peace and Friendship. The description is a universalization of the Alciati emblem called "Concordia." The love and hate she unites are not only moral but physical and metaphysical concepts. She is the force that binds all natures and the universe together and is a branch of charity, the highest virtue in the tree of virtues. She is described at some length because the concept she represents is so basic to the world Spenser knew and because she is our introduction to that even more basic concept Venus. Spenser places Concord at the gate of the Temple of Venus to make sure that our vision of Venus will not be restricted to any tiny area of what he considered love.

The statue of Venus is set in the middle of a temple in which the symbolism of one hundred or perfection is reiterated. The statue is covered with a veil and at her feet is a snake, "whose head and tail were fast combyned." It is possible that this snake owes its existence to the *Hieroglyphics* of Horapollo. It has been variously allegorized as "Charitas," "Aeternitas," and "Vita humana,"[43] all of which conceptions are united in Spenser's picture of Venus, for she is one of Spenser's most basic descriptions of the Love that moves the world. She is veiled not

> for womanish shame,
> Nor any blemish, which the worke mote blame;
> But for, they say, she hath both kinds in one,
> Both male and female, both vnder one name:
> She syre and mother is her selfe alone,
> Begets and eke conceiues, ne needeth other none.
>   (4.10.41)

This statue is another version of the Venus of the *Hymn of Love* and *Colin Clout* already discussed in connection with the Garden of Adonis. What is represented there as eternal cyclic reproduction is here represented as an immutable artifact. They are both aspects of the same Love, and this Love includes all those things that have ever been conceived to spring from Love, which is why Spenser introduces his adaptation of Lucretius's *Alma Venus*.

Lest his description of Love should become a mere treatise in praise of Venus's power, Spenser makes his Lucretian adaptation a song sung by a lover apparently in the same condition as Scudamour, and we are immediately back in the

[43] See Filippo Picinelli, *Mundus Symbolicus*, Cologne, 1687, pp. 486ff. and Giovanni Piero Valeriano, *Hieroglyphica*, Lyons, 1602, p. 138E. The passage in Horapollo can be seen in George Boas's edition, New York, 1950, p. 57.

Petrarchan setting of Spenser's cosmic figures. Scudamour's progress to the center of the temple is marked by his encounters with Doubt, Delay, and Daunger, and after his vision of Concord and Venus he passes immediately to the conquest of Amoret. The situation might very well have been developed along the lines of Marlowe's *Hero and Leander*, for the paradoxes are the same: a virgin devoted to the service of Venus's temple. Needless to say, Spenser's treatment has little to do with Marlowe's ambiguous irony. Instead Spenser uses the paradox of the situation as another instance of *discordia concors*. The extreme reluctance of Amoret to leave the temple is overcome by the picture of Cupid on Scudamour's shield and by Scudamour's hold on her hand, which recapitulates the clasped hands of Love and Hate earlier in the canto. From this initial discord of the lovers will grow their love. As a pledge of this faith they both pass from the temple, now safe from the power of Daunger, and Scudamour has moved beyond the realm of Petrarchan contraries to the reality and unity of love, justifying his earlier statement: "Much dearer be the things, which come through hard distresse."

(c) The Original Endings of 1590

In the revised version of 1596 Amoret is not reunited with Scudamour after her trial in the House of Busyrane but journeys with Britomart until, briefly wandering, she is captured by Lust. The episode is less important for the development of the figure of Amoret than it is for the relationship of Belphoebe and Timias, and therefore I shall defer discussion. After this point Amoret is no more than a shadowy figure in the background of the poem. She has fulfilled Spenser's purpose of defining the nature and problems of Christian marriage. Undoubtedly there was to be a reunion of Amoret and Scudamour in the twelfth book, but there is no necessity to speculate on the unwritten conclusion of *The Faerie*

Queene, for the original ending of Book III provides the most simple, the most satisfactory conclusion for the allegorical education of Amoret.

> There did he [Scudamour] see, that most on earth him ioyd,
>   His dearest loue, the comfort of his dayes,
>   Whose too long absence him had sore annoyd,
>   And wearied his life with dull delayes:
>   Straight he vpstarted from the loathed layes,
>   And to her ran with hasty egernesse,
>   Like as a Deare, that greedily embayes
>   In the cool soile, after long thirstinesse,
> Which he in chace endured hath, now nigh breathlesse.
>
> Lightly he clipt her twixt his armes twaine,
>   And streightly did embrace her body bright,
>   Her body, late the prison of sad paine,
>   Now the sweet lodge of loue and deare delight:
>   But she faire Lady ouercommen quight
>   Of huge affection, did in pleasure melt,
>   And in sweete rauishment pourd out her spright:
>   No word they spake, nor earthly thing they felt,
> But like two senceles stocks in long embracement dwelt.
>
> Had ye them seene, ye would haue surely thought,
>   That they had beene that faire *Hermaphrodite,*
>   Which that rich *Romane* of white marble wrought,
>   And in his costly Bath causd to bee site:
>   So seemd those two, as growne together quite. . . .
>
> Thus doe those louers with sweet counteruayle,
>   Each other of loues bitter fruit despoile.
>
>   (1590: 3.12.44-47)

It has been suggested that the "shocking" image of the hermaphrodite was the cause of Burleigh's displeasure with

Spenser.⁴⁴ If so, then Burleigh simply did not understand the Biblical metaphor, which is the basis for the comparison: "For this cause shall a man leave his father and mother, and shall be joined unto his wife, and they two shall be one flesh." "For that is the meaning of the daring simile," as C. S. Lewis has pointed out.⁴⁵ He is wrong only in calling it a daring

Reusner, *Aureolorum Emblematum*, Strassburg, 1591, sig. Diii.

simile, for it appears in at least two emblem books with a woodcut, the one "In sponsalia Ioannis Ambij, & Albae Rolleas," the other illustrating the epigram:

> Vna caro, mens vna duobus: separet ambos
> Concretos nec mors, nec torus aut tumulus.⁴⁶

---

⁴⁴ *Var.*, 3.303-304.
⁴⁵ Lewis, *Allegory of Love*, p. 344.
⁴⁶ Johannes Sambucus, *Emblemata*, Antwerp, 1564, pp. 124-125. The tradition of symbolizing this Christian concept by a hermaphrodite is still current. I know one couple, who after a formal Church engagement, were presented with medals almost identical with the Renaissance woodcuts. The concept is extended to include friends by de la Primaudaye: "Whereby it appeareth vnto vs, that a friend is a second selfe, and that whosoeuer would take vpon him this title in regard of another, he must transforme

There can be no doubt that Spenser was using the simile to illustrate the mystical significance of Christian marriage and in using it he grants to his lovers a unity akin to that Venus which is the source and end of their love.

V · BELPHOEBE AND TIMIAS

Belphoebe's part in the narrative action of the poem is confined almost entirely to the three cantos that describe Timias's rescue, rejection, and final reconciliation. Very briefly, Timias, in pursuit of the forester who was threatening Florimell, is beset by the forester and his two wicked brothers. Although he dispatches them promptly, he collapses from a severe wound. Belphoebe chances on him and cures his wound only to inflict the deeper wounds of love. This much of the story is told in Book III. Book IV, canto 7, takes up their story where Timias rescues Amoret and Belphoebe kills Lust. On her return she mistakes Timias's ministrations to Amoret for lust and rebukes him. Disconsolate he retreats into the forest and pines away, not to be recognized even by Arthur. A mourning dove joins him and eventually flies off with a heart-shaped ruby amulet, by which she leads Belphoebe to Timias, where the reconciliation occurs.

Amoret's encounter with Lust might almost be considered merely the catalyst for the development of the Belphoebe-Timias story, if it were not that this encounter brings Arthur into the action of Book IV for the first time. Amoret's encounter with Lust has been interpreted as a "failure in integration" and the lack of true chastity.[47] Both these criticisms imply that Lust is an interior quality, a psychological state of Amoret's mind, but Spenser's usual identification of lust with

---

himselfe into his nature whom he purposeth to loue, and that with a steadfast and setled minde to continue so for euer. Hereupon one of the auncients speaking of him that loueth perfectly, saith that he liueth in another man's body" (p. 57).

[47] A. S. P. Woodhouse, "Nature and Grace in *The Faerie Queene*," *ELH*, 16 (1949), p. 215; F. M. Padelford, *Var.*, 3.326.

pure bestiality is entirely lacking from his description of Amoret.[48] This Lust is an external quality, more specifically, rape, and the episode is an exemplum of the dangers of unprotected beauty. In the cave of Lust Amoret meets Aemylia, whose sad tale of going to meet her lover, the Squire of Low Degree, and of finding Lust instead may mean either that she was consumed with lust on meeting the Squire or that the Squire attempted to rape her. Perhaps it means both. Amoret's situation is different; she wanders off from Britomart "for pleasure, or for need." Wandering is usually a danger signal in Spenser, meaning that the wanderer has put himself in the way of temptation. In Amoret's case, however, she herself is the temptation. She is a married woman, separated from her husband, and at this time unprotected by Britomart, the visible symbol of her chastity. In short, she has made herself a prey for Lust, whose description is phallic in the extreme.[49]

Amoret's rescue from this monster is won in three stages: the rescue proper by Timias, the killing of Lust by Belphoebe, and the cure by Arthur. The pity of Amoret's situation is that even the honorable Timias inflicts a wound, all the more grievous because unintentional. The wound from Timias is a wound to Amoret's reputation of chastity. It differs from the wounds inflicted by Lust, but it has the same effect.

The only person able to destroy Lust is Belphoebe. She is the only person in the poem for whom Lust is not a possible temptation. As the Neoplatonic heavenly Venus and as Elizabeth she must destroy the dishonorable, the bestial, the socially disruptive forces that Lust represents. Yet not even

---

[48] See *Hymne of Loue*, ll. 176-189 and the description of Ollyphant, 3.11.3-4. Also Amoret receives no instruction on avoiding lust from Arthur, which one might expect if it were her own failure. There is not a hint of reprisal on this point even in Sclaunder's hut.

[49] Rarely outside the House of Alma and *The Purple Island* are anatomical details given such graphic description. Spenser's Lust is clearly emblematic of the male genitalia (4.7.5-6).

BELPHOEBE AND AMORET

Belphoebe can distinguish between Lust and the sincere ministrations of Timias; Amoret's wounds are all the same to Belphoebe. From a distance it is difficult to perceive that line which separates lust from love or human care, and Amoret is left behind rescued but uncured. The consequences of this rescue treated purely as narrative of chivalry are disappointing, since they lack anything resembling a proper narrative conclusion. The cause and its consequences are never reconciled; Amoret never recalls Belphoebe and Timias, and they never refer to her.

The lack of narrative finesse almost defies the allegorical interpretation that Amoret's plight obviously requires and has given rise to a number of interpretations, all of which focus on aspects of the episode that minimize the moral allegory and its significance in the structure of Books III and IV. Perhaps it would be well to dispense right now with one interpretation, very seldom explicit but nonetheless prevalent, that Belphoebe really should have returned Timias's love and that the reconciliation really should have been a happy, romantic wedding.[50] This is absolutely wrong. The figure of Belphoebe as virginity makes this ending impossible, a violation of character, allegory, and decorum. In part this is due to the Venus-Diana ambivalence Spenser uses to characterize Belphoebe.

When Belphoebe rescues the wounded Timias in Book III, canto 5, she takes him to a hidden pavilion in the wood.

> Into that forest farre they thence him led,
>   Where was their dwelling, in a pleasant glade,
>   With mountaines round about enuironed,
>   And mighty woods, which did the valley shade,
>   And like a stately Theatre it made,
>   Spreading it selfe into a spatious plaine.
>   And in the midst a little riuer plaide

[50] *Orlando Furioso*, 19.1-40. See McMurphy, p. 39.

Emongst the pumy stones, which seemd to plaine
With gentle murmure, that his course they did restraine.

Beside the same a dainty place there lay,
  Planted with mirtle trees and laurels greene,
  In which the birds song many a louely lay
Of gods high prayse, and of their loues sweet teene,
As it an earthly Paradize had beene:
  In whose enclosed shadow there was pight
  A faire Pauilion, scarcely to be seene,
The which was all within most richly dight,
That greatest Princes liuing it mote well delight.
                         (3.5.39-40)

This description might have been lavished on the trysting place of any young lovers, but this is not the case. The central ambivalence is given in the two kinds of trees that surround the pavilion. Traditionally the myrtle is the tree of Venus as the laurel is the tree of Diana and Apollo.[51] The same ambivalence is noticed in the birds' songs—some turned to the praise of God and some to the praise of their true loves. This Diana, as her pavilion suggests, is a virgin, not coldly and inwardly contemplative, but filled with a charitable compassion for her partners in humanity. Belphoebe combines the best qualities of both Venus and Diana: contemplatively active, lovingly chaste, and when one considers she represents an aspect of Elizabeth, the virgin queen married to her kingdom.

The ambivalence is partially resolved by the image of the rose at the end of canto 5:

  That dainty Rose, the daughter of her Morne,
    More deare then life she tendered, whose flowre
    The girlond of her honour did adorne:
    Ne suffred she the Middayes scorching powre,

---

[51] See Panofsky, *Studies in Iconology*, p. 161n., and Cartari, p. 343, marginal gloss "myrtus veneri sacra."

Ne the sharp Northerne wind thereon to showre,
But lapped vp her silken leaues most chaire,
When so the froward skye began to lowre:
But soone as calmed was the Christall aire,
She did it faire dispred, and let to florish faire.

Eternall God in his almighty powre,
  To make ensample of his heauenly grace,
In Paradize whilome did plant this flowre;
Whence he it fetcht out of her natiue place,
And did in stocke of earthly flesh enrace,
That mortall men her glory should admire:
In gentle Ladies brest, and bounteous race
Of woman kind it fairest flowre doth spire,
And beareth fruit of honour and all chast desire.
(3.5.51-52)

At least two traditions of rose symbolism are fused in these stanzas glorifying Belphoebe—the rose exemplified by the *Roman de la Rose* and all its descendants and the *Rosa mystica* of the litany of the Blessed Virgin. The concept of the rose changes as the description progresses, from the rose symbolizing physical virginity to the rose of spiritual virginity and spiritual love. It is quite clear from the stanza preceding that the opening lines refer to Belphoebe's virginity and love. She has cared for the physical wounds of Timias,

But that sweet Cordiall, which can restore
A loue-sick hart, she did to him enuy;
To him, and to all th'vnworthy world forlore
She did enuy that soueraigne salue, in secret store.
(3.5.50)

It is equally clear from the development of the stanza that the image changes almost immediately to the spiritual aspects of virginity. Virginity becomes her "daughter," whom she protects and shelters from the ravages of life. Her virginity is a kind of fruition of the spirit, "of honour and all chast desire." This rose becomes the emblem of the spiritual life to be emulated by "Faire ympes of beautie."

> With this faire flowre your goodly girlonds dight,
> Of chastity and vertue virginall,
> That shall embellish more your beautie bright,
> And crowne your heades with heauenly coronall,
> Such as the Angels weare before Gods tribunall.
>
> (3.5.53)

The physical beauty of Belphoebe is emblematic of her spiritual beauty and virtue; it is more closely related to the worship of the Blessed Virgin than it is to secular traditions. Vestiges of the old religious litany were commonly applied to Elizabeth, for example, in the praise of virginity by Sir John Davies:

> The Christall Glasse that will no venome hold,
> The mirror wherein Angels loue to looke,
> *Dianaes* bathing Fountaine cleere and cold,
> Beauties fresh Rose, and vertues liuing booke.[52]

But Spenser's praise of virginity is religious awe become poetic myth, the poetic myth of the virgin mistress of England, the Tudor rose, in whose person was combined the beauty of Venus and the chastity of Diana.[53] Historical conditions were right for this Virgin Queen to adopt the terms of praise formerly applied to the Virgin Mary, that figure of contemplation whose care is the children of this world—the Christian Diana and the mother of Love. Spenser's poetic myth of Belphoebe as Venus-Diana is an example of the old religious veneration turned to the praise of Elizabeth, the

---

[52] From "A Contention betweixt a Wife, a Widow, and a Maid," quoted in E. C. Wilson, *England's Eliza*, p. 192; reprinted in Gerald Bullett, ed., *Silver Poets of the Sixteenth Century*, London, 1947, p. 411.

[53] *Batman uppon Bartholome*, Liber XVII, chap. 136, quoted in Wilson, *England's Eliza*, p. 219n.

type *par excellence* of temporal beatitude. Virgil's Venus, Dante's Beatrice, Spenser's Belphoebe are examples of the virgin-mother type in the Christian culture, a type that existed in classical times disparately as Venus and Diana. Having established Belphoebe as a representative of the Heavenly Venus in her first and second appearances, Spenser drops the ambivalence noted in his description of her. In canto 6 he analyzes the Venus-Diana type into its components: the birth of Belphoebe *and* Amoret, the flyting of Diana *and* Venus, the forest *versus* the Garden of Adonis, firmly establishing the figures of Belphoebe and Amoret and allowing him to use this figure of Belphoebe for other allegorical purposes in Book IV, cantos 7 and 8.

The most common interpretation of the Timias-Belphoebe episode is that it is an "historical" allegory of Ralegh's difficulties with the Queen over his marriage to Elizabeth Throgmorton. The problems of this historical identification have been thoroughly treated by A. H. Gilbert, who concludes that there may be "political allusions" to Ralegh in the hope that the reconciliation of Belphoebe and Timias might influence the Queen to receive Ralegh back into favor.[54] Whether Spenser intended Timias to refer to Ralegh or not is hardly the primary question to ask about this episode. A more basic question is: does this episode add something to Spenser's concepts of chastity and friendship, and is the episode integrated to the figure of Belphoebe? If these questions cannot be answered affirmatively, the episode must be regarded as an artistic flaw.

One possibility, suggested by Professor Gilbert, has not been exploited. At one point in his argument he mentions that

---

[54] Allan H. Gilbert, "Belphoebe's Misdeeming of Timias," *PMLA*, 62 (1947), pp. 622-643. Although I cannot agree with Professor Gilbert that *The Fairie Queene* is primarily a chivalric rather than an allegorical poem, I am inclined to think his evidence does point to Timias as an allusion to Ralegh, especially in light of the opening stanza of canto 8.

the etymology of Timias is the Greek *timios*, "honored."⁵⁵ There is the strong possibility that this episode between Belphoebe and Timias is an allegory of honor. Consider for a moment the use of the word "honor" in these cantos. Timias, named only Squire in Books I and II, suddenly becomes Timias in Book III when he pursues the wicked forester, the adventure that leads to his rescue by Belphoebe. Spenser apostrophizes the young squire lying wounded:

> Now God thee keepe, thou gentlest Squire aliue,
> Else shall thy louing Lord thee see no more,
> But both of comfort him thou shalt depriue,
> And eke thy selfe of honour, which thou didst atchiue.   (3.5.26)⁵⁶

Timias is about to be deprived of his due honor when he is rescued by Belphoebe—the same Belphoebe, who on her first appearance gives a speech on honor to Braggadocchio, the type of dishonor and vainglory.⁵⁷ The concept of honor is introduced five more times in canto 5, twice referring to the problem of honor in Timias's love for Belphoebe and three times in the rose image of Belphoebe's virginity.⁵⁸ It is introduced again when Belphoebe rejects Timias:

> He seeing her depart, arose vp light,
> Right sore agrieued at her sharpe reproofe,

---

⁵⁵ Gilbert, p. 638; see also John W. Draper, "Classical Coinage in the 'Faerie Queene,'" *PMLA*, 47 (1932), p. 104.

⁵⁶ The mention of the bond between Arthur and Timias at this point recalls the bond between Medoro and his lord Dardinello. Medoro is wounded in an attempt to bury his dead lord (*Orlando Furioso*, 18.164ff.). His rescue and eventual marriage to Angelica is interpreted by Harington as an allegory of honor: "*In* Angelicas *wedding of* Medoro *I gather this Allegorie,* Angelica *is taken for honor, which braue men hunt after, by blood, and battells, and many hardie feats, and misse it: but a good seruant with faith and gratefulnesse to his Lord gets it.*" (sig. N5). This interpretation, if it were current, may be the reason that Spenser chose to imitate the early part of the Ariosto episode.

⁵⁷ Braggadocchio is associated with dishonor on his first entrance. See *FQ* 2.3.4, 10, 24.

⁵⁸ *FQ*, 3.5.26, 45, 49, 51, 52, 54.

BELPHOEBE AND AMORET

> And follow'd fast: but when he came in sight,
> He durst not nigh approch, but kept aloofe,
> For dread of her displeasures vtmost proofe.
> And euermore, when he did grace entreat,
> And framed speeches fit for his behoofe,
> Her mortall arrowes, she at him did threat,
> And forst him backe with fowle dishonor to retreat.
>
> (4.7.37)

The situation can be glossed by a passage from Ashley, *Of Honour*: ". . . yt appeareth that men of witt and complement are drawne with nothing more then with honour, nor feared with any thing so much as reproach. . . . yt ys much better to die with Honour then to liue with shame."[59] Yet it is this latter alternative that Timias must face.

Timias's extreme reaction to Belphoebe's reproach can be understood as the excess of the romantic, but if subjected to analysis it is not a convincing display. To understand Timias's desperation it is necessary to understand the nature and significance of the reproach. Belphoebe says simply, "Is this the faith?" and flees. Despite its ambiguity the concept of honor suggests a reason for Belphoebe's remark and explains Timias's reaction. Ashley writes that honor "respecteth not so much the greatnes and propagacion of yt self (which glorie doth especially) as the desertes of vertue: for yt ys of glorie when any mans name ys magnified amongst many and ys much spoken of in euery bodyes mouth as renowned and very rare. Honour on the contrary being content with the ample approbacion of the better sort, yea, and peradventure with a few, doth neither seeke after fame nor magnificence, nor affecteth great prayses."[60] Timias's honor as well as his

---

[59] Ashley, *Of Honour*, p. 50, and ". . . glory ys not only of the living but also of the dead; whereas honour perteyneth properly to those which are alive, because yf yt be geven for vertue to some one, and that vertue be not in him when he ys dead, howsoeuer yt were before, by reason that the accion of vertue ceasinge, the prayse therof ceaseth therwith. Truly honour ys peculiar to those that are alive." (Ashley, p. 36.)

[60] Ashley, p. 36.

life have been rescued by Belphoebe; she is the "few," "the better sort," of whom Ashley speaks. Timias is content to live in the forest not only because of his love but also because his honor consists of Belphoebe's opinion of him.[61] As his soliloquy on love indicates, Timias is willing to serve Belphoebe forever, willing to submit to her judgment of him. Her judgment and approbation of him is dependent on his virtue, possibly on his defeat of the three evil foresters. This is the relation that exists between them.

Belphoebe's "Is this the faith?" may refer to her changed judgment of his virtue. In her opinion he is not now virtuous but lustful, and she rejects him. The reader is well aware that this is Belphoebe's error, but the consequences are the same for Timias. His honor is gone, since the judgment by which he was honored has been changed. Timias is faced with an impossible love and honor destroyed; the result is flight from the world:

> There he continued in this carefull plight,
>   Wretchedly wearing out his youthly yeares,
> Through wilfull penury consumed quight,
>   That like a pined ghost he soone appeares.
>   For other food then that wilde forrest beares,
> Ne other drinke there did he euer tast,
>   Then running water, tempred with his teares,
>   The more his weakened body so to wast:
> That out of all mens knowledge he was worne at last.
>
> (4.7.41)

His honor gone, he is not even recognized by Arthur, nor does he try to take up his old allegiance as Arthur's squire. This too is impossible. Arthur leaves him "Till time for him should remedy prouide, And him restore to former grace againe."

[61] Ashley's definition: "*Honour* therefore ys a certeine testemonie of vertue shining of yt self, geven of some man by the iudgement of good men" (p. 34). See also p. 36.

BELPHOEBE AND AMORET

This remedy and reconciliation is described in canto 8, where Belphoebe's "grace" is extended to him again through the agency of a dove and a ruby. The dove as the symbol of widowed fidelity is the companion of his "penaunce sad And pensiue sorrow" and throws an interesting light on the "faith" that existed between Belphoebe and Timias.[62] His relation with Belphoebe was the fidelity of marriage; his rejection becomes a shameful, living death,[63] and the dove is an appropriate companion and symbol of his spiritual condition. Timias becomes like the dove a mourner, chaste, sorrowful, and faithful. The heart-shaped ruby amulet hardly needs a commentary; it is a symbol for his lost love. Finally Belphoebe is led to him by the dove and in pity asks,

> Ah wofull man, what heauens hard disgrace,
> Or wrath of cruell wight on thee ywrake
> Or selfe disliked life doth thee thus wretched make?
>
> (4.8.14)

For the first time since his rejection Timias speaks and names the causes of his "languishment": heaven, "Enuying my too great felicity," and Belphoebe's "high displesure, through misdeeming bred." Belphoebe offered another alternative—"selfe disliked life"—which Timias ignores. Since Spenser does not take the opportunity of correcting him, the reader must assume that Timias is blameless in the affair. On the other hand it should be observed that Timias does not blame Belphoebe or heaven. She has made a mistake, but like heaven "none may it redresse or blame, Sith to his powre we all are subiect borne." Timias's only plea is "That when your pleasure is to deeme aright, Ye may redresse, and me restore to light."

---

[62] See *The Book of Beasts*, trans. T. H. White, New York, 1954, pp. 145-146 and Camerarius, *Symbolorvm & Emblematvm*, Frankfurt, 1654, Liber III, symb. LXIII, "Turtur."

[63] He is twice described as a ghost: 4.7.41; 4.8.12.

BELPHOEBE AND AMORET

> Which sory words her mightie hart did mate
> With mild regard, to see his ruefull plight,
> That her inburning wrath she gan abate,
> And him receiu'd againe to former fauours state.
> (4.8.17)

His honor is restored, and Timias once more joins Belphoebe in the forest, "Fearlesse of fortunes chaunge or enuies dread."

The episode ends happily, but the reader may well question the morality, may even question whether there is any, like Mrs. Barbauld and *The Ancient Mariner*. From Timias's point of view, persevering virtue is finally rewarded by long-due honor, but by modern standards Belphoebe's error should receive some reprisal, some poetic judgment. There is none, and here *the figure of the Queen looms behind Belphoebe*. She can do no wrong: Timias makes it quite clear that his restoration is entirely at her pleasure. But the apparent flouting of morality goes further; Timias never returns to Arthur, is "all mindlesse of his owne deare Lord," to which Spenser adds:

> The noble Prince, who neuer heard one word
> Of tydings, what did vnto him betide,
> Or what good fortune did to him afford,
> But through the endlesse world did wander wide,
> Him seeking euermore, yet no where him descride.
> (4.8.18)[64]

It seems strange that Timias should quit his allegiance to the hero of the poem to become the "servant" of Belphoebe, and yet not so strange as Spenser's taking the time to wind up a thread of the plot that comes to nothing, when his usual habit is to leave even important incidents unfinished.

The episode of Timias and Belphoebe takes on a new

---

[64] This is another of Spenser's narrative slips because Timias is once more with Arthur in 6.5.23.

dimension if it is interpreted as an attempt to relate further the private and public persons of the Queen in the poem. At the beginning of the poem Timias is Arthur's squire; at the end of his career he has forgotten Arthur and become a servant to Belphoebe, and Spenser implies that this is a fruition rather than a falling away. The explanation seems to be in a parallelism between Timias and Belphoebe, Arthur and Gloriana. Arthur's quest for Gloriana has always been interpreted as a quest for glory. Is it not possible to see in Timias's happy service to Belphoebe a minor analogy to Arthur's unfinished quest for Gloriana? The quotations from Ashley make it abundantly clear that honor is the virtue of the private individual, glory the virtue of the public.

Spenser does not stress this aspect of the Timias-Belphoebe relationship, but in *The Ruins of Time* occurs a curious passage:

> Then did I see a pleasant Paradize,
> Full of sweete flowres and daintiest delights,
> Such as on earth man could not more deuize,
> With pleasures choyce to feed his cheerefull sprights;
> Not that, which *Merlin* by his Magicke slights
> Made for the gentle squire, to entertaine
> His faire *Belphoebe*, could this gardine staine.
>
> (519-525)

Of this paradise we hear nothing in *The Faerie Queene*, but perhaps it is just as well. Belphoebe's paradise cannot compare with Gloriana's Faeryland, and if Merlin's work for Timias is slighted in the poem, it is only to do justice to his other creation:

> Both shield, and sword, and armour all he wrought
> For this young Prince, when first to armes he fell;
> But when he dyde, the Faerie Queene it brought
> To Faerie lond, where yet it may be seene, if sought.
>
> (1.7.36)

vi · CONCLUSION

The adventures of Belphoebe and Amoret take them farther and farther away from their common origin; it is only the reader who realizes that they are two complementary aspects of love, for not even they are aware they are twins. For this reason it is all the more important to emphasize the relationship between them. With considerable psychological insight Spenser describes in Belphoebe and Amoret the two alternatives of Christian love. Amoret's adventures are types of the education of a wife and the evils that beset marriage, but for Belphoebe Spenser went to the highest example of virginity known to him and made her adventures an allegory of honor.

It is this typicality that distinguishes Belphoebe and Amoret from Britomart, who represents that chastity or purity of life that is possessed by all Spenser's heroines, indeed by all who live pure lives. The choice that Belphoebe and Amoret represent has been made for Britomart by Providence or Merlin's magic glass, for the fruit of her marriage will be a long line of kings. In this respect she differs from Amoret, for whom no such glorious future is assured. Because the choice has been made for her there is no need for Britomart ever to encounter Belphoebe. The three heroines go their separate ways, each representing different solutions to the problem of love, the central issue of the middle books of *The Faerie Queene.*

Chapter Three
Florimell and Marinell

The earth may glide diaphanous to death;
But if I lift my arms it is to bend
To you who turned away once, Helen, knowing
The press of troubled hands, too alternate
With steel and soil to hold you endlessly.

—CRANE, *For the Marriage of Faustus and Helen*

IN contrast to the figures and adventures treated in chapters I and II, Florimell and Marinell are not related to the real world of history like Britomart, nor to Elizabeth like Belphoebe, nor to other major figures in the poem like Amoret; indeed they can hardly be said to belong to the world of the Faery court. Florimell and Marinell are surrounded by the mysterious deities of the sea and remain to the very end beautiful, elusive, and passive. Their story begins with Florimell's flight from the "griesly Forster" in the first canto of Book III and ends with their marriage in Book V. Between these two points their adventures are slight and for the most part solitary. Marinell is overcome and wounded by Britomart; Florimell, fleeing from the Hag's hut, is pursued successively by the beast, the old fisherman, and Proteus. It is only through the happy accident of the marriage of the Medway and the Thames that their narrative is brought to any conclusion. There are hardly enough events to account for their existence in the poem, yet without dropping overt clues, Spenser emphasizes their importance by the structural position their story occupies and by the simple fact that theirs is the only marriage consummated in *The Faerie Queene*.

Oddly enough this very lack of overt significance has led most critics to draw Florimell and Marinell back into the world of history, to explain away their elusiveness by identification with historical figures. To say with Upton, to take one example, that Florimell is Mary Queen of Scots is to say nothing about the figures in the poem.[1] This is not to deny that *The Faerie Queene* is filled with allusions to historical figures, but one is left (if lucky) with a parallel set of names, about whose personalities we know much less than those in the poem.[2] The whole tradition of the fall of princes demonstrates conclusively that the rise or fall of a prince—that is, the history of an individual—was considered subordinate to a larger concept of history, the universal history of mankind moving through time toward Apocalypse. Spenser could not, if he wanted to, simply portray Mary Queen of Scots under the guise of Florimell. Those actions that he did portray would be recognized as acts of a larger significance, universal rather than particular. Thus the true significance of the historical actions of Mary as disguised in the narrative of Florimell could be learned only from the text of the poem, and we are immediately faced with the problem with which we began: what does Florimell mean?

The only other serious attempt to treat the images of Florimell and Marinell is the mythic interpretation of Northrop Frye, in which they become the types of the Proserpine-Adonis, Ishtar-Tammuz myth, the vegetation myth of decay

---

[1] Upton, *Var.*, 3.263-264. What has been said applies equally to the theories of Pauline Henley, *Spenser in Ireland*, Dublin, 1928, pp. 137-138, and Isabel E. Rathborne, "The Political Allegory of the Florimell-Marinell Story," *ELH*, 12 (1945), pp. 279-289.

[2] Allegory as Spenser intended the word means the *significacio* or *sentence* of any episode. This allegory could be enriched with allusions to historical figures and events, but this would not replace the moral *sentence*. What is known today as "historical" or "political" allegory would probably have been called "allusion," which Harington defines: "The Allusion: of fictions, to be applied to some things done, or written of in times past, as also where it may be applied without offence to the time present. But these happen in verie few bookes." (*Orlando Furioso*, 1591, "Advertisement to the Reader," sig. Ai.)

and regeneration.[3] The value of this kind of interpretation as opposed to the school of historical allegory is that a poem retains its own peculiar moral *sentence* at the same time that it corresponds to a more general mythic structure; it does not try to replace the *significacio*. In this case, however, Frye's suggested myth is more general than Spenser's structure demands, and hence is less illuminating about the specific narrative pattern established by the Florimell cantos. Spenser is using a myth to control the adventures of Florimell and Marinell, but he specifies the exact significance of his Florimell by making the structure of these cantos conform to the narrative pattern of the alternate myth of Helen of Troy—type of beauty *par excellence*.[4]

i · FLORIMELL AND THE CHASTE HELEN

> Helen's cheek, but not her heart.
> (*As You Like It*, 3.2.153)

The most common source for the alternate Helen myth is Euripides's account, but his is only the most familiar of a long series of attacks on and defenses of Helen's part in the Trojan war.[5] After Homer a new attitude toward Helen sprang up, begun by Hesiod and associated early with the blindness of Stesichorus. Plato refers to it twice:

---

[3] Frye's interpretation is cited in *Anatomy of Criticism*, p. 153.

[4] Alfred B. Gough, ed., *The Faerie Queene, Book V*, Oxford, 1918, pp. 193-194, 197, suggested Plato's reference to the Stesichorus version of the myth in *Republic* 586 and also Euripides. H. M. Belden suggested also the Euripides story as source of Proteus's capture of Florimell, *MLN*, 44 (1929), pp. 526-531. Isabel E. Rathborne simply alludes to the relation of the two Florimells to the two Helens. J. W. Bennett, *Evolution*, p. 140, dismisses the suggestion rather summarily, claiming only the influence of Ariosto.

[5] For a full account and interpretation of the development of the Helen myth in all its aspects up to the time of Euripides see Frank J. Groten, Jr., "The Tradition of the Helen Legend in Greek Literature," unpublished Princeton Ph.D. dissertation, 1955. I am indebted to Dr. Groten for most of the references to the alternate myth before the time of Euripides.

"There is an ancient purgation of mythological error which was known not to Homer but to Stesichorus. For when Stesichorus was deprived of his eyesight because of his slander of Helen, he was ignorant like Homer, but like a seer he knew the reason and composed as follows:

> This is not the true story;
> You did not embark on well-benched ships,
> Nor did you go to the citadel of Troy.

"And when he had composed all of the so-called palinode, he suddenly regained his eyesight."[6]

And again in *Republic* IX, 586C: "Just as Stesichorus says that the eidolon of Helen was fought for by those in Troy in ignorance of the truth." The legend to which Plato is referring is the basic alternate myth. Helen did not go to Troy; Paris in fear of pursuit sailed to Egypt, where King Proteus demanded that Helen be left. In some versions Paris sailed on to Troy with an *eidolon* of Helen; in others he sailed on alone. At the end of the war Menelaus journeyed to Egypt, where he recovered Helen from the protection of Proteus.

This alternate myth meant two things to later Greek writers. It meant first that the great, heroic war of Troy was the supreme example of human futility. If the Trojans had the *eidolon*, they were cheated in their honorable war of defense; if they did not have it, the Greeks' demands for Helen's return could not be answered, and the war becomes utterly futile for both sides. But the myth has a less cynical side; it meant that Helen's chastity was preserved, a fact that provided an effective rebuttal to her detractors. This myth was continued with various morals drawn from it by Herodotus, Isocrates, Lycophron, Apollodorus, and in the Christian era by Philostratus, Hyginus, Servius, Tzetzes and the other scholiasts on Lycophron, to mention but a few.[7]

---

[6] Groten, p. 250 (Groten's translation).
[7] Euripides, *Helene*, 31-51, 582ff., 669ff.; *Electra*, 1280ff.; Herodotus,

The alternate myth was overshadowed in the Renaissance by the "face that launched a thousand ships," but the myth of the false Helen who accompanied Paris to Troy was still current. The fact that Servius mentioned it twice in his famous commentary on the *Aeneid* assured it an authority known to all scholars and readers of poetry. Servius calls the false Helen a *phantasma*, thus making the vague Greek *eidolon* more specific. Servius may have been influenced by the account in Apollodorus, who writes that "Alexander repaired to Troy with a phantom of Helen fashioned out of clouds."[8] It is recorded by Natalis Comes and Charles Stephanus, both of whose accounts seem to be derived from Herodotus.[9] Harington alludes to it in the forty-sixth canto of *Orlando* in connection with a tent woven by Cassandra given by Menelaus to Proteus in return for Helen, and Ralegh relates the myth in his *History of the World*.[10]

Spenser might have read any or all of these sources with the exception of Ralegh, from whom he could have learned of the myth first-hand. The problem is not, however, where Spenser got the myth but what he made of it. In the matter of details he diverges from the myth as much as he follows it. Florimell is not raped but flees from the Court. Instead of a Paris there is a succession of much less attractive figures, culminating in the old fisherman. Proteus is not the hospitable king of the myth, and Marinell is certainly not a Menelaus figure.[11] But the larger resemblances make clear that Spen-

---

2.112-120; Isocrates, *Helen*, 64-65; Lycophron, *Alexandra*, 110-127, 820-827; Apollodorus, *Epitome*, 3.5; Philostratus, *Vita Apolloni*, 4.5; Hyginus, *Fabula* LXXIX in *Opuscula Mythologica*, Amsterdam, 1688; Servius, *Aeneid*, 1.651, 2.592; Tzetzes, *Antehomerica*, Lipsiae, 1798, 147ff. and *Schol. on Lycophron*, 110ff., 820ff.; for other references see Groten *passim*.

[8] Apollodorus, *Epitome*, 3.5.

[9] Natalis Comes, Lib. 6.23, "De Paride"; Charles Estienne (Stephanus), *Dictionarium* . . . , Geneva 1660, col. 1677 (s. v. "Proteus").

[10] Harington, *Orlando*, sig. L15ᵛ (canto 46, st. 66); Ralegh, *History of the World*, 1614, 1.2.14.3, pp. 383-384.

[11] The confusion of Proteus the sea-god with Proteus the king of Egypt can be attributed to poetic license and is duplicated in a sixteenth century

ser's basic archetype is this alternate Helen myth. Without obtruding the myth, Spenser makes his heroine borrowed from Ariosto conform to the pattern. Florimell is rescued from rape by Proteus, who keeps her until she is released by her true love; while a false Florimell is created to impersonate her. Spenser's choice of the alternate Helen myth as the basis of these episodes implies that he is exploring the effect of beauty true and false on love and lust. His moral allegory, therefore, should account for the differences between the adventures of Florimell and his structural archetype. Like the analogies between the *Odyssey* and Joyce's *Ulysses*, the moral issues involved in these episodes become clearer against the background of the alternate Helen myth.

Beginning with her flight from the Court, Florimell is subjected to a continual dehumanization of her surroundings.[12] She moves from the Court to the country to the sea, from the protection of the Knights of Maidenhead to the rocky prison of the sea god Proteus. The original motive for flight—her love for the wounded Marinell—is changed to fear, when she is beyond the protection of the Court.

The inappropriateness of Florimell's surroundings is caught at once in the reaction of the witch and her churlish son.

> She was astonisht at her heauenly hew,
> And doubted her to deeme an earthly wight,
> But or some Goddesse, or of *Dianes* crew,
> And thought her to adore with humble spright;
> T' adore thing so diuine as beauty, were but right.
>
> (3.7.11)

Italian poem "Proteus Abdvcente Helenam Paride," *Io. Baptistae Pignae Carminvm Lib. Qvatvor* . . . , Venice, 1553, pp. 187-188.

[12] From the time of Plato's image of the soul as a team of horses, writers have used the horse as a symbol of human passions. Florimell's surrender of the reins to her palfrey (3.7.2) is the romance writer's way of saying that reason is no longer in control of the passions. See Harington's remarks on the hippogriff in *Orlando*, canto 4, and *passim*.

Her beauty even causes the churl to change his slothful ways, but in a mind so low beauty can inspire only lust. Fearing that familiarity might breed contempt and she become a prey to his lust, Florimell escapes pursued by the witch's hyena-like monster. She is driven farther and farther away from the norms and protection of society and escapes into the apparent protection of the fishing boat. Like the symbolism of her former escape on the palfrey, this boat is a symbol that Florimell has subjected herself to the realm of fortune and the vagaries of this mutable life as represented by the sea.[13] Once again Florimell's beauty is the cause of lust, this time in the withered old fisherman, whose attempted rape exemplifies the debasement to which she has subjected herself.

> Beastly he threw her downe, ne car'd to spill
> Her garments gay with scales of fish, that all did fill.
>
> (3.8.26)

Spenser interrupts his narrative at this point to apostrophize the knights of the Faery Court:

> O ye braue knights, that boast this Ladies loue,
> Where be ye now, when she is nigh defild
> Of filthy wretch? well may shee you reproue
> Of falshood or of slouth, when most it may behoue.
>
> But if that thou, Sir *Satyran*, didst weete,
> Or thou, Sir *Peridure*, her sorie state,
> How soone would yee assemble many a fleete,
> To fetch from sea, that ye at land lost late;
> Towres, Cities, Kingdomes ye would ruinate,
> In your auengement and dispiteous rage,
> Ne ought your burning fury mote abate;

---

[13] The symbolism of the storm-tossed bark is so common in classical, medieval, and Renaissance literature that it is hardly necessary to cite other examples. Britomart's complaint to the sea in 3.4 is a compendium of all the things symbolized by this escape of Florimell.

> But if Sir *Calidore* could it presage,
> No liuing creature could his cruelty asswage.
>
> (3.8.27-28)

Spenser surely has in mind the Greeks, who did "assemble many a fleete, To fetch from sea" the Helen who had been stolen away, but this Helen has put herself beyond their power and delivered herself into the hands of the natural in its more bestial aspect. Sir Calidore the knight of courtesy is certainly the proper champion to avenge Florimell's ill-usage, but at this point Spenser wants to emphasize not the wrong to society but the wrong to nature. This is why Sir Satyrane is introduced in the middle of canto 7.

Satyrane represents the best elements of nature and society combined, the honesty and integrity of the naturally unified man, "For both to be and seeme to him was labour lich" (3.7.29). He is equally at home in the Court and in the world to which Florimell has fled, but at his arrival she has abandoned herself to the sea. He is able to subdue the dark powers of the witch's beast with the aid of Florimell's girdle. At this point we must indulge in a cautionary digression about the allegorical significance of this apparently irrelevant episode.

Neither Florimell's loss of the girdle nor Satyrane's subduing the beast should be read psychologically. Neither girdle nor beast are part of the interior "life" of Florimell or Satyrane. She does not lose her chastity when she loses the girdle; she loses the outward sign of her chastity, a sign known and respected at the Court but no longer operative in the world to which she has fled. In this respect the girdle is like Cinderella's slipper, a visible sign of her true station that can be fitted to her only by those who recognize the value of both slipper and scullery maid as part of the same being. In a similar way the beast does not indicate that Satyrane has passions that must be subdued but that there are in this world such things as passions that can be subdued by such forces as Satyrane. Spenser is exemplifying the moral ramifications of Florimell's plight.

As if to demonstrate that Satyrane's victory can be only temporary, Spenser introduces the exemplum of Argante and the Squire of Dames, which illustrate respectively sexual perversions in nature and in society. What perversions Argante and Ollyphant do not think of, the Squire's anti-social Lady will. The bestiality of Argante can be continually pursued by Sir Palladine, the knight of wisdom, but only the unified spirit of Satyrane can see through the hypocritical, false chastity of the Squire's Lady. These women are the female counterparts of the men who attack Florimell, perverters of beauty and of chastity alike. At the end of the episode Satyrane returns to find the beast escaped and the girdle broken, and this leads to the creation of the false beauty of the False Florimell and Satyrane's tournament to replace Florimell.

Spenser cannot allow Satyrane to rescue Florimell, but following the pattern of the alternate Helen myth he makes Proteus her dubious salvation. From the point of view of "character" Florimell's encounter with Proteus is filled with moral ambiguities, for his rescue of her represents both a further debasement and at the same time an exaltation, in that he is a god. The sources provide no satisfactory explanation for Proteus's behavior to Florimell. The ambiguities disappear, however, if we consider Proteus not as a character with human or divine motivations but as a force, a figure, an image whose actions spring from that quality of being that is his essence. In short, Proteus should be viewed as a complicated personification, whose actions in the poem are required only to figure forth what he represents. The significance of his treatment of Florimell is to be understood by differentiating his rescue from that of the churl and the fisherman.

Unlike the churl's ineffectual bawling and the fisherman's

rude endeavors, Proteus uses all the resources in his power to win Florimell's *willing* consent. A further contrast between the two rescues and that of Proteus is that they were really offenses against chastity, while Proteus's is clearly an offense against Florimell's love for Marinell. It is not until Florimell is in his power that the original motive for her leaving Court is reintroduced. Marinell was of no concern to the interests of the churl and the fisherman; Proteus wants to replace Marinell in Florimell's affection (just as Busyrane wanted to replace Scudamour in Amoret's). His treatment of Florimell is unmannerly in terms of man or god, but his wooing of Florimell springs not from human need or interest but from that essential quality that he represents in the poem.

The main attribute of Proteus as a god of the sea was his ability to change shapes. This ability is described in his more literary appearances, but the popularity of the notion made it a common adage—*Proteo mutabilior*.[14] The commentators allegorized Proteus, offering a number of interesting and often conflicting interpretations. As usual Abraham Fraunce provides a compendious list: "Cornelius Gemma *in his booke de diuinis naturae characterismis allegorically expoundeth this tale out of the fourth of* Virgils *Georgicks, making* Proteus *a type of nature.* Plato *compareth him to the wrangling of brabling sophisters: and some there be that hereby vnderstand, the truth of things obscured by so many deceauable apparences: Lastly there want not others, which meane hereby the vnderstanding and intellectual parte of mans minde, which vnles it seriously and attentiuely bend it selfe to the contemplation of things, shall neuer attaine to the truth, as* Proteus *would neuer reueale his propheticall knowledge, but first did turne and winde himselfe euery way to escape, vntil with bands he were enforced therunto. . . .*"[15] More popular among the interpretations were those that made Proteus a

[14] *Var.*, 3.270.
[15] Fraunce, *Third part. . .* , sigs. F4^v-G.

type of nature or the truth of things obscured by material appearance. Gyraldi cites Ponticus Heraclides, Proclus, and the Orphic hymns to this effect.[16] Alciati's emblem of Proteus is accompanied by a quotation from Clement of Alexandria comparing Proteus "ad cupiditatem animi humani in varias sese mutantem formas."[17] Bocchi's emblem is entitled "vnam videndam veritatem in omnib(us),"[18] and Charles Stephanus refers to him as "naturam rerum."[19]

Proteus represents the whole world of mutable nature and man insofar as man's body is independent of but not opposed to his soul. He represents on the cosmic level what Satyrane represents as a knight, and like Satyrane he introduces the theme of appearance and reality, which is the basic meaning of Florimell and her false double. In this respect the episode of Florimell and Proteus is Spenser's analysis of the nature of beauty and its effect on love. It works on two levels, the personal and the cosmic. Florimell as a beautiful woman is in love with Marinell. Proteus, representing all other possible lovers, tries to win Florimell. But this is impossible according to Spenser's Neoplatonic theory of love.

> Then wrong it were that any other twaine
> Should in loues gentle band combyned bee,
> But those whom heauen did at first ordaine,
> And made out of one mould the more t'agree:
> For all that like the beautie which they see,
> Streight do not loue: for loue is not so light,
> As streight to burne at first beholders sight.
>
> (*Hymne of Beautie*, 204-210)

[16] Giraldi, *Historiae Deorum*. . . . s. v. "Marini Dei," vol. 1, 168c-169: "informem rerum materiam" (Ponticus), "in se complectentem omnes rerum formas in mundo genitarum" (Proclus), "totius naturae exordia, & multiformibus speciebus materiam mutare" (Orpheus).

[17] Alciati, *Emblemata*, Antwerp, 1581, pp. 629ff. Alciati also calls Proteus "materia informis" and "multiformis."

[18] *Achilles Bocchi Bonon, Symbolicarum . . . Libri Quinque*, Bologna, 1555, Liber II, symbolum LX, p. 124 (symbol 61 in ed. of 1574).

[19] Stephanus, *Dictionarium*, s.v. "Proteus."

Spenser keeps this from becoming merely sentimental by making these same figures also represent the relation of beauty to the mutable world. Florimell as Beauty is wooed by Proteus, the mutable forms of this life, but Spenser makes it quite clear that the source of beauty is not the material or the flesh.

> How vainely then doe ydle wits inuent,
> That beautie is nought else, but mixture made
> Of colours faire, and goodly temp'rament
> Of pure complexions, that shall quickly fade
> And passe away, like to a sommers shade,
> Or that it is but comely composition
> Of parts well measurd, with meet disposition.
>
> And who so list the like assayes to ken,
> Shall find by tryall, and confesse it then,
> That Beautie is not, as fond men misdeeme,
> An outward shew of things, that onely seeme.
>
> For that same goodly hew of white and red,
> With which the cheekes are sprinckled, shal decay,
> And those sweete rosy leaues so fairely spred
> Vpon the lips, shall fade and fall away
> To that they were, euen to corrupted clay.
> That golden wyre, those sparckling stars so bright
> Shall turne to dust, and loose their goodly light.
> But that faire lampe, from whose celestiall ray
> That light proceedes, which kindleth louers fire,
> Shal neuer be extinguisht nor decay....
> (*Hymne of Beautie*, 64-70,88-101)

The soul is the cause of beauty; Florimell is Spenser's figure of the spiritual beauty of the soul manifested through physical beauty. When she is considered in this light, Proteus's wooing is really the physical attempting to claim beauty for its own. What sustains Florimell is her love for Marinell; indeed beauty is always sustained by love. Spenser is telling the reader that beauty and love are above the physical, mutable realm of Proteus. This is part of the allegorical meaning of the marriage of Florimell and Marinell, but Spenser does not choose to complete the allegory at this point in his narrative. Instead he breaks off his praise of Florimell to return to the adventures of Satyrane.

It is only now that the reader can begin to understand why Spenser did not follow the details of the alternate Helen myth, why he did not introduce a Paris, for in canto 9 Paridell comes riding up to Satyrane. Together they set out to the Castle of Malbecco, where Paridell is to take another Helen, the Helen whom Spenser and Shakespeare recognized as a whore. It is possible now to see that by juxtaposing his versions of the alternate and Homeric Helen myths Spenser is presenting a Neoplatonic explanation of the Troy story and that his two Florimells are really the philosophic prototypes of the conflicting Helen myths—true and false beauty. Spenser's assurance that Florimell would not succumb to the power of Proteus did not prevent his belief in the existence of the adventures of the False Florimell, who dishonors Satyrane's tournament, the prototype of the Trojan war and all wars for false values.

ii · THE FALSE FLORIMELL

False Florimell requires little explanation to the age of the "pin-up"; she is composed of sonneteers' epithets and represents the same type of wish-fulfillment and debasement of the female form as her modern counterpart. She differs from her modern descendants in being a fiend incarnate. Her beauty is only physical and has the power to inspire only lust. She is incapable of true physical love, which Spenser like all Neoplatonists derived from the soul. Spenser sees her as the *eidolon*, the "Idole faire," for whom the Greeks and Trojans destroyed Troy, and therefore she is the fitting counterpart for the Helen Hermes made of clouds to deceive Paris.

Her career is a complete parody of the true Florimell's. She dallies with the delighted Churl "Enough to hold a foole in vaine delight: Him long she so with shadowes entertained" (3.8.10). Since she cannot love, her companions make no difference, and she passes in rapid succession from the Churl to Braggadocchio to Ferraugh to Blandamour—from the sub-human, to the type of empty vainglory, to a knight probably derived from Ferrau in Ariosto, to a knight whose name means "the blandishments of love." They are indistinguishable to her; and her progress from one to another is less important than that she is a constant source of discord and a debasement of the true Florimell whom she impersonates.

As a source of discord she figures most prominently in the first half of the fourth book, which is dominated by the power of Ate. The fight of Britomart and Arthegall in Book IV, canto 6, has already been treated as a resolution of Ate's power and a major example of the theme of *discordia concors*, a theme most generally stated in the battle and reconciliation of Cambell and Priamond, Diamond, and Triamond. Between these two cantos is Satyrane's tournament and the contest for Florimell's girdle where the forces of discord temporarily rout the forces of concord, and it is in these two "wars" that the False Florimell exerts her greatest power of destruction.

Satyrane is the ideal knight to sponsor this tournament, for in him there is no distinction between appearance and reality, no outer feigned personality masking an inner evil. His one shortcoming is his inability to rise above the natural reason. Unfortunately this is exactly what is required to overcome the discord inspired by Ate and her crew. The themes of appearance and reality and *discordia concors* merge in the events of his tournament and clarify the issues at stake.

From the opening of Book IV the forces of concord and discord have been gathering, and when the Squire of Dames announces the tournament to the strange group of knights and ladies whose journeys have brought them together, they set off to the tournament as to a focus. Cantos 1 and 2 present an almost symmetrical pattern of this convergence of the good and the evil. Canto 1 initiates the theme of discord with the appearance of Blandamour and Paridell accompanied by Ate and Duessa. Canto 2 presents a parallel group—Cambell, Triamond, Cambina, and Canacee—representing the forces of concord. These groups are met at various points by three couples, of whom one member is always disguised in some way. Britomart and Amoret are the first; Amoret has just discovered that her knight is really a woman but no one of the discord group is aware of this. At the end of canto 1 Scudamour and Glauce meet this group, the old nurse disguised as a squire. And finally in canto 2 Ferraugh rides up with the False Florimell, whom everyone accepts as the true.

Britomart and Amoret can escape unharmed from the discord group because they know each other in truth, but Scudamour, unaware that Britomart is a woman, is harmed by the malice of Ate. Ferraugh is downed immediately by Blandamour, but the real power behind his defeat is the evil of the False Florimell, which "made him thinke him selfe in heauen, that was in hell" (3.8.19). Inspired by Ate, the evil power of False Florimell is about to destroy Blandamour and Paridell when the Squire of Dames announces the tournament. The grouping is complete when they all meet another solitary figure, Braggadocchio, representing here the evil of egotism, which knows neither true nor false friendship and like the False Florimell exists entirely in the world of appearances.[20]

The tournament itself presents another pattern of sym-

[20] This aspect of Braggadocchio's character has been suggested to me by Dr. Eric Rothstein, who points out the appropriateness of vainglorious egotism's winning the False Florimell since neither one can get beyond himself.

metry, a symmetry which will not fall into the simple pattern of good and evil. Satyrane and the knights of maidenhead are united on one side to defend their right to possess the girdle of Florimell. The opposing side is the entire group that has been gathering in cantos 1 and 2. This confusion is only apparent, for to a certain extent the morality of the situation is referable to the chivalric rules of the tournament: the evil fight, the good play. But Spenser goes further in dissociating his good figures from their evil partners. In each case that a good figure fights on the opposing side he is disguised. On the first day Triamond grabs the spear of the hesitant Braggadocchio and is finally wounded by Satyrane. The second day is won for the opposition by Cambell in Triamond's armor and Triamond in his armor, and on the third day they are rescued from total defeat at the hands of Satyrane by the appearance of Arthegall disguised as the Salvage knight. Of course, the day is won by the sudden appearance of Britomart, who has been disguised from her first appearance.

These disguises are Spenser's way of specifying the allegorical meaning of the tournament. The participants are not only knights but allegorical figures in their own right. The allegorical significance of Satyrane, Britomart, and the evil figures *en masse* is appropriate to Spenser's allegorical intentions for the tournament, but that of the other major figures is not. Their disguises are intended to show that their allegorical personalities are not operative in this canto. In canto 3 Cambell and Triamond represent a very special allegory already described in the Introduction; here they work only tropologically as an exemplum of friendship. Arthegall's defeat and consequent behavior is at variance with the concept of justice; his disguise shows that he is playing another role for the moment, a role which has been explained in connection with his encounter of Britomart.

The outcome of the three days' tournament is really an emblem of the progress of Books III and IV, in which the first day is won by the champion of Chastity, the second by Friendship, and the third by Britomart as the supreme example of Chastity, who progresses from the role of chaste maiden to that of chaste wife of Justice in Book V. The tournament is the first triumph of concord over discord, for chastity and friendship are not really opposed and the enmity of Britomart and Arthegall is soon to be resolved by recognition and love.

From the point of view of Satyrane and Britomart the tournament illustrates also the deficiency of Satyrane as a defender of chastity and beauty. He has been referred to above as the natural man. As Una in Book I must finally leave his benevolent protection, so Florimell passed from his realm to that of Proteus, and so too must the girdle. He is incapable of saving the third day of the tournament; he cannot pass beyond the chastity of natural reason. The higher chastity of Britomart is required, the chastity aided by the grace of God. Like Proteus he cannot grasp the true significance of Beauty; he can see only its exterior, and for this reason he is deceived by the false beauty of the False Florimell at the contest for the girdle.

The climax of the theme of appearance and reality is the point where False Florimell wins the girdle. But the girdle will not fasten; its magical virtues are not deceived. The effect is so absurd,

> That all men wondred at the vncouth sight,
>   And each one thought, as to their fancies came.
> But she her selfe did thinke it doen for spight,
>   And touched was with secret wrath and shame
> Therewith, as thing deuiz'd her to defame.
>   Then many other Ladies likewise tride,
>   About their tender loynes to knit the same;
> But it would not on none of them abide,
> But when they thought it fast, eftsoones it was vntide.

FLORIMELL AND MARINELL

> Which when that scornefull *Squire of Dames* did vew,
> He lowdly gan to laugh, and thus to iest;
> Alas for pittie that so faire a crew,
> As like can not be seene from East to West,
> Cannot find one this girdle to inuest.
> Fie on the man, that did it first inuent,
> To shame vs all with this, *Vngirt vnblest*.
> Let neuer Ladie to his loue assent,
> That hath this day so many so vnmanly shent.
>
> (4.5.17-18)

The tournament has ended like a medieval *fabliau* in ribald laughter and scorn of chaste beauty. Even when Amoret succeeds in tying the belt, the crowd assents to False Florimell's keeping it. Virtue and concord have been defeated, but the seeds of eventual victory are evident in the unity of the good characters. Britomart refuses to take False Florimell as her lady, "For that strange Dame, whose beauties wonderment She lesse esteem'd, then th'others (Amoret's) vertuous gouernment" (4.5.20). Arthegall has departed in rage, and Triamond and Cambell will not give up their loves. Satyrane, however, who cannot see through to the lack of virtue in the lady, accepts her. Once again inspired by Ate the discord group wrangles over Satyrane's prize and once more are about to destroy themselves, when False Florimell finds the appropriately empty companion, Braggadocchio, the knight of appearances and no real substance. They rush off and are not seen again until the marriage of Florimell and Marinell in Book V.

iii · THE MARRIAGE OF THE THAMES AND MEDWAY

> The sea lifts, also, reliquary hands.
> (Crane, *Voyages III*)

The marriage of the Thames and the Medway occupies a climactic position in Book IV. From a purely structural point of view it is contrasted to the House of Busyrane in Book III. As Amoret, imprisoned by a wall of flame, is rescued by Britomart; so Florimell, imprisoned by walls of waves, is rescued from Proteus through the occasion of this marriage of rivers.[21] Within its own book the reluctant consent of the Medway (4.11.7) recapitulates Scudamour's winning of Amoret in the preceding canto and anticipates the awakening of Marinell in the next. The marriage is both a commentary and analogue of reluctance transformed to consent in a young lady and a young man—one more example of the theme of *discordia concors*. In another sense it is a cosmic symbol of the power of the Temple of Venus and on the social level is paralleled by Marinell's sudden love for Florimell.

Although these structural parallels are important in pointing out a significance for the marriage greater than the usual praise of its descriptive beauty, although they direct the reader's attention to the marriage as a symbolic statement of the meaning of the Temple of Venus and the love of Marinell and Florimell, they do not tell why Spenser chose the river marriage to express these parallels. To do that we must study with some care the structure and symbolism of the canto and relate Spenser's marriage to the concept of river marriages and their literary precedents.

A little more than a century after Spenser published *The Faerie Queene* Daniel Defoe writes in a rather characteristic vein: "I shall sing you no Songs here of the River in the first Person of a Water Nymph, a Goddess (and I know not what) according to the Humour of the ancient Poets. I shall talk nothing of the Marriage of old *Isis*, the Male River, with beautiful *Thame*, the Female River, a Whimsy as simple as the Subject was empty, but I shall speak of the River as Occasion presents, as it really is *made glorious* by

---

[21] Amoret like Florimell is imprisoned for seven months, 3.11.10 and 4.11.4.

the Splendor of its shores. . . ."[22] One can begin to understand Defoe's irritation with the convention of the river marriage as it is exemplified by Drayton's great unread classic, *Poly-Olbion*, and in a sense there is something artificial and merely poetical about the conception. Two rivers join and flow to meet the ocean. And yet to dismiss the river marriage as a legitimate device for poetry is to ignore its significance in the history of English literature.

The river marriage, which must be carefully distinguished from the Ovidian metamorphosis of a nymph into a stream, is a subject peculiar to the Renaissance in England, where it was first used as a formal device by antiquarian scholar-poets, culminating in Drayton's monumental work. The nineteenth century gives us such examples as Shelley's delightful *Arethusa* and Peacock's laborious *The Genius of the Thames*. In the twentieth century there has been a resurgence of interest, especially among the more symbolic or mythic writers. One has only to think of the lyrical "riverrun" in *Finnegans Wake*, or Hart Crane's description of the Mississippi in *The Bridge*, or Eliot's allusions to Spenser's river marriages in "The Fire Sermon" to be convinced that the river marriage has once more become an important poetic device.[23]

These disparate works of art have two characteristics in common. They describe actual rivers, and these descriptions are used symbolically. The all but endless enumeration of English rivers in *Poly-Olbion* builds up a marvellous picture of England, its history and geography. As Douglas Bush

[22] Daniel Defoe, *A Tour thro' the whole Island of Great Britain* . . . , ed. G. D. H. Cole, 2 vols., London, 1927, vol. 1, p. 173.

[23] Crane's description occurs at the end of the section called "The River." I am indebted to Professor Northrop Frye for calling my attention to "The Fire Sermon" as a frustrated river marriage. Mr. William Hollis has pointed out that Ezra Pound includes an oriental version in the marriage of the Wei and Han (canto 91). The concept has influenced even civic statuary. Professor Hal Smith has told me that the "marriage" of the Missouri and the Mississippi at St. Louis is commemorated by a statuary group, whose expression of impending connubial bliss shocked the local citizens.

reminds us, "The best translation of the title is simply 'Merry England.' "[24] *Poly-Olbion* creates unity from diversity and evokes a symbol of England by amassing minute particulars. The modern writers have reversed the situation. Whereas Drayton's patternless enumeration of rivers eventually creates a symbol of unity, the modern writer starts with a pattern that can best be symbolized by the marriage of rivers. The river marriage becomes for the modern writer a symbol of one part of the eternal pattern of flux in time. Northrop Frye has described this pattern of process in treating *The Waste Land*: "... although there is a fire sermon and a thunder sermon, both with apocalyptic overtones, the natural cycle of water, the Thames flowing into the sea and returning through death by water in the spring rains, is the containing form of the poem."[25] The "Doublends Jined" of *Finnegans Wake* repeat the same pattern in the endless Viconian cycle of Anna Livia Plurabelle.

Spenser stands somewhere between these two types and is in many ways the progenitor of both. The marriage of the Thames and the Medway leads to Drayton through its enumeration of river names and to Joyce and Eliot through its symbolism. Spenser is the great poet of mutability in English. Blake and Shelley, Yeats and Joyce and Eliot have all learned from him. They are all intensely aware of the tension between the temporal and the eternal and the ultimate resolution of this tension in some kind of Apocalypse. The marriage of the Thames and Medway is part of Spenser's mythology of mutability, but its greatness both as poetry and as part of *The Faerie Queene* cannot be fully appreciated until it is seen contrasted to the shallow background of antiquarian verses that were its antecedents.

The first poem built around the concept of the river mar-

[24] Douglas Bush, *English Literature in the Earlier Seventeenth Century*, Oxford, 1945, p. 79.
[25] Frye, *Anatomy of Criticism*, p. 323.

riage is Leland's *Cygnea Cantio*, written in Latin hendecasyllables and published in 1545.[26] Its 699 lines are frankly inspired by antiquarian interests and describe a journey of swans "reviewing the beauties and antiquities of various sites down along the Thames—Reading, Windsor, Eton, Richmond, Kew, London, Greenwich, and Deptford. Then, from speaking of England's ships and prowess by sea, it begins a eulogy of Henry VIII, and a review of his works and exploits, which occupy the rest of the poem. At the end, the swan bids its mates farewell, in preparation for its journey to heaven."[27] Leland's poem is paralleled in the next generation of antiquarians by Camden's fragments *De Connubio Tamae et Isis*, which are scattered throughout his *Britannia*.[28] These fragments follow the same pattern as the Leland poem and very probably were to celebrate Elizabeth, as Leland's poem celebrated Henry.[29]

Before these two poems I have been unable to find trace of another poem constructed around a river marriage. The lack of evidence points to the possibility that the concept may be entirely native to England.[30] Camden in describing the

[26] The poem is reprinted in the ninth volume, pp. 9-25, of *Leland's Itinerary*, ed. Thomas Hearne, 9 vols., Oxford, 1769, and is accompanied by over seventy pages of Latin commentary.

[27] Charles G. Osgood, "Spenser's English Rivers," *Transactions of the Connecticut Academy of Arts and Sciences*, 23 (1920), p. 102.

[28] Professor Osgood's statement that the fragments consist of 93 Latin hexameters is incorrect. About 100 more lines are included in various editions of the *Britannia* and one more line is recorded by Ben Jonson, *Works*, ed. Herford and Simpson, vol. 7, p. 92. The same line is recorded in John Nichols, *Progresses of James*, 4 vols., London, 1828, vol. 1, p. 384. The history of the passages quoted in the *Britannia* is treated by Leicester Bradner, *Musae Anglicanae*, New York, 1940, pp. 40-42.

[29] The subject matter of the fragments suggests that Camden's principle of organization was to trace the progress of both the Tame and the Isis until they merged into the Thames and then to follow its course. Since the last passage we have is the praise of Hampton Court, we cannot be certain whether Camden continued his poem to London and a possible meeting with an allegorical representation of Elizabeth or to the Thames's entry into the sea.

[30] I have searched with no success through probable classical sources.

merging of the Tame and the Isis to form the Thames supports this possibility: "A little beneath this towne (Dorchester) *Tame* and *Isis* meeting in one streame become hand-fast (as it were) and ioyned in Wedlocke: and as in waters, so in name, they are coupled, as *Ior* and *Dan* in the Holy Land, *Dor* and *Dan* in France, whence come *Iordan* and *Dordan*. Forever after this, the river by a compound word is called, *Tamesis*, that is *Tamis*. Hee seemeth first to have observed this, who wrot the book entituled *Eulogium Historiarum*."[31] This medieval etymology, for lack of other evidence and analogues, seems to be the source of English river marriages. It may be that the concept of river marriages would never have been popular in the Renaissance if the Thames had not been the most important river in England and if its parent streams had not been called Tame and Isis. In any case, the etymology forms the basis of both Leland's and Camden's poems and as a poetic device retained its popularity until the eighteenth century.[32]

Ovid has nothing comparable to the river marriage, and Plutarch's treatise, "The Names of Rivers and Mountains," yields not a hint. Hilda Taylor, "Topographical Poetry in England during the Renaissance," Unpub. Univ. Chicago Ph.D. dissertation, 1926, brings nothing to light; in fact, she does not mention the concept. It may have its source in Italian or French Renaissance poetry unknown to me, but Professor Erwin Panofsky informed me that the concept was unknown to him outside of Spenser and suggested a possible source in ancient or Renaissance coins. This also yielded no results.

[31] William Camden, *Britain*, trans. Philemon Holland, London, 1610, p. 384. The author to whom Camden refers is William of Malmesbury, the twelfth century monk, who writes as follows about this marriage: "Tama isa [*sic*] est amnis dividens partem Angliae Orientalem, et Fluit per Londoniam, et cadit in Mare Boreali; capit autem originem de uno fonticulo juxta Cirencestriam et ibi vocatur Tame, et est ibi nomen compositum de duobus rivis, et vocatur Tamise, ab illo composito." *Eulogium (historiarum sive temporis)* . . . , ed. Frank Scott Haydon, 3 vols., London, 1858, 1860, 1863, vol. 2, p. 8. The work is attributed to William, although additions were made from the time of his death until 1366. I have not been able to trace the source of the etymologies of Jordan and Dordan; several references are given in Robert R. Cawley's *Milton and the Literature of Travel*, Princeton, 1951, p. 108 and note.

[32] This etymology was undoubtedly one cause of Defoe's annoyance with

Professor Osgood calls attention to William Vallans's *A Tale of Two Swannes*, published in 1590, and now available only in Hearne's edition of Leland's *Itinerary*.[33] Written in English, it differs from the two earlier examples only in language and setting and does not trace the growth of the Thames, but its main purpose is antiquarian, having a full commentary "Of certaine proper names used in this tale." It is a slighter poem than the elegant Latin eulogies of Leland and Camden despite its being one of the early examples of blank verse, but its freer use of the device of the swans and the introduction of Mercury and Venus do not indicate a greater interest in the symbolism of river marriages. These three poems are the only instances available of the river marriage before Spenser, and they show only traces of the symbolism that characterizes Spenser's poem.

With so few examples of a type any generalizations are bound to be only partially correct. Nevertheless, one can generalize to the extent of saying that the river marriage was employed as a device by learned Court poets,[34] that it was used as a frame to unite political praise with descriptions

---

river marriages. There are two poems from his period that take the etymology as a kind of poetic exercise. The anonymous "In Amorem Tami & Isidis" and its imitation in English appeared in 1714 in *Poetical Miscellanies. . . . Publish'd by Mr. Steele*, pp. 290-291. William King includes the following poem as part of his works:

> So the God Thame, as through some pond he glides,
> Into the arms of wandering Isis slides:
> His strength, her softness, in one bed combine,
> And both with bands inextricable join;
> Now no Coerulean Nymph, or Sea god, knows
> Where Isis, or where Thame, distinctly flows;
> But with a lasting charm they blend their stream,
> Producing one imperial River—Thame.

Original Works of William King, ed. John Nichols, 3 vols., London, 1776, vol. 3, p. 259. I am indebted to Dr. John Meagher for calling these two late examples to my attention.

[33] William Vallans, *A Tale of Two Swannes*, in *Leland's Itinerary*, ed. Hearne, vol. 5, pp. v-xxxii.

[34] See Vallans in *DNB*.

both historical and geographical. A few years after the publication of Vallans's poem Spenser brought out the second installment of *The Faerie Queene*. Here the river marriage is loaded with symbolic import; only the place names remain from the old antiquarian poems, and all overt patriotic pride is converted to a subtle symbolism implicit in bringing the Thames and the Medway into the epic structure of *The Faerie Queene*.

After the publication of this second installment and before the publication of *Poly-Olbion* there are more numerous allusions to river marriages, always basically symbolic. In 1600 E(dward) W(ilkinson) brought out a modest poem entitled *Thameseidos*, which was obviously influenced by Spenser. The poem is a mythological pastoral, which disguises the adventures of Diana and Calisto, the amours of Jupiter, and other classical gods under the names of Thames, Isis, and Medway. The sea gods especially play an important part, and at one point Wilkinson makes an allusion to Florimell.[35] Wilkinson was evidently trying to "overgo" Spenser and certainly did in the confusion of mythological references and narrative abruptness. The poem is not great poetry, but it is much better than many other mythological pastorals of the period. For our purposes it is interesting to note the immediate impact of Spenser's poem on the literary fashion. Drayton too cites Spenser as the original of his treatment of the Medway and the Thames:

And but that *Medway* then of *Tames* obtain'd such grace,
Except her country Nymphs, that none should be in place,

---

[35] *E. W. his Thameseidos*, London, 1600, sig. E^v-E2. Thames lying in a meadow is surprised by Neptune and is compared to Diana seen by Actaeon. She flees:
>Not halfe so fast distressed *Florimel*
>Fled from the sight of that *Hiena* fell,
>Which the despightful Witch after her sent,
>To bring her back and her in peeces rent.

More Rivers from each port, had instantly been there,
Then at this marriage, first by *Spenser* numbred were.[86]

Whether it is a case of direct Spenserian influence or simply an historical coincidence, rivers and river symbolism became an important part of pageants about this time, and it is almost impossible to decide how responsible Spenser is for the fashion of river symbolism. This is the best answer Hilda Taylor could give in her interesting thesis on topographical poetry in the Renaissance: "The influence of the pageants upon Drayton's *Poly-Olbion* is unquestionable; the case of Leland, Vallans, and *Spenser is less clear, since recorded examples of the particular kind of allegory in question in English pageants of the earlier date are neither so numerous nor so striking as in these later pageants which may conceivably have been affected by the poems."*[37] It would be rash to go beyond this statement in assessing Spenser's influence on later river symbolism. In light of the slim evidence it will be better to turn to the examples of river marriages in Spenser, for like the general subject of river marriages they have received hardly any critical attention.

Spenser first mentions the Thames and the Medway in the July eclogue of *The Shepheardes Calender*:

> Here has the salt Medway his sourse,
>   wherein the Nymphes doe bathe.
> The salt Medway, that trickling stremis
>   adowne the dales of Kent:
> Till with his elder brother Themis
>   his brackish waues be meynt.   (79-84)

[86] *Poly-Olbion*, in *Works of Michael Drayton*, ed. J. W. Hebel, *et al.*, 5 vols., Oxford, 1961, vol. 4, p. 366 (Song 18).

[37] Hilda Taylor, "Topographical Poetry in England...," p. 109. Jean Rousset, "L'Eau et les Tritons dans les Fêtes et Ballets de Cour (1580-1640)," *Les Fêtes de la Renaissance*..., ed. Jean Jacquot, Paris, 1956, pp. 235-245, argues that the eventual literary source of the water fetes is Colonna's *Hypnerotomachia Polyphili*, Venice, 1499, which was extremely popular during the Renaissance and part of which was translated into English before 1600.

The symbolism, if Spenser intended anything more than a personification, is missed by E. K. in his gloss: "The name of a Ryuer in Kent, which running by Rochester, meeteth with Thames; whom he calleth his elder brother, both because he is greater, and also falleth sooner into the Sea." In itself the reference to the two rivers is unimportant, but the passage in its context provides a basis for two generalizations about Spenser's river marriages. With one exception they all fall into the same mythic pattern and they describe one of two localities—either the Thames-Medway country or Ireland.[38]

We know that shortly before the publication of *The Shepheardes Calender* Spenser was secretary to John Young, Bishop of Rochester, and was therefore familiar with the Medway country he describes in the marriage of the Thames and Medway. On two occasions he turns to the countryside around Kilcolman, his estate in Ireland, as the source of his poetry. Both of these passages are river marriages. The first is the myth of Old Father Mole's revenge on the river Bregog for loving his daughter Mulla (*Colin Clout*, ll. 88-155), and the second is the myth of Arlo Hill in canto 6 of the *Mutabilitie Cantos*, in which Molanna, Mulla's sister and a nymph of Diana, is enticed by Faunus to betray her mistress. Since these river marriages each treat localities that he knew, it has been supposed that they are merely masks for historical allegory and allusion. Attempts to prove such historical connections have been unconvincing, and with the exception of *Colin Clout*, which overtly states its references to the court world, these passages offer more interesting prospects than historical hide-and-seek.

Such a one is their mythic significance. All Spenser's river marriages deal with the problem of mutability. The context

[38] Only the *Prothalamion* does not correspond to this pattern, and it obviously uses the river marriage as a framework as the earlier examples did, and even its symbolic value is lessened by the fact that the symbol turns into the thing symbolized: the swans turn into brides, and it becomes a poem about a real marriage.

of the passage from the July eclogue is a speech by Morrell the goatherd, who represents the forces of pride and modernity in the Church. In his rebuke to the humble Thomalin he justifies his sitting on a hill with the assertion that hills are holy places to saints, that the muses dwell on a hill and that Christ himself sanctified Mount Olivet.

> Besyde, as holy fathers sayne,
>   there is a hyllye place,
> Where *Titan* ryseth from the mayne,
>   to renne hys dayly race.
> Vpon whose toppe the starres bene stayed,
>   and all the skie doth leane,
> There is the caue, where *Phebe* layed,
>   the shepheard long to dreame.
> Whilome there vsed shepheards all
>   to feede theyr flocks at will,
> Till by his foly one did fall,
>   that all the rest did spill.   (57-68)

This passage, which comes just before the Thames-Medway reference, contains in embryonic form all the elements of Spenser's Irish river myths. Titan running "hys dayly race" calls to mind Spenser's constant concern with passing time, the cyclical repetition of day and night, spring and fall, summer and winter. The same impulse draws him to the "natural cycle of water" where rivers are constantly changing and ever the same. The physical cycle describes a perfect circle: Ocean to cloud to rain to river and back to Ocean—"eterne in mutability." The ocean is the girdle of the earth, the analogue to eternity.[39] The tension between this temporal cycle and eternity is evoked by the cave where Diana, the Titan's twin, laid Endymion "long to dreame." We need hardly be reminded that Arlo Hill is the favorite haunt of Diana until

---

[39] See Sir John Davies, *Orchestra* in *Some Longer Elizabethan Poems*, ed. A. H. Bullen, Westminster, 1903, pp. 17-18, 21 (stanzas 49-54, 63). See also *FQ*, 6, Pr. 7.

the folly of Faunus brings "an heauy haplesse curse" and Diana deserts the hill forever. The result of this fall is the marriage of Fanchin and Molanna. If the consequence of the Fall seems slight, we must remember that even Milton allowed that his First Transgressors "hand in hand with wandring steps and slow/ through Eden took thir solitarie way." Mulla and Bregog, Molanna and Fanchin, Medway and Thames—all Spenser's river marriages—with differing emphasis, are myths about love in a fallen world. The pattern is the same: Eden—the Fall—love in marriage. Spenser is trying to show that the only way to retain the vestiges of our pre-Fall Eden is through the union of lovers, of friends, of rivers. Robert Frost's comment in another poem about the Fall is appropriate to Spenser.

> The question that he frames in all but words
> Is what to make of a diminished thing.

With this in mind we may turn to the structure and symbolism of the marriage of the Thames and Medway to see how Spenser varies the mythic pattern and how he relates this marriage to the structure of Book IV.

Spenser begins by reminding the reader that he has left Florimell languishing in a dungeon since Book III, canto 8, and that Marinell's mother is still searching for a cure of the wound inflicted by Britomart in Book III, canto 4. The marriage is the occasion for bringing these two threads of the narrative together.

> It fortun'd then, a solemne feast was there
>   To all the Sea-gods and their fruitfull seede,
>   In honour of the spousalls, which then were
>   Betwixt the *Medway* and the *Thames* agreed. . . .
>
> So both agreed, that this their bridale feast
>   Should for the Gods in *Proteus* house be made;
>
> (4.11.8-9)

With this apparently tenuous connection between his main narrative and this episode Spenser invokes the aid of the muse and begins the procession.

The procession has been compared to the masque because of its pageant-like descriptions, but the effect is not that of a masque—it can hardly be called a procession, for the main effect is that of a static picture. The participants do not move. The poet describing the procession moves through his description in the same way that one "reads" a medieval painting, moving from scene to scene within the frame of one picture.

The actual description is 43 stanzas long and orderly in the extreme. Neptune and Amphitrite, preceded by Triton (11-12), are followed by their offspring, the sea-gods (13-14) and the founders of nations (15-16). Next come Ocean and Tethys, preceded by Nereus (18-19) and followed by the famous rivers of the world (20-21). After a brief digression in praise of women (22) Arion (23) leads in the procession of the bridegroom (24-44), including his parents Tame and Isis with their "grooms" (24-26), his tributaries (29), his "neighbour floods" (30-39), and the Irish rivers (40-44). Last comes the procession of the bride attended by her two pages and handmaids (40-42) and followed by the fifty Nereids (43-51), of whom one is Cymoent (Cymodoce), Marinell's mother.

It should be evident that the procession is really composed of four smaller processions, each with its own focal point: Neptune-Amphitrite, Ocean-Tethys, the bridegroom Thames, and the bride Medway. The first three of these are preceded by mythical figures, which are clues to the meaning of that particular procession. Within each procession the order of names is dependent on many factors, of which rhyme and meter is not the least important.[40] In the case of the English

---

[40] Lotspeich cites Natalis Comes, 2.8 as the source of the list of sea-gods. Natalis lists almost 100 proper names as the sons of Neptune, of which

rivers Spenser names the tributaries of the Thames, and then follows a counter-clockwise order, beginning with the Severne and ending with the Lindus; P. W. Joyce contributes a slightly more complicated order for the Irish rivers.[41] Order there is, and order implies design and meaning, and the meaning of this orderly structure is our next concern.

The first of the sub-processions is that of the sea-gods and founders of nations. It is led by Triton, half-man and half-fish. He represents that part of the sea that is fertile and brings prosperity and concord to the land. He is Neptune's trumpeter, and when he blows his trumpet, "it is a signe of calme and fayre weather."[42] He is the appropriate symbol of the lawful and orderly aspects of the sea, ruled by Neptune, who has the power over the foundations of buildings. He leads in those gods who govern the sea and those who have established order on the land. This group is followed by the older generation of sea-gods represented by Nereus, the old man of the sea, and Oceanus and Tethys, who represent the fertility of the sea and the primary substance that eventually leads to the law and order preceding them in the procession. Lotspeich cites Natalis Comes, 8.1, as the source of Spenser's

---

Spenser chooses only 26. Natalis accounts for all the names in Spenser except Glaucus, Inachus, and Albion. The first two occur second in the lists of the sea-gods and founders of nations respectively, although I can see no significance in this. For the Irish rivers Frank P. Covington, Jr., cites Alexander Neckham, *De Laudibus Divinae Sapientiae*, which is quoted in Camden, "Spenser and Alexander Neckham," *SP*, 22 (1925), 222-225. Two sources have been cited for the list of Nereids. J. W. Bennett cites a Latin translation of Hesiod by Boninus Mombritius, editions from 1474-1574, and Lotspeich cites Natalis. Spenser differs slightly from both sources, and neither scholar disproves the other, *Var.*, 4.274-275.

[41] P. W. Joyce, "Spenser's Irish Rivers," *Fraser's Magazine*, n.s. 17 (1878), p. 321: "Beginning at the Liffey, the poet proceeds south and west till he reaches the Shannon; starting next from the Boyne, he goes north and west, naming the rivers in the exact order of position—Boyne, Ban, Awniduff (or Blackwater), Liffar (or Foyle), and Trowis,—curiously omitting the Erne: he then returns southwards, and finishes off the stanza with his own two rivers."

[42] Fraunce, *Third part. . .* , sig. F3.

conception of Ocean: "Oceanus, qui fluviorum et animantium omnium et Deorum pater vocatus est ab antiquis, . . . quippe cum omnia priusquam oriantur aut intercidant, indigeant humore: sine quo nihil neque corrumpi potest, neque gigni."

These two great principles of the symbolism of the sea bring in their wake Arion, the herald of the wedding party. He represents the power of order and harmony to curb the cruel and unlawful aspects of the sea. As Spenser writes in *Amoretti* 38:

> *Arion*, when through tempests cruel wracke,
> He forth was thrown into the greedy seas:
> through the sweet musick which his harp did make
> allu'rd a Dolphin him from death to ease.

Arion reintroduces the theme of *discordia concors* and precedes the bride and groom, who have been united after an initial disharmony.

The essential purpose of this procession is to show the unity underlying the multiplicity of life, as symbolized by the world of the sea. After the emergence of Tame and Isis instead of the expected geographical descriptions in the manner of the antiquarian poets Spenser asserts his independence, abandoning the usual iconographical attributes of rivers:

> But he their sonne full fresh and iolly was,
>   All decked in a robe of watchet hew,
>   On which the waues, glittering like Christall glas,
>   So cunningly enwouen were, that few
>   Could weenen, whether they were false or trew.
>   And on his head like to a Coronet
>   He wore, that seemed strange to common vew,
>   In which were many towres and castels set,
> That it encompast round as with a golden fret.
>
> Like as the mother of the Gods, they say,
>   In her great iron charet wonts to ride,

> When to *Ioues* pallace she doth take her way;
> Old *Cybele*, arayd with pompous pride,
> Wearing a Diademe embattild wide
> With hundred turrets, like a Turribant.
> With such an one was Thamis beautifide;
> That was to weet the famous Troynouant,
> In which her kingdomes throne is chiefly resiant.
>
> (4.11.27-28)

Two aspects of these stanzas demand special comment, the more obvious of the two being the comparison to Cybele. She is the great mother of the gods and first taught men to fortify cities. This is why she wears a turreted crown. Spenser describes her in the sixth sonnet of *The Ruines of Rome*, a sonnet translated from du Bellay, which ultimately owes its source to Virgil.[43] The principles of law and order and ancient fertility represented by the first two groups in the procession are drawn together in this simile. Cybele is a symbol of ancient civilization and fertility, of which Troynouant is the latest example. Spenser is going beyond the patriotic zeal of the antiquarian poets to show that his nation partakes of the ancient order of civilization, that its youthful fertility, symbolized by the Thames, is the inheritance of the beginning of civilization, of Troy and Rome, and thus generalizes the Trojan imagery woven into the third and fourth books. This brief simile implies his belief in the destiny of Britain and its ultimate roots in the glories of the past.

To emphasize this point he etherealizes the substance of his river: "few Could weenen, whether they [the waves] were false or trew." And similarly the description of the Medway makes her something more than a river:

> Then came the Bride, the louely *Medua* came,
>   Clad in a vesture of vnknowen geare,

---

[43] The reference is given by Professor Rathborne, p. 29, and by Merritt Y. Hughes, *Var.*, 4.253. The Virgil reference is *Aeneid*, 6.784ff.

FLORIMELL AND MARINELL

> And vncouth fashion, yet her well became;
> That seem'd like siluer, sprinckled here and theare
> With glittering spangs, that did like starres appeare,
> And wau'd vpon, like water Chamelot,
> To hide the metall, which yet euery where
> Bewrayd it selfe, to let men plainely wot,
> It was no mortall worke, that seem'd and yet was not.
> (4.11.45)

The two rivers are described as that curious state where sunlight and waves become nothing and everything all at once, where things are just about to become ideas—the realm of mythic vision. The most commonly known analogue to this state is Shelley's *To a Skylark*.

> Keen as are the arrows
>   Of that silver sphere
>   Whose intense lamp narrows
>   In the white dawn clear,
> Until we hardly see, we feel that it is there.

Just at that point where the day star becomes invisible its significance becomes clear. The pageant of the Thames and Medway is the highest expression of the joy and fullness of Spenser's conception of marriage. The reader is, as it were, enveloped in the vision along with the poet until he too can feel the significance of the unifying power of love and can return shortly to the complete concord and unity of the prelapsarian world where man is most himself when he has given most of himself. Unity has momentarily emerged from the diversity of mutability.

This is the significance of the marriage of the Thames and Medway for Spenser, for Book IV, and for the reader who is attuned to the subtle power of his symbols. Their subtlety is not derived from picayune differences; rather it is always a rich and vibrant variation on some basic theme—in this case the theme of mutability and the relation of order to chaos, of time and eternity. Although it is not stated in the poem, the reader knows that this marriage must dissolve itself in the multiplicity of the sea and that this act of union will occur and dissolve again and again, and ultimately from his knowledge of the physical world that the act of union and dissolution are the same and inseparable. Like the paradox of the procession of Mutabilitie,[44] whose apparent multiplicity is the expression of the principle of universal order Spenser's river marriage ends abruptly with the incantatory effect of the names of the Nereids, the individualized spirits of fertility, among whom is Cymodoce. The reader is once more in the world of Marinell and Florimell, although in reality—the reality of the mythic vision—he has never left it, for Spenser's canto of the marriage of the Thames and the Medway is simply a universal expression of the love that moves the universe and lovers alike.

iv · MARINELL AND THE RELUCTANT ACHILLES

> The thin-lipped armorer,
>   Hephaestos, hobbled away:
> Thetis of the shining breasts
>   Cried out in dismay
> At what the god had wrought
>   To please her son, the strong
> Iron-hearted man-slaying Achilles
>   Who would not live long.
>   (Auden, *The Shield of Achilles*)

---

[44] Mutabilitie's procession contains within it the answer to her claims. The procession describes the orderly cycle of toil in man's life and all those things that give point and meaning to the mutability of man's existence. Nature's judgment of Mutabilitie's claims is based on this implicit order, which is represented by the iconographical details of the procession. See Sherman Hawkins, "Mutabilitie and the Cycle of the Months," in *Form and Convention in the Poetry of Edmund Spenser*, ed. William Nelson, New York, 1961, pp. 76-102.

I have deferred discussion of Marinell until this point because of the peculiar delineation Spenser gives him. The figure of Marinell is even less articulated than that of Scudamour, and there are curious inconsistencies even in the few details given. On his first appearance in the poem he is a doughty, rich young man, guarding his rich treasures on the seashore. The wound he receives from Britomart renders him completely passive, and the narrative moves on to the hysterical ministrations of his over-protective mother. He might very well be one more of the many incidental characters, except that in canto 5 we learn that Florimell's precipitate flight in canto 1 was occasioned by the news that her loved one Marinell was wounded (3.5.7).[45] Through this report we know that the adventures of Spenser's Helen are to be related to those of this reluctant bachelor.

Marinell's predicament, it has been pointed out by several critics, parallels the course of Achilles's life, but here again one runs into inconsistencies.[46] Spenser at one point in writing apparently wanted Arthegall to be an Achilles figure, for in Britomart's first vision of Arthegall she reads on his shield *"Achilles armes, which Arthegall did win"* (3.2.25). Spenser does not develop this possibility, which he undoubtedly

[45] This information presents a crux in the narrative. Florimell's flight in canto 1 occurs before Marinell receives the wound from Britomart. The problem would have been solved if Spenser had included the wounding of Marinell as part of the flashback story Britomart tells Red Cross in cantos 2 and 3.

[46] Upton, *Var.*, 3.239-240; Lotspeich, *ibid.*; Isabel E. Rathborne, "The Political Allegory of the Florimell-Marinell Story," pp. 279-289. Professor Rathborne feels that Marinell's encounter with Britomart becomes the new battle of Achilles with Penthesilea, but in the New Troy Penthesilea is the victor. She interprets this victory of Britomart as the praise of "nascent British imperialism," but it is specifically mentioned immediately after the defeat of Marinell that Britomart scorns the wealth that Marinell has heaped up on the Rich Strond. She would not stay "For gold, or perles, or pretious stones an howre, But them despised all; for all was in her powre" (3.4.18). Professor Rathborne forgets that Britomart also represents chaste love; and far from being a glorification of British imperialism, Marinell's wealth is what selfishly keeps him from loving Florimell.

borrowed from Ariosto's Ruggiero, and it may be that he intended Marinell's career to parallel those of Achilles. Like Achilles, Marinell's parentage is half mortal, half immortal; like Achilles, he has an over-protective mother and a fatal weakness. But Marinell's fatal weakness leads not to death but to marriage with the woman whom Spenser intends as his version of the chaste Helen. If the Achilles archetype is to be significant for the figure of Marinell, it will have to explain the marriage of Florimell and Marinell.

Such a passage, I believe, occurs in Pausanias. It tells of Achilles's marriage to Helen after his death and of the island sacred to them: "I know that the people of Crotona tell another story about Helen, and that the people of Himera agree with them. I will record it also. In the Euxine Sea there is an island over against the mouths of the Danube: it is sacred to Achilles, and it is called the White Isle. . . ." The first man who visited this island returned and told: "that he had seen Achilles, and Ajax the son of Oileus, and Ajax the son of Telamon. And Patroclus and Antilochus, he said, were with them; and Helen was wedded to Achilles, and she had bidden him sail to Himera, and tell Stesichorus that the loss of his eyesight was a consequence of her displeasure. Therefore Stesichorus composed his palinode."[47]

Here is the alternate Helen myth in association with an account of Achilles that takes him beyond the incidents of the Trojan War and makes him an apotheosized lover. This is especially true of the account in Philostratus where Helen and Achilles gaze lovingly at each other "a Parcis conciliati."[48] I am not certain that Spenser saw either of these accounts, and I have been unable to find other more likely sources of the story, but these stories will serve as a convenient analogue to Spenser's marriage of Florimell and Marinell.

Marinell's threat to the world of Britomart and chastity,

[47] Pausanias, *Description of Greece*, Book III, chapter 19, sections 11-13.
[48] Philostratus, *Heroica* in *Opera*, Paris, 1608, pp. 720-722.

already treated in chapter I, is analogous to Achilles's threat to the Greeks, and it is conditioned by his mother's knowledge. He is "loues enimy," because Proteus's prophecy "Bad her [Cymoent] from womankind to keepe him well: For of a woman he should haue much ill, A virgin strange and stout him should dismay, or kill" (3.4.25). Cymoent's interpretation of this prophecy does not take into account the possibility of a Britomart figure where love and power are combined. Spenser comments:

> This was that woman, this that deadly wound,
> That *Proteus* prophecide should him dismay,
> The which his mother vainely did expound,
> To be hart-wounding loue, which should assay
> To bring her sonne vnto his last decay.
> So tickle be the termes of mortall state,
> And full of subtile sophismes, which do play
> With double senses, and with false debate,
> T'approue the vnknowen purpose of eternall fate.
>
> (3.4.28)

The "vnknowen purpose" is "approued" and made known when Marinell falls in love with Florimell, and it becomes clear that for Spenser one of the purposes of fate is that no man should eschew love. One may become a dedicated virgin like Belphoebe, but one cannot take the middle ground of neutrality and simply ignore love. Marinell to be saved must undergo a "sea-change," and he is taken to his mother's bower where Liagore and Tryphon minister to his wound.

Tryphon's skill as a "leach" soon cures Marinell's wound, but Marinell is subjected to his mother's care "like her thrall; Who sore against his will did him retaine, For feare of perill, which to him mote fall, Through his too ventrous prowesse proued ouer all" (4.11.7). Once again Cymoent's over-anxious care brings Marinell to the very danger that she wants him to avoid. The marriage of the Thames and the Medway leads him to the prison where Florimell is similarly held captive by Proteus. And here Marinell did "learne to loue, by learning louers paines to rew" (4.12.13). The wound of love is even more grievous than the wound from Britomart, and once again Cymoent's angry, stumbling maternal care leads her to reverse the decrees of fate, for her meeting with Apollo and Neptune exactly reverses the roles of these two gods in the death of Achilles.

As Ovid tells the story of Achilles's death in the twelfth book of the *Metamorphoses*, Neptune and Apollo as the founder and protector of Troy turn against Achilles, who has slain and despoiled Hector and in their anger point the arrow of Paris toward the vulnerable heel.[49] Homer says that Apollo assumed the shape of Paris to kill Achilles,[50] and later writers speak of Achilles, ambushed in the temple of the Thymbraean Apollo by Deiphobus and Paris, led to his destruction by his love for Polyxena.[51] Most of these versions would have been known to Spenser, and his version of this "death" seems to be a conflation of all of them. Marinell is "ambushed" at the house of Proteus, the scene of a sacred wedding, and both Neptune and Apollo are required to explain this strange "love-death."

This wound cannot be healed or fathomed by Tryphon, and Cymoent

> rested not so satisfide,
> But leauing watry gods, as booting nought,
> Vnto the shinie heauen in haste she hide,
> And thence *Apollo* King of Leaches brought.
> *Apollo* came; who soone as he had sought
> Through his disease, did by and by out find,

---

[49] *Metamorphoses*, 12.580ff.

[50] Homer, *Odyssey*, 24.42. Robert Graves cites also Hyginus and Apollodorus.

[51] Dares and Dictys, Mythographus II, Rawlinson, as well as Servius, are cited by Robert Graves, *The Greek Myths*, 2 vols., Baltimore, 1955, 2.319, note 23.

FLORIMELL AND MARINELL

That he did languish of some inward thought,
The which afflicted his engrieued mind;
Which loue he red to be, that leads each liuing kind.
(4.12.25)

Apollo's diagnosis given, Cymoent's legalistic mind is thrown into confusion and even more so when she learns that it is Florimell whom Marinell loves. Her only recourse is to Neptune. Like Merlin's recognition of Glauce's feminine circumlocution Neptune's attitude toward Cymoent is that of benevolent authority. She cannot bring herself to name Florimell but describes her in Renaissance legal terms usually reserved for goods and cattle (4.12.29-32). Neptune mildly rebukes her for her lack of insight and immediately orders Proteus to release Florimell, and Book IV ends with the meeting of Florimell and Marinell after their captivities in the sea. Spenser's description of Marinell's predicament is a free rendition and reversal of the fate of Achilles and morally a panegyric to the power of love and beauty.

V · *POTENTIA AMORIS*

The marriage of the Thames and the Medway, it must be remembered, occurs at the house of Proteus. Florimell's prison becomes the occasion for her release. In this sense the marriage of these two rivers, following the course of nature, is an answer to the claims of Proteus. Its orderly process is the denial that the protean—the mutable—reigns in this world, and the marriage becomes simply another statement of the *Mutabilitie Cantos*. It is a fitting occasion to bring Florimell and Marinell together. Florimell's refusal of Proteus has been interpreted as an allegorical statement that beauty is not entirely of the body, that its source is really the soul, manifested not only in her physical beauty but also in her constant love for Marinell. Neither this nor the archetypes of Achilles and Helen, however, tell the reader why it is appropriate allegorically for Florimell to love Marinell or for them to be married. For this there is no simple explanation, but the etymology of their names is a good starting-place.

Florimell means "flower-honey," and it is obvious that she represents beauty. Marinell is related to the Latin "marinus," of the sea, but it is difficult to see exactly how this relates to beauty. Obviously Marinell represents some power of the sea, and the reader can be sure that it will be a power equivalent in generality to beauty. A clue to this general meaning is given in one of the woodcuts in Whitney's *Choice of Emblemes*. It is a picture of a naked Cupid holding in one hand a fish and in the other a flower. The title is *Potentia Amoris* or *Vis Amoris*, and it is accompanied by the following quatrain:

> Here, naked loue doth sit, with smilinge cheare,
> No bended bowe, nor quiver he doth beare:
> One hande, a fishe: the other houldes a flower:
> Of Sea, and Lande, to shewe that he hath power.[52]

The woodcut is taken from Alciati's *Emblemata*, and the quatrain is a translation of the verses accompanying Alciati, ultimately derived from a Greek epigram.[53] The commentaries on Alciati give abundant analogues from the classics: Virgil's *omnia vincit amor* and Lucretius's *Alma Venus* being the most popular.[54] The French bilingual edition of Paris,

---

[52] Whitney, *Choice of Emblemes*, p. 182.

[53] The emblem occurs in all the editions of Alciati I have seen: p. 116 (Lyon, 1551); p. 109 (Paris, 1561); pp. 322-323 (Lyon, 1573); pp. 374-376 (Antwerp, 1581); pp. 346-347 (Paris, 1583). The Greek epigram ultimately responsible for the emblem is to be found on p. 458 of *Epigrammatvm Graecorvm* with notes by Johannes Brodaeus, Basle, 1549. The emblem is also included in a selection of Alciati, *Diverse Imprese...*, Lyon, 1551. A description of the emblem under *Forza d'Amore* is included in Ripa, *Iconologia*, pp. 251-262. A reference to Alciati is part of the emblem "Et in aequore flamma est" in Jacob Cats, *Silenus Alcibiades, sive Proteus, Humanae vitae ideam*, Amsterdam, 1619, pp. 30-31.

[54] *Omnia Andreae Alciati v.c. Emblemata: cum commentariis, Per*

Alciati, *Emblemata*, Augsburg, 1531, sig. D8.

1561, is a little more specific on the significance of the flower and the fish: "Tous animaux viuans en la terre portāt fleurs, & en la mer portant poissons, sont naturellement subiects à

Alciati, *Emblemata*, Padua, 1661, sig. Ee8.

Clavdium Minoem, Paris, 1583, p. 347; *Francisci Sanctii Brocensis* . . . . Comment in And. Alciati Emblemata. . . , Lyon, 1573, pp. 322-323.

amour de son per, tāt pour volupté, que pour generation. Parquoy Amour regne par tout."[55] The resemblance of the flower and the fish, in the symbolic sense used here, to the names of Florimell and Marinell is more than striking. One might object that even if Florimell is a flower, Marinell is never compared to a fish, but this is not the point. The association of flowers and the sea with beauty is too common to be dwelt on, but the sea is not easily represented pictorially, particularly as an iconographical attribute held by an allegorical figure. Hence the sea is represented by a fish, or some other small object associated with the sea. For example, in the *Hypnerotomachia Polyphili* at the height of the high priestess's prayer to Venus and Mars she throws into the ritual flames roses and sea shells.[56] It has never been explained, but her action is undoubtedly an allusion to the *potentia amoris*, the universal sway of love. Cartari makes roses and shells attributes of Venus: "Interdum eadem concham manu tenens, roseo serto redimita effingebatur; nam rosae ei sunt dicatae. . . : concha autem, eam ex mari ortam innuit."[57] The ultimate linking of beauty and the sea is the myth of the birth of Venus, the myth to which Spenser turns at the conclusion of the marriage of the Thames and the Medway, complaining of the "endlesse worke . . . To count the seas abundant progeny,"

So fertile be the flouds in generation,
So huge their numbers, and so numberlesse their nation.

[55] *Emblemes d'Alciat, en Latin et François* . . . , p. 109.
[56] *Hypnerotomachia Polyphili*, Venice, 1499, sig. O8: "Dalle sancte oratione & pio interuento gli sancti labri non piu praesto occlusi furono, che la orante Antistite degli sacri peritissima prēdette delle rose odorose praeparate, & assai cortici di conchule, o uero ostree marine, & cum le mundissime mano implete, quelle cerimoniosamente sopra dillara, īcircuito dillo ignitabulo sparse, Et posto in uno cortice di ostrea, dilaqua marina dilla Irnella asperse tota la diuina Ara."
[57] Cartari, pp. 340-341.

FLORIMELL AND MARINELL

> Therefore the antique wisards well inuented,
> That *Venus* of the fomy sea was bred;
> For that the seas by her are most augmented.
>
> (4.12.1-2)

It is to this myth that one must turn for the significance of Florimell and Marinell, for like Venus both Florimell and Marinell are born again from the sea through a baptism of beauty and love.

Florimell is rescued from the dark night of imprisonment in Proteus's dungeon through Cymodoce's sought confrontations with the gods just as Marinell is rescued from the prison of parental possession. Her love has won his love, and beauty is born again from the sea with her sea-treasure husband. Marinell is half-man, half-god. He rules the seashore, the boundary of land and sea, and has garnered the wealth of the sea to enrich his life on the land. He represents the fertility and force of the sea deprived of its terror. As Florimell's constancy in love asserts the *potentia amoris*, her marriage to Marinell asserts a beauty protected by love and its union with fertility. This is the meaning of Spenser's marriage of Helen and Achilles.

Their marriage does not take place in either the Book of Chastity or of Friendship but in the Book of Justice. They have left behind the elusive world of the sea and are returned to the world of Faeryland. The tone of high romanticism characteristic of their former adventures is gone; in its place are the "solemne feasts and giusts" of retribution and justice, in which Marinell is again the strong defender, in which false beauty is unmasked and vanishes, in which sham honor and vainglory are punished. On first reading it is a disappointment; one wants more of the world of the sea, but this is not Spenser's intention. Beauty must be restored its girdle of virtue and its rightful place in society. If the adventures of Florimell and Marinell end disappointingly, if their allegory seems to disappear, one must think of Shakespeare's late romances, whose atmosphere and structure are so intimately bound up with the world of the sea, whose miraculous climaxes always return us to the real world where the problems of beauty and constant love and the over-protective parent ultimately must be resolved after their anatomy in the depths of the sea.

Conclusion: Structure as Meaning

THE preceding chapters of this book have treated the adventures of the four heroines of Books III and IV as separate allegorical incidents; they have purposely avoided the problem of Spenser's placement of these incidents in his poem, and hence the problem of the unity and integrity of these books. My violence in wrenching the episodes even further apart than Spenser was purposeful in that I wanted to show that the adventures of the individual heroines do constitute a fictional line. Britomart's adventures rely on the theme of her quest for Arthegall. Amoret's present the training and trials of woman as beloved and wife. Belphoebe's present the image of virginity and its relation to society in the allegory of Timias. Florimell's rely on the theme of flight and her eventual union with Marinell. The reader must decide whether individual violences were justified, but a general justification can be offered by showing that these separate adventures are indeed yoked together in Spenser's poem not by violence but by a decorum that transcends clarity of narration. However, more general problems about unity arise and must be answered before the integrity of Spenser's method can be assessed.

The first of these problems is twofold: the process of composition as hypothesized by Professor Bennett and the dates of publication of the two installments. Clearly Spenser was not ready to publish Book IV in 1590, for he would not have had to change the original ending of Book III to accommodate the further adventures of characters continued in Book IV. Clearly there are indications that the process of composition did not succeed entirely in smoothing out contradictions in the narrative. The fact remains that Spenser did publish

CONCLUSION

the second installment with only slight revision in the first. He thought his poem was ready, and unless we are willing to deny him a sense of his craft, we should be prepared to accept his offering as a fiction arranged with some regard to form evidenced within the fiction itself. Thus, when Professor Bennett remarks, "Whatever the history behind any single episode, it is evident that Book III was arranged rather than written as a book of Britomart" or complains that Book IV was constructed out of the leftovers from the hastily made Book III, my sense of Spenser's poem is not troubled.[1] In formal analysis arrangement of material is as important as the writing of it, and thrift and speed should only increase our wonder.

A second problem arises in the Letter to Ralegh where Spenser himself seems to be undermining the unity I would like to ascribe to his poem: "*But by occasion hereof, many other aduentures are intermedled, but rather as Accidents, then intendments. As the loue of Britomart, the ouerthrow of Marinell, the misery of Florimell, the vertuousnes of Belphoebe, the lasciuiousnes of Hellenora, and many the like.*" By the *occasion* of Britomart's rescue of Amoret, which Spenser has just described as the climactic adventure in his third book, almost every other incident becomes an *Accident* rather than an *intendment*. These are strange words and small comfort as an elucidation of the poem we find in front of us. Surely Spenser cannot mean that the first ten cantos of this book bear no relation to his stated theme; even a casual reading of the poem must discount this possibility. Having turned away my head so often from earlier interpretations of Spenser's plan, I would like to offer yet one more hypothetical conjecture.

The Letter describes Book III as if it were following the

[1] Bennett, *Evolution*, pp. 152, 155. I am not for a moment denying the value of Professor Bennett's extraordinary work, but after careful consideration I cannot see that it has any relevance to the problem of the final disposition of the poem, which is the subject of this chapter.

model of Books I and II: Sir Scudamour, hearing of Amoret's plight, sets out to rescue her and at a particularly difficult point is aided by Britomart, just as Red Cross and Guyon in performing their tasks are aided by Arthur. I have already suggested that Britomart and Arthegall replace Arthur in the historical fiction, and the Letter (it seems to me) suggests that Britomart replaces Arthur in aiding the individual knights. It will, I hope, be immediately objected that the poem is not about the task of Scudamour's rescue of Amoret, for the objection is undeniably true. Scudamour's adventure of chastity touches the poem only at that point where Britomart comes to his aid. Spenser chose to develop his legend of chastity by presenting the adventures of Britomart *intermedled* with other incidents. Just as in the other books we know of Arthur's quest for Gloriana but see it only at those points where Spenser allows him to come to the aid of the individual knights, so here the individual knight is allowed to enter only when Britomart, the replacement of Arthur, needs to help him. Spenser solves the problem he has created by making Britomart the titular heroine of Book III. I think there is no contradiction. I suggested in the Introduction that the poem is organized around the tasks imposed by Gloriana, and so (I still believe) it is. But in Books I, II, V, and VI the knight upon whom the task is imposed is also the titular hero; in Books III and IV it is not. What Spenser would have done with Scudamour's failure to rescue Amoret we cannot know because it lies in that great unwritten conclusion, but it is important to distinguish between the role Spenser describes but did not write for Scudamour and the poem he did write about Britomart and all those *Accidents*.

These *Accidents* are not *intendments*, but Spenser's other use of this latter word do not help us much in determining his meaning here.[2] He cannot mean that these episodes were not

---

[2] Spenser uses the word *intendiment* (intendment) on four other occasions. The *OED* cites *FQ* 3.5.32 as an example of the first meaning, "understand-

CONCLUSION

intended, in our modern sense of the word, but he can mean that they are not parts of his narrative design, that design he has been outlining in the Letter. This *fact* has been noticed by all who have compared the Letter to the poem. Let us suppose that Spenser is making just such a simple statement. If this is the case, then the word *Accidents* cannot have its meaning of chance occurrence. I would like to suggest that Spenser is thinking of the meaning of this word in logic to denote that which is a property or quality, an attribute, as distinguished from the essence of a thing. This meaning will fit the present context.

Spenser is thinking, at this point, of the narrative design of his poem as its essence, and since the poem does not follow this design, the episodes of Book III become accidents or attributes. More important for our purposes, he was also probably thinking of the virtue his episodes were to present, in which case his *intermedled* adventures become the attributes of that essence he is trying to adumbrate.

Neither the dates of publication, nor the process of composition, nor the description of the poem in the Letter to Ralegh discount the possibility that Books III and IV can be read as a unified structure, and it is to this possibility that I now turn in order to justify the intermeddling of Spenser's episodes. How does the apparent surface disorder achieve that order and coherence that make it a great allegorical poem? The answer lies in the intricate structuring that Spenser's allegorical intention dictated. In a poem so vast as *The Faerie Queene* it would be ludicrous to talk about *the* structure. What we usually mean by structure is that pattern we

---

ing" (to which we might add *Tears of the Muses*, 144) and *FQ* 1.12.31 as an example of the third meaning, "attention, attentive consideration." The only other use, *FQ* 3.12.5, suggests, like the Letter, *OED* 2, "intention, purpose," which refers the reader to "intendment," 5: "The act or fact of intending; will, purpose, intent, that which is intended, an intention; a design, project. Obs." See George Puttenham's use of the word in *The Arte of English Poesie*, Book III, chap xviii.

abstract from the total experience of the poem. We may observe a structure as geometrically precise as Spenser's division of the poem into books or as hazily significant as the fact that Amoret and Florimell are imprisoned for seven months in walls of flame and walls of water respectively in parallel parts of Books III and IV. No one can say definitively that these formal and verbal facts are structurally vital, are as real as the amazingly rich temporal experience of the poem as one reads it. In fact, one can positively say that the narrative of these episodes that constitute Books III and IV begins in Book II, canto 3, where Belphoebe makes her first appearance and pushes on into Book V, where Florimell and Marinell are married, where Britomart and Arthur must rescue Arthegall, and even into Book VI, where Timias makes his last appearance. But the linear progression of the poem for all its enticing power does *not* constitute understanding. Understanding almost requires the momentary staying of the onward push of the poem to make those significant moments or phrases (that become our own vision of *the* structure) our limited means of attempting to hold the total poem. The problem is analogous to that simple configuration of lines used by E. H. Gombrich in his book, *Art and Illusion*, to figure a rabbit and a duck:

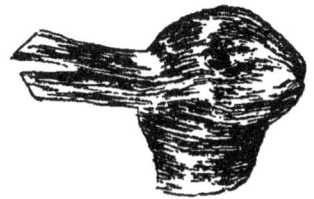

As the eye moves from left to right, the beak of the duck almost magically becomes the ears of a rabbit, and almost frighteningly, as the eye moves back, those ears become the same old beak. It never fails, but this figure is an artifact of only a few ink scratches, not a poem of many thousands of lines.

Let us begin with the division of the poem into books. The first three books present the virtues of holiness, temperance, and chastity; the second three the virtues of friendship, justice, and courtesy. The two halves of the poem are like a diptych in that they maintain their individuality and at the same time are united. The first half presents those virtues that pertain particularly to individuals; the second half those virtues that pertain to two or more individuals. One might call them the personal and the social virtues. The pattern is even more complex, for a mirror relationship exists between individual books in each half: holiness:courtesy, temperance:justice, chastity:friendship. That virtue, which in individuals is called holiness, manifests itself socially as courtesy, as Spenser's profoundly ambiguous use of the three graces on Mount Acidale is intended to suggest. The proper ordering of the claims of the body is called temperance; the proper ordering of the body politic is called justice. Chastity and friendship are merely Spenser's names for the proper use of love in individuals and between human beings, which goes far to explain the often heard complaint that the virtues of these books are hard to differentiate. It might also suggest that Spenser knew what he was doing when he arranged the material of Books III and IV after the manner of Ariosto. The manner does set them off from the others. So much so, in fact, that another kind of structural pattern begins to emerge: three pairs of two books each. Woodhouse saw many years ago that Book I could be differentiated from Book II as the order of grace is differentiated from the order of nature. It would not be difficult to imagine a similar differentiation between Books V and VI: the claims of law and right on society as opposed to society's courteous attention, lovingly offered, to go beyond the minimal demands of duty. Whether we see the poem as one set of six books, two sets of three books, or three sets of two books, the relationship of Books III and IV is the hinge on which all these structural patterns depend. The fitness of that hinge is the subject of this chapter.

Before approaching that problem, let us consider the possibility of structural patterns *within* each book. Certain cantos tend to have certain kinds of events happen in them. For example, Professor Rathborne has pointed out that in canto 10 of each book the knight receives a vision of his virtue—the House of Holinesse, Alma's Castle, the Temple of Venus, Mercilla's Court, Mount Acidale.[3] Similarly Arthur's first appearance in the various books occurs in either canto 7 or 8 (except in Book VI). The appearances are usually planned to rescue the knight of that book and to help him to complete his task. Canto 3 in all but Book I occupies a strange position in either changing the direction of the book or introducing an important theme. In Book VI, canto 3, is the point where Calepine "replaces" Calidore until his re-entry in canto 10. In Book II Belphoebe encounters Braggadocchio, who has just stolen Guyon's horse. The episode introduces the theme of honor and vainglory. Beyond this single appearance Belphoebe and Braggadocchio have nothing to do with the narrative of Book II. In Book V occurs the marriage of Florimell and Marinell. Like Belphoebe and Braggadocchio they do not figure in any other episode of this book. By placing these four figures in canto 3 of both Book II and Book V, Spenser is attempting to call attention to these episodes and to link the virtues of the separate books together. The theft of Guyon's horse, treated as an act of intemperance in Book II, is not resolved until the marriage of Florimell and Marinell in Book V, where justice is meted out. The emphasis Spenser gives to canto 3 in other books should make us conscious of its importance in Books III and IV; in both it introduces important themes in episodes that depart from the main stream

[3] Rathborne, *The Meaning of Spenser's Fairyland*, p. 129. Mercilla's Court is in canto 9. The point is still valid nevertheless.

of the action—in Book III, Merlin's prophecy, which announces the theme of Troy and British destiny, and in Book IV, the battle of Cambell and Triamond, which establishes the theme of *discordia concors*.

In other respects, however, Book III does not follow the interior structural pattern I have suggested; Book IV does. Arthur's appearance in Book III is not a rescue; the transformations of Malbecco and Hellenore are not a vision or an instruction except in a negative sense. On the other hand, Arthur does rescue Amoret in Book IV, canto 8, and the Temple of Venus episode in canto 10 is intended (I believe) as instruction and vision. The reason for this deviation is the nature of Books III and IV. They function both as individual books and at the same time as one continuous legend of chastity and friendship. They may be treated as separate entities, but to understand the form of either they must be viewed as a continuous twenty-four-canto unity with correspondences between each half. The deviation from the pattern set up by the other books can be explained by the necessity of uniting the two books formally. The progress of these two books is composed of four movements of six cantos each, moving from the inception of love to marriage. The first movement is initiated by Britomart's quest and ends with the vision of the Garden of Adonis. Its subject, if we must name one, is love. The second movement begins with the adventures of Florimell and ends with the triumph of Britomart over Busyrane. Its subject is beauty and the lust inspired by it. The third movement progresses from the inception of Ate's power to the confrontation of Britomart and Arthegall, where the destructive forces of discord run rampant. The fourth movement begins with the capture of Amoret by Lust and ends with the union of Florimell and Marinell. Its subject is the emergence of concord from discord, personal, social, and cosmic. Each movement is either initiated or concluded by the next development in Britomart's quest. Her parallelism to Arthur, reinforced by their parallel laments at the beginning and end of Book III, canto 4, made it unnecessary for Arthur to have an active part in aiding the virtue of Book III, and this is why he makes his usual rescue only in the latter stages of Book IV and why this rescue is not that of the titular hero, since that function has been fulfilled by Cambina in uniting Cambell and Triamond in canto 3. Thus Britomart's quest is the narrative thread by which the other episodes hang together. This, I believe, is the structural pattern of these two books, but it does not constitute the meaning of Spenser's allegory. To see why Spenser's form does unify the two books we must translate structure into meaning.

Canto 1 presents Britomart at the moment when she becomes aware of love as a reality outside herself and escapes from Malecasta's Castle. The next two cantos present in flashback the nature and end of the love that has driven Britomart to her quest. Cantos 4 and 5 present two further problems of love. Marinell exemplifies the reluctant bachelor and receives from Britomart a wound that will eventually lead him to a new birth in his love for Florimell, in spite of over-protective parental love. Timias's wound from the forester leads him to the protection of Belphoebe and finally to the attainment of a love different from all the others in the poem. On the other hand, these cantos present the extremes of love. Marinell is frozen chastity in the conventional sense of that word. Britomart (as well as Arthur) is questing chastity, demonstrating in every action the positive or active qualities of Spenser's virtue. Belphoebe is the extreme form of the virtue, destined by a gift of grace to remain the virgin huntress. Finally the Garden of Adonis—the central episode of the book—is a universal praise of chaste love and the fated multiplication and increase of mankind. To show that all these kinds of chastity are related, Spenser introduces us to the Garden of Adonis through the occasion of the birth of Belphoebe, the most extreme form of his virtue.

CONCLUSION

The first half of Book III deals with several types of love in the individual. Love, its negation and sublimation, are the central issues. The second half of the book presents the motive for love, "That same is Beautie, borne of heauenly race." The adventures of Florimell frame the first six cantos, as it were, with the problem of beauty; the second six cantos develop the idea of beauty, the true and the false and their uses in this world. In cantos 7 and 8 Florimell's sad plights re-enact the myth of the chaste Helen, and in cantos 9 and 10 Spenser presents his version of the unchaste Helen and her Paridell. The two are related as the two halves of a diptych. From the psychology of love in the first half of the book we progress to the abuses of marriage and beauty. Possession is the governing idea. In various ways the witch, her son, the old fisherman, and Proteus want to possess Florimell. Paridell wants to possess Hellenore in the same way that the gallimaufry of knights wants the False Florimell. Malbecco possesses Hellenore in the same way he possesses his hoarded gold, which complements Marinell's "Rich strond" in the first half. In this kind of marriage love is unknown. From Malbecco we pass to Busyrane, who represents another kind of possession—the possession of the mind and the abuse of a true marriage. Malbecco is destroyed by his possessive jealousy; Amoret is almost destroyed by a fear of this very kind of possession.

The book ends with the triumph of marriage and chastity but no reunion. Whether we call Book III Britomart or chastity, it describes the movement of courtship and its perils, that interaction of love and beauty defined by the figures of Venus and Adonis, eternal and ever-changing, transcending the material yet dependent on it. As if to stress the importance of this paradox to human love, Spenser plays with the theme of appearance and reality throughout the book.

The theme is introduced in canto 1 with the sudden appearance and flight of Florimell, who is not identified, whom no one of the characters recognizes. Arthur rides off in pursuit. Overtaken by night, he wonders whether this apparition may have been his Faery Queen. Like Britomart, Arthur is led on by a vision, the reality of which can be tested only within himself. Thus, the fleeting apparition of Florimell means for Arthur not only the chance for a noble deed but also the possibility of achieving the end of his quest. But Florimell is not Gloriana, and the disillusionment that follows finds an outlet in his complaint to the power of night and darkness to obscure and hide the truth of the vision. Again like Britomart, whose despair is dissipated by the attack of Marinell, Arthur recovers with the opportunity presented by Florimell's dwarf, and Arthur is not seen again in Book III.

The theme of appearance and reality, however, branches out and envelops the whole book. Arthur's error is only the fallibility of the senses; there has been no intentional deceit. But Florimell rides on, and the true falsehood of appearances is made real in the creation of the False Florimell, who deceives all men. The two Florimells are simply the most obvious examples of this theme. Cymoent understands only the surface and not the reality of Proteus's prophecy. Malbecco with his one eye can see only the appearances of things and is deceived. To Paridell the realities of the three Troys are nothing compared to the sensuous appearance of Hellenore. Amoret takes the perversions of Busyrane for the reality of marriage. Structurally the theme is illuminated by the tapestries of Venus and Adonis in Malecasta's Castle and the House of Busyrane. Halfway between these two episodes is the reality of the Garden of Adonis, a reality unknown and unwanted in these false appearances.[4] Of all the characters in Book III only Britomart rides forward on her quest; only she can see through the appearance of Malecasta and Busy-

---

[4] It may be of some significance that at the very end of the Garden of Adonis episode Spenser mentions the sad plight of Amoret, which he would describe in canto 12. This could be an indication that even Spenser was aware of a structural pattern within his poem.

CONCLUSION

rane; only she can see that the realities of the three Troys are more real than the parodies of those values feasting at Malbecco's castle. Appearance may mask either good or evil, but it does mask. It is the lot of human perception to know the real or to be deceived.

The third movement of these books begins with the inception of Ate's discordant power. The carefully arranged pairs of riders signify the shift from the Book of Chastity to the Book of Friendship, from the concept of love in the individual to love as a social phenomenon, and as a confirmation of this shift the movement ends with the recognition and reconciliation of Britomart and Arthegall. What began as the quest of an individual in Book III ends in the middle of Book IV with that union of opposites that is the beginning of society. Between these two points the problems of love and beauty and the theme of appearance and reality are complicated by the disruptive forces of discord, symbolized by Ate and the ever-increasing group of discordant "friends." Canto 3 establishes allegorically the possibility of overcoming discord in the story of Cambell and Triamond, set off from the main narrative both by its priority in time and by the artifice of consciously invoking and completing Chaucer's unfinished tale. Canto 3 once more takes on the responsibility of changing the direction of the narrative. Cantos 4 and 5, as I have already suggested, through its deployment of characters already known and through their disguises, adumbrates the progress of the two books in awarding the victories in the three-day battle to Satyrane, Cambell-Triamond, and Britomart, to chastity, to friendship, and finally to that character who has progressed from chastity to friendship. Through the victory of False Florimell in canto 5 the personal victories of canto 4 are almost negated, enforcing the cruel fact that the rightful victories of individuals need not be respected by society. All these paradoxical bafflements of the good and the bad are resolved in canto 6 in the battle and reconciliation of Britomart and Arthegall with its strongly suggested hint about the ultimate source of reconciliation, the *imago Dei*, a hint we have already seen symbolized in canto 3 in the figure of Cambina. Thus the third movement urges us into the increasing entanglements of discord but always with the hope that concord will indeed emerge from discord, a hope witnessed by the allegorical exemplum of Cambell and Triamond, the moral victories in Satyrane's tournament, and the reconciliation of Britomart and Arthegall.

The fourth movement begins with Britomart's departure from Arthegall to take up her "second care," Amoret, and ends with Marinell's winning of Florimell, whose flight had initiated the action of Book III. Although Britomart's protection of Amoret is not developed in the narrative, it is an appropriate beginning for this fourth movement, because it emphasizes the essential lovingness of friendship in making Britomart turn away from her hard-earned love to help Amoret find Scudamour. The first major incident in this movement is Amoret's capture by Lust, described in all his horror but basically viewed in his effect on society. Canto 7 presents the effect of lust on woman in the persons of Amoret and Aemylia. But Lust, as Spenser conceives it, "The shame of men, and plague of womankind," affects more than the woman, and Spenser presents the effect of lust on man in the figure of Corflambo, who kills all "by the powre of his infectious sight." *Intermedled* between these two incidents is the falling out and reconciliation of Belphoebe and Timias, which I have already discussed as an allegory of honor. The incident's appearance at this point in the narrative suggests the social implications of Amoret's plight and lends support to the theory that the Belphoebe and Timias episode alludes to the Queen's displeasure at Ralegh's marriage to Elizabeth Throgmorton. Arthur's rescue of Amoret immediately after this episode provides the solution for lust: grace to restore Amoret's wounds (for the three companions can escape the subjection of Sclaunder's vilifications) and stern measures to destroy Corflambo and his power over Amyas. The social implications are further demonstrated in Arthur's ability to bring concord out of discord. He first rescues the *two* women, Amoret and Aemylia, then brings into more proper social accord the *four* lovers, Aemylia, Amyas, Placidas, and Poeana, and finally he can pacify the *six* knights quarreling over their lost love, False Florimell. Into the momentary lull of hostilities Scudamour can relate his winning of Amoret in the Temple of Venus, that massive symbol of the Love that is the ground of all human loves. The Temple of Venus presents the theme of *discordia concors* as a social phenomenon; the marriage of the Medway and the Thames in canto 11 presents the same theme as a natural phenomenon and leads the reader to view the union of Marinell and Florimell as the decorous emblem of the union of society and nature in marriage.

The coherence of meaning that I find in the four movements of Books III and IV is supported by the structural pattern of Britomart's quest at the beginning and end of Book III and in the middle of Book IV. Other structural patterns within the books supplement the basic pattern. In particular Glauce's concern for Britomart's love in cantos 2 and 3 is paralleled by Cymoent's concern for Marinell in canto 4, framed by the laments of Britomart and Arthur, who are here presented as parallels in their quest for love. The chaste and reverential love of Belphoebe and Timias leads into the description of the Garden of Adonis, to which it is a contrasting parallel. Cantos 7-8 and 9-10 are also contrasting parallels in making the stories of Florimell and Hellenore follow the pattern of the myths of the true and false Helens.

The narrative of Book IV also supports the basic pattern. At the beginning of the third movement Scudamour falls under the influence of Ate until he is rescued by Britomart. At the beginning of the fourth movement Amoret falls prey to Lust until she is rescued by Arthur. Scudamour's trials in the House of Care are paralleled by Amoret's experience in the House of Sclaunder. The disposition of these episodes in the adventures of the four characters, it seems to me, is not without design. Similarly the allegorical exemplum of Cambell and Triamond in canto 3 is balanced by the exemplum of Amyas and Placidas in canto 9.[5]

Not only is there evidence of structure within each book but also between the two books, bridging that six-year gap in publication so extrinsic to the poem. Both books begin with a female figure, whose appearance in the poem will affect the development of the action. Florimell, fleeting, solitary, leads Arthur, Timias, and indirectly Britomart into that series of adventures that defines them. Ate, riding with Blandamour, Duessa, and Paridell, breeds that discord which will send all the characters on the road to divisive and mistaken enmity. These figures are extremely decorous in symbolizing the problems of each book. In Book III characters are solitary, and the action imitates the interior and solitary battle of love within the individual. In Book IV characters ride in couples or foursomes, and the action imitates the struggles of love in society. Cantos 2 and 3 are also parallel both in being flashbacks and in the protective female figure concerned for the titular hero or heroine. Glauce's concern for Britomart is balanced by Agape's concern for her triune son. Both visit sages to solve their problems, and both are granted some prophetic message. In keeping with the personal and social concerns of each book Merlin's prophecy pertains solely to Britomart, while the Fates' boon to Agape, finding expression in the mystical battle of Cambell and Triamond, pertains not only to the characters involved but to all men who would understand the paradox of *discordia concors*. The final adven-

---

[5] This parallel is mentioned by Notcutt, *Var.* 4.299-300. Other well-conceived designs, such as the disposition of the tournaments in cantos 4 and 5 and the inclusion of the Belphoebe and Timias reconciliation, have been discussed earlier.

tures in each book are also parallel. Amoret is held prisoner for seven months within walls of flame; Florimell for seven months within walls of water while both Busyrane and Proteus are trying to win them from their true love.

This last parallel I called "hazily significant" in the beginning of this chapter, and so it is. We learn nothing more about the meaning of these episodes from the parallelism; the same thing may be said of many of the parallels I have pointed out.[6] What we do learn from the parallels is that Spenser did not assemble the middle books of his poem without special concern for the way in which the individual episodes fit the general design of the poem and the purpose of presenting a particular virtue. When the structure of these books varies from what we might expect, having read the other books, it is not that Spenser has lost control but that he is preserving decorum, that innate sense of what is poetically fitting.

The bewildering array of characters and adventures in the manner of Ariosto is fitting in this way. When Spenser chose to present the virtue of holiness, he had at hand a well-defined Christian myth that approximated the development of holiness in all men. As a result the structure can depend on the quest of one man and still be true to the nature of that virtue. Although there is no comparable myth for temperance, the nature of the virtue allowed it to be presented as the quest of one man. The same cannot be said of love because of the variety and multiplicity of forms inherent in that virtue. We

[6] One of the main difficulties with most recent studies of Spenser is the indiscriminate pointing out of "parallel passages" within the poem, whether these are derived from a basic archetype or myth or from the formal pattern of the poem *without regard to the author's intention*, explicitly stated or undeniably evidenced within the structural balance of the poem. All readers of the poem should be continually reminded of C. S. Lewis's warning about skinning the eyes for symbol in reading Spenser. Although my study disagrees with Lewis's theory of allegory, his chapter on Spenser in *The Allegory of Love* is still the best introduction to the poem and by far the most dutiful and sensitive reading.

may talk of love true and false, good and bad, human and divine, parental, sexual, philanthropic, and a good many more that would be absurd to apply to holiness and temperance. Spenser's third and fourth books do not lack structure, but where that structure is not immediately and intellectually apparent we are seeing the amazing richness of that virtue presented fittingly and properly within the conventions of the romance, the form of which mirrors the multiplicity of the virtue of love. Far from being a defect, the structure of Books III and IV is the reason why Spenser's allegory of love is so extremely profound. It opens out the multiple possibilities inherent in the virtue and defies definition (which is just another form of the search for structure). We shall never be able to define Spenser's conceptions of chastity and friendship more than he has done in the poem, for we would be forced to use discursive language, which would take us into the realm of ethics and metaphysics, whose truths Spenser was trying to present in the manner of an allegorical poet.

Too often allegory has been misjudged by those who feel like a cynical friend of mine about the eighteenth century: "the same old things but ne'er so well expressed." The two parts of this phrase must go together. If one chooses to emphasize the same-old-thing-ness of allegory, one will be bored—not by the allegory but by the ideas that inform it. If one chooses to emphasize the expression, one is in danger of missing the forest for the trees. But if one takes the phrase as a unity, one will *begin* (and the word must be emphasized) to understand the beauty, economy, and even the structure of allegory where new arrangements of old figures call forth new perceptions of old realities. The middle books of *The Faerie Queene* burgeon with such meaning.

Index

Abbot, Robert, 106n.
Abraham, 43n.
accidents, 196-198
Achates, 100
Achilles, 89, 184-189
Acrasia, 3, 11
Actaeon, 115, 174n.; allegory of, 111-113
Adam, 34, 43n., 91
Adonis, 123, 151, 204, 205; garden of, 34, 72, 104, 110, 116, 117-128, 130, 142, 202, 203, 205, 208
Aemylia, 137, 207, 208
Aeneas, 32, 37, 44, 64, 65, 99, 100
Agape, 19-22, 209
Albion, 44
Alciati, Andreas, 17-18, 111n., 160, 190-191
Alençon, Duc d', 100
allegory, v; basis of, 7; character in, 52; definition of, 4; dependence of on narrative, 4; historical, 151, 152; mixed, 16 and n.; nature of, 3ff.; psychological reading of, 14 and n., 51-52, 53, 73n., 116-117, 129n., 136-137, 157-158; relation of to narrative, 31; senses of, 5-8, 50
Allen, Don Cameron, 126n.
Alma, Castle of, 91n., 119, 128n., 137n., 201
Alpers, Paul, 23n., 73n.
Amoret, v, 51, 52, 53, 55, 67, 72, 73, 74, 75, 77, 78, 80, 83, 86, 87, 88, 96-149, 150, 164, 167, 168, 195, 196, 197, 199, 202, 204, 205, 207, 208, 209, 210
Amphisa, 106
Amphitrite, 179
Amyas, 208, 209
Ancient Mariner, The, 147
Angela, 61
Angelica, 11-15
Apocalypse, 50, 151, 170

Apollo, 84, 177, 188, 189
Apollodorus, 81n., 153, 155
appearance and reality, theme of, 204-206
Apuleius, 125, 126
Archimago, 19, 98
Argante, 158
Arion, 179, 181
Ariosto, Ludovico, 3, 14, 26-27, 32, 97, 138n., 143n., 152n., 155, 163, 186, 200, 210
Arlo Hill, 176, 177
Arthegall, v, 47, 48, 51, 52, 53, 55, 59, 60, 62, 64, 66, 69, 71, 81, 88-95, 163, 165, 167, 185, 195, 197, 199, 202, 206, 207
Arthur, vi, 3, 11, 13, 14, 34, 35, 43, 45, 47, 49, 50, 62, 88, 116, 136, 137, 143n., 145, 148, 197, 199, 201, 202, 203, 204, 205, 207, 208, 209; Arthur and Britomart, parallel, 48
Ashley, Robert, 40n., 144, 145
Astolfo, 32
Atalanta, 24, 26n.
Ate, 15, 88, 95, 129n., 163, 164, 167, 202, 206, 208, 209

Babylon, 41
Bacchante, 67
Barbauld, Anna Letitia, 147
Baron, Hans, 42n.
Basciante, 67
Batman, Stephen, 141n.
Beatrice, 142
Beaumont, Francis, 74, 75
beauty, 202, 204; allegory of, 160-162, 189
Belden, H. M., 152n.
Bellay, Joachim du, 182
Belphoebe, v, 46, 67, 80, 96-149, 150, 187, 195, 199, 201, 203, 207, 208
Bembo, Pietro, 112n.
Bennett, Josephine Waters, 3, 38,

213

INDEX

66n., 104n., 117n., 120, 123, 152n., 180n., 195, 196
Berger, Harry, Jr., 45n., 98
Blake, William, 170
Blandamour, 163, 164, 209
Blatant Beast, 47
Boas, George, 132n.
boat, symbolism of, 156
Boccaccio, Giovanni, 9, 17, 18, 35, 126
Bocchi, Achilles, 160
Bodenham, John, 103n.
Boethius, 42n.
Boiardo, Matteo, 15
Book of Common Prayer, 105
Bonduca, 44n.
Bouelles, Charles de, 36n.
Bower of Bliss, 47, 72
Bradner, Leicester, 171n.
Braggadocchio, 98, 100, 104, 143, 163, 164, 165, 167, 201
Bregog, 176, 178
Britomart, v, 6, 11, 14, 46, 51-95, 96, 102, 103, 149, 150, 156, 163-168, 185-188, 195, 196, 197, 199, 202, 203, 205, 206, 207, 208; armor of, 56, 61-62, 66; imagery of light, 56-61, 90; stages in quest, 52
Britomartis, 54-55
Britons (Brutans), 44
Bruce, J. Douglas, 110n.
Brutus, 37, 44
Bryskett, Lodowick, 39, 41, 42n.
Budge, Sir Ernest A. T. Wallis, 81n.
Bullinger, Heinrich, 127n.
Burleigh, Lord, 134-135
Bush, Douglas, 111n., 112n., 170
Busiris, 81-83
Busyrane, 6, 73, 79-83, 87, 88, 95, 116, 129, 129n., 159, 202, 204, 205, 210; house of, 51-53, 72-88, 111, 116, 117, 168

Cador, 48n.
caduceus, 23, 28
Cadwallader, 44n.
Caesar, Julius, 44
Calepine, 201
Calepino, Ambrogio, 4n.
Calidore, 47, 157, 201
Calisto, 174
Calvin, John, 41, 106n.
Cambell, 11, 15, 17, 22, 30, 55, 163-165, 167, 202, 203, 204, 207, 209
Cambina, 15, 22-28, 164, 203, 207
Camden, William, 171, 172, 173
Camerarius, Joachim, 146n.
Canacee, 15, 22, 30, 164
Captivity, the, 43n.
Care, House of, 209
Carme, 54
Cartari, Vincenzo, 24n., 139n., 192
Cassandra, 154
Cassibelane, 44n.
Castelain, Maurice, 19n.
Castle Joyous, 53, 56, 67-72
Cats, Jacob, 190n.
Cawley, Robert R., 172n.
Chapman, George, 26
chastity, v, 51-53, 67, 81, 95, 100, 103, 115, 142, 149, 153, 166, 186, 200-211
Chaucer, Geoffrey, 11, 15 and n., 68n., 74, 206
Christ, 44n.
Christine de Pisan, 81n.
chronicle of British kings, 33, 43, 45, 47, 61
Chrysogonee, 106-109, 113-115
churl, 163, 204
Cinderella, 157
Cinthio, Giraldi, 39, 42n.
Ciris, 53-54
city, the third, 41. *See also* St. Augustine.
civil life, ideal of, 38-43, 46, 64, 114
Cleopolis, 34-38, 42
Coleridge, S. T., 33
Colin Clout, 124
Conan, 48
Concord, figure of, 17-18, 23-28, 130-133
Constantine II, 44n.
Constantius, 48

214

INDEX

Corflambo, 207, 208
Coronis, 84
cosmology, Neoplatonic, see three worlds.
courtesy, 200
Coverdale, Miles, 105
Covington, Frank P., Jr., 180n.
Cox, Robert, 112n.
Crane, Hart, 169
Crantz, F. Edward, 41n.
Crueltie, 74, 75, 78
Cupid, 24, 68n., 74-76, 83-88, 109-113, 122-127, 129n., 133, 190
Cybele, 24, 26-27, 182
Cymbeline, 44n.
Cymoent (Cymodoce), 178-179, 184-189, 205, 208

Damon, 131
Dante, 32, 118, 142
Daphne, 84
Dardinello, 143n.
Daunger, 73, 78, 133
David, 43n., 131
Davies, Sir John, 141, 177n.
Davis, Walter, 112n.
Defoe, Daniel, 168-169, 172n.
Delay, 133
Demiurge, 19
Demogorgon, 17-19
Despight, 74, 75, 78
Desyre, 73
Diamond, see Priamond
Diana, 54, 97-101, 104, 109-115, 128, 139, 141, 174-178
Dido, 65, 99-100
Diodorus Siculus, 81n.
Dionysius the Areopagite, 7
discordia concors, 17, 20, 23, 26, 27, 55, 56, 61, 63, 66, 95, 129 and n., 133, 163, 164, 167, 168, 181, 202, 206, 207, 208, 209
Displeasure, 74
Dissemblance, 74
Doubt, 73, 133
dove, 136, 146
Draper, John W., 143n.
Drayton, Michael, 169-170, 174-175
Duessa, 19n., 164, 209

E. K., 176
Ease, 73, 74, 87
Eden, 178
Egypt, 153
Elfant, 37
Elfe, 34-36
Elficleos, 34
Elfin chronicle, 34-43, 45, 123n.
Elfinan, 37
Eliot, T. S., 118, 169, 170
Elizabeth I, 46, 47, 49, 51, 60, 62, 97, 99, 100, 101, 128, 137, 141, 142, 147, 150, 171, 207
Endymion, 177
Erasmus, 120n.
Euripides, 152
Eve, 35, 109

Fabyan, Robert, 43n., 44n.
Faeryland, 32, 34-50, 96, 102, 148
False Florimell, 158, 162-167, 204, 205, 206, 208
Fanchin, 178
Fancy, 73
Fates, 20, 209
Faunus, 176, 178
Faustus, 19
Fay, 34
Feare, 73, 78
Ferraugh, 163, 164
Ferrex, 44
Feuillerat, Albert, 111n.
Ficino, Marsilio, 101-102
fisherman, 156, 204
Flesh, 126
Fletcher, John, 74-75
forester, 11, 13-14, 143, 150, 203
Florimell, v, 11, 13, 14, 67, 88, 136, 150-194, 195, 199, 201, 202, 203, 204, 205, 207, 208, 209, 210; girdle of, 157, 163-167
Fraunce, Abraham, 26n., 112-113, 159, 180
Free-Will, 126
friendship, v, 142, 166, 200, 202, 206, 207, 211
Frost, Robert, 178
Frye, Northrop, 33, 151-152, 169n., 170

215

INDEX

Fucilla, Joseph G., 110n.
pseudo-Fulgentius, 126
Fury, 74

Gardante, 67, 70-72, 95
Genesis, 90
Geneva, 41
Genius, 120
Gesippus, 131
Giants, 44
Gilbert, Allan H., 67n., 142, 143n.
Giraldi, Lilio Gregorio, 120n., 160
Glauce, 11, 51-53, 59, 61, 164, 189, 208, 209
Gloriana, 34-35, 46-50, 148, 197, 205
glory, 46, 49-50
Golden Bowl, The, 5
Gombrich, E. H., 199
Gorboduc (Gorbogud), 44
Gorboduc, 44n.
Gorlois, 48n.
Gough, Alfred B., 152n.
grace, order of, 107, 200
Graces, 74
Grafton, Richard, 44n.
Groten, Frank J., Jr., 152n.
Graves, Robert, 188n.
Grief, 74
Guazzo, Stefano, 42n.
Guyon, 3, 6, 11, 13, 14, 18, 34, 45, 47, 62, 72, 98, 197, 201

Harding, Thomas, 114
Harington, Sir John, 5-6, 8, 12-15, 143n., 151n., 154, 155n.
Harper, Carrie Anna, 44n., 48n.
Harrison, T. P., Jr., 117n.
Hartt, Frederick, 127n.
Hawkins, Sherman, 184
Hector, 100
Helen of Troy, 26, 27, 62-64, 186, 193, 204, 208; alternate myth of, 152-162
Hellenore, 66, 162, 202, 204, 205, 208
Hengistus, 44
Henley, Pauline, 151n.
Hercules, 131
hermaphrodite, 134

Hermes, 163
Herodotus, 81n., 153-154
Hesiod, 152
Heywood, Thomas, 81n.
Hieatt, A. Kent, 129n.
Hippomenes, 24, 26n.
Holbein, Hans, 121-122
holiness, 200, 210; House of, 128n., 201
Holinshed, Raphael, 43n., 44n.
Hollis, William, 169n.
Homer, 26, 32, 152, 153, 155, 162, 188
honor, 100, 104, 149, 201; allegory of, 143-148, 207; different from glory, 144
Hope, 74, 78
Hopkins, G. M., 31
Horapollo, 132
horse, symbolism of, 155n.
Huckabay, Calvin, 56n.
Hughes, Merritt Y., 53, 99, 100, 101, 182n.
Hutton, James, 67n., 110n.
Hyacinth, 84
Hyginus, 153
Hylas, 131
Hypnerotomachia Poliphili, 175n., 192

Igerne, 61
imago Dei, 90-94, 207
Incarnation, the, 43n., 105-109, 114
intendment, 196-197
Ireland, 176
Irena, 47
Ishtar, 151
Isis (goddess), 59, 81; Temple of, 59-60
Isis (river), 172, 174, 179, 181
Isocrates, 81n., 153

Japhet, 44
Jerusalem, 41, 42; allegory of, 40
Jewel, John, Bp., 114-115
Jocante, 67
Jonathan, 131
Jonson, Ben, 112n., 120n., 171n.
Jortin, John, 16
Joyce, James, 5, 155, 169, 170

216

INDEX

Joyce, P. W., 180
Judgment, Day of, 43n.
Jupiter, 84, 85, 174
justice, 165, 200

Kilcolman, 176
King, William, 173n.
Kristeller, Paul, 125n.

laurel, 139
Lawrence, D. H., 52
Leland, John, 171-175
Lemmi, C. W., 101-102
Lewis, C. S., 33, 59, 68, 78, 108, 109, 111, 114, 117, 135, 210
Liagore, 187
lions, 23-24
London, 34, 37, 38
Lotspeich, H. G., 26, 179n., 180, 185n.
love, 202, 204, 210; as war, 55; courtly, 109-111
Lovelace, Richard, 59
Lucius, 44n.
Lucretius, 24n., 132, 190
Lud, 37
Lust, 136-137, 202, 207, 209; Cave of, 116-117
Luther, Martin, 106n.
Lycophron, 153

magnificence, 50
Maidenhead, knights of, 88, 155, 165
Malbecco, 62, 66, 162, 202, 204, 205
Malecasta, 12, 67-70, 203, 205
Maleger, 36
Mammon, 3
Marinell, v, 67, 71, 150-194, esp. 184-189, 195, 199, 201, 202, 203, 205, 207, 208
Marle, Raimond van, 121n.
Marlowe, Christopher, 19n., 99, 111n., 133
marriage, 103, 106, 107, 114, 115, 133, 149, 150, 183, 195, 204
Marrou, H. I., 41
Mars, 85, 192
Martianus Capella, 126

Mary Queen of Scots, 151
May Games, 112n.
McClennen, Joshua, 3
Meagher, John, 173n.
Medea, 85
Medoro, 143n.
Medway, 150, 167-184, 208
Menelaus, 62, 153-154
Mercilla, Court of, 128n., 201
Mercury, 27, 173
Meres, Francis, 112n.
Merlin, 47, 59-61, 91n., 148, 149, 189, 202, 209
Milton, John, 19n., 26, 32, 58, 118, 119, 178
Minos, 54
Mnemon, 65
Molanna, 176, 178
Mole, Old Father, 176
Mommsen, Theodor E., 41
Morrell, 177
Moschus, 110
Mount Acidale, 128n., 200, 201
Mount Olivet, 177
Mulla, 176, 178
Mulmutius Donwallo, 44 and n.
myrtle, 139

Narcissus, 71
narrative, 3, 138, 198, 203
Nashe, Thomas, 59
Natalis Comes, 26, 120n., 154, 180
nature, order of, 108, 200
Nausa, 63
Neoplatonism, 101, 107, 108, 120, 123, 125n., 127, 137, 160, 162
nepenthe, 26-27
Neptune, 44, 85, 179, 180, 188, 189
Nereids, 179, 184
Nereus, 179-180
Nichols, John, 171n.
Nisus, 53
Noah, 43n., 44
Noctante, 67-68
Norman invasion, 44
Notcutt, H. C., 209n.

Oceanus, 179-181
Oenone, 63
Ollyphant, 158

217

INDEX

Orestes, 131
Orphic hymns, 160
Osgood, C. G., 171n., 173
Osiris, 59, 81
Ovid, 24n., 26n., 81, 82, 111, 169, 188
Ovide moralisé, 112

Pactolus, 94
Palazzo del Te, 127
Palladine, 158
Palmer, 11
Panofsky, Erwin, 123n., 125n., 139n., 172n.
Paridell, 62-66, 91n., 162, 164, 204, 205, 209
Paris, 63-64, 153-154, 162, 188
Parius, 63
Parlante, 67
Paros, 63-64
Pasiphae, 85
Pausanias, 186
Peacham, Henry, 4
Peacock, T. L., 169
Penthesilea, 100
Perseus, allegory of, 8-10
Petrarch, Francesco, 88, 99, 129, 130, 133
Petrus Comestor, 35
Pettie, George, 42n.
Philostratus, 153, 186
Piccolomini, Alessandro, 42n.
Picinelli, Filippo, 132n.
Pico della Mirandola, 7, 21
Pigna, Johannes Baptista, 155n.
Pirithous, 131
Placidas, 208-209
Plato, 153, 155n.
Pleasance, 74
Pleasure, 122-123; allegory of, 126
Plutarch, 5, 81n., 172n.
Poeana, 208
Ponticus Heraclides, 160
Porrex, 44
Potentia amoris, 189-194
Priamond, Diamond, Triamond, 11, 15-31, 56, 163-167, 202, 203, 204, 207, 209
Primaudaye, Pierre de la, 8, 21, 92, 135n.

Proclus, 160
Prometheus, 24-36, 123n.
Proserpine, 151
Proteus, 150-155, 166, 168, 187, 189, 204, 205, 210; allegory of, 158-162
Psyche, 122, 123, 127; allegory of, 125-126
Ptolemy, 7
Purple Island, The, 137n.
Puttenham, George, 16n., 198n.
Pylades, 131
Pythias, 131

Radigund, 60
Raggio, Olga, 35, 36
Ralegh, Sir Walter, 81n., 142, 154, 207
Rathborne, Isabel E., 34, 41, 43n., 48n., 81n., 151n., 152n., 182n., 185n., 201
Red Cross Knight, v, 6, 12, 42, 47, 72, 185n., 197
Repentance, 74, 76, 78
Reproach, 74, 76, 78
Rice, Eugene, 42n.
Ripa, Cesare, 23, 26n., 190n.
river marriage, 167-184
Rollins, Hyder, 112n.
Roman de la Rose, 74, 102, 140
romance, 3, 32, 56, 67, 72, 80, 138, 194, 211
Rome, 37-38, 65, 82
Romano, Giulio, 127
Romulus, 37, 65
Rosa mystica, 140
Rothstein, Eric, 164
Rousset, Jean, 175n.
Rubinstein, Nicolai, 42n.
ruby amulet, 136, 146

St. Augustine, 40-41, 45, 105n.
St. Bernard, 105n.
St. Clement of Alexandria, 160
St. Paul, 115
Sala di Psiche, 127
Salutati, Colluccio, 18n., 42n.
Sambucus, Johannes, 111n., 135
Samothes, 43
Satyrane, 88-89, 157-158, 160, 162-

218

163, 165-166, 206; Tournament of, 163-167
Saturn, 85
Saxon heptarchy, 44
Scarlet Letter, The, 5
Schübring, Paul, 112n.
Sclaunder, 208; House of, 209
Scudamour, v, 52, 53, 67, 72, 77, 80, 83, 88, 89, 94, 102, 128-133, 164, 168, 185, 197, 207, 208, 209
Scylla, 53-54
Servius, 153-154
Seznec, Jean, 112n.
Shakespeare, William, 60, 120n., 194
Shame, 74, 76, 78
Shelley, P. B., 169-170, 183
Sidney, Sir Philip, 82
Simier, Jean de, 100
Slatyer, William, 43n., 44n.
Smith, Hal Hampson, 169n.
Song of Solomon, 4n., 31
Spenser, use of imagery, 58

WORKS

Amoretti, 55, 60, 92, 93, 181
Colin Clout, 123, 125, 132, 176
Epithalamion, 60
Faerie Queene
  as epic, 32
  division into books, 200-201
  parallel structure of III and IV, 209-210
  process of composition, 195
  structure of, v, vi, 32, 66-67, 104, 152, 167-168, 178, 195-211
  structure within books, 201-202
  time of, 47
  two installments, 195-196

  Book I, 3, 11, 197
  Book II, 3, 197
    canto 3, 98-101, 199, 201
    canto 10, 34ff.
  Book III, 196-197, 203-206
    canto 1, 11-14, 203, 204
    canto 2, 53-55
    cantos 2 and 3, 185n., 201, 203, 208
    canto 4, 185-187, 203, 205, 208
    cantos 4 and 5, 203
    canto 5, 107, 136, 138-142
    canto 6, 103-128, 203, 205
    cantos 7 and 8, 152-162, 204, 208
    cantos 9 and 10, 62-66, 91n., 201, 204, 208
    cantos 11 and 12, 72-88, 196, 199, 205
    original ending, 116, 133-136, 195
  Book IV, 196, 206-208
    cantos 1-5, 88, 163-167, 206
    cantos 2 and 3, 11, 15-30, 201, 203, 206
    canto 6, 66, 88-95, 207
    canto 7, 80, 116-117, 136-137, 207
    canto 8, 136, 202, 207
    canto 9, 208
    canto 10, 128-133, 201, 208
    canto 11, 167-184, 208
    canto 12, 109, 187-189, 199, 208
  Book V, canto 3, 193-194, 199, 201
Fowre Hymnes, 16, 124, 132, 137n., 160-161
Letter to Ralegh, v, 46, 47, 80n., 97, 196-198
Mutabilitie Cantos, 60, 109, 176, 184, 189
Prothalamion, 176
Ruines of Rome, 182
Ruines of Time, 148
Shepheardes Calender, 60, 99, 175-177
Teares of the Muses, 198n.
Squire of Dames, 158, 164
Squire of Low Degree, 137
Statius, 19
Steele, Richard, 173n.
Stephanus, Charles, 154-160
Stesichorus, 152-153
Stirling, Brents, 104n., 117n., 120
Suspect, 74
Swanus, 44

INDEX

Talus, 60
Tame (river), 172, 179, 181
Tammuz, 151
Tanaquil, 34
Tasso, Torquato, 32, 40-42, 97, 99
Taylor, Hilda, 172n., 175
Telamond, 16
temperance, 200, 210
Tethys, 179-180
Thames, 150, 208; marriage with Medway, 167-184
Theodontius, 18
Theseus, 131
Thomalin, 177
three worlds, 7, 16-17, 21, 30, 125, *see* Priamond
Throgmorton, Elizabeth, 142, 207
Time, 119, 122
Timias, v, 11, 13, 67, 80, 136-148, 195, 199, 203, 207, 208, 209
Titus, 131
Triamond, *see* Priamond
Trinity, 91
Triton, 179-180
Trompart, 98, 100
Tros, 37
Troy, 37-38, 62, 65, 66, 100, 153, 182, 188, 202, 205
Troynovant, 64-66, 182
Tudor, Henry, 44
Tudors, 34, 38, 45-50
Tuve, Rosemond, 30, 59, 81n., 103
Tryphon, 187
Tzetzes, 153

Ulysses, 63

Una, 47, 166
Upton, John, 63, 100, 105, 111, 151, 185n.
Uther, 47, 61

Valeriano, Giovanni Piero, 132n.
Vallans, William, 173-175
Venus, 68, 70, 72, 85, 99, 101, 102, 104, 109, 110, 111, 113, 115, 118, 119, 122-127, 130, 132, 133, 137, 141, 142, 173, 192, 193, 204, 205; Temple of, 23, 55, 78n., 110, 116, 117, 119, 128-133, 168, 201, 202, 208
Virgil, 3, 32, 53-54, 66, 97, 99-101, 142, 182, 190
Virgin Mary, 140-141
virginity, 46, 103, 106-107, 114, 116, 128, 138, 140, 149, 195

Warton, Thomas, 81-82
White, T. H., 146n.
Whitney, Geoffrey, 111n., 190
W(ilkinson), E(dward), 174
William the Conqueror, 44
Williams, Arnold, 43n., 90-92, 126n.
Wilson, E. C., 115n., 141n.
Wilson, Thomas, 4n.
witch, 150, 156, 204
Woodhouse, A. S. P., 117n., 126, 136, 200
Woolf, Virginia, 52

Ydelnesse, 74
Yeats, W. B., 170
Young, John, Bp., 176

GPSR Authorized Representative: Easy Access System Europe - Mustamäe tee
50, 10621 Tallinn, Estonia, gpsr.requests@easproject.com